The

Construction

Net

The Construction Net

Online information sources for the construction industry

E & FN SPON
An Imprint of Chapman & Hall

London · Weinheim · New York · Tokyo · Melbourne · Madras

Alan H. Bridges

**Published by E & FN Spon, an imprint of
Chapman & Hall, 2—6 Boundary Row, London SE1 8HN, UK**

Chapman & Hall, 2—6 Boundary Row, London SE1 8HN, UK

Chapman & Hall, GmbH, Pappelallee 3, 69469 Weinheim, Germany

Chapman & Hall USA, 115 Fifth Avenue, New York, NY 10003, USA

Chapman & Hall Japan, ITP-Japan, Kyowa Building, 3F, 2-2-1 Hirakawacho, Chiyoda-ku, Tokyo 102, Japan

Chapman & Hall Australia, 102 Dodds Street, South Melbourne, Victoria 3205, Australia

Chapman & Hall India, R. Seshadri, 32 Second Main Road, CIT East, Madras 600 035

First edition 1996

© 1996 Alan H. Bridges

Printed in Great Britain by The Alden Press, Osney Mead, Oxford

ISBN   0 419 21780 0

A catalogue record for this book is available from the British Library

Publisher's Note This book has been prepared from camera ready copy provided by the author.

Contents

Contents

Preface

ABOUT THIS BOOK

This book is a guide to using Internet tools to find construction industry related information. It contains instructions on the use of the tools together with a large number of information sources. It is:

- for builders and designers who, having got an Internet connection, are wondering what to do next. It does not discuss connecting to the Internet (there are several metres of book shop shelf devoted to that already) or the development of World Wide Web pages to make publicly available through the Internet.
- a Guidebook. Although not an Internet reference, there is an overview of some aspects of the Internet. An understanding of the organisation of these 'Internet Navigator Tools' will help in making effective use of the resource guide and searching for other sources.
- a Resource Catalogue. The main purpose of the book is to provide a resource catalogue of Construction Industry (and related) information sources.

The Internet is continuously evolving. This book was correct at the beginning of 1996 but detailed parts (such as locations of some resources, for example) could be out of date almost before the book was printed. However, the Guide provides sufficient information to enable the finding of up-to-date information from the most reliable source – the Internet itself.

As several writers have observed, survival in the Information Age requires finding a balance between discovering the information that is useful and filtering out the mass of the data that is irrelevant. The filtering process is, however, time-consuming and, when connecting to the Internet by public telephone lines, costly. This book attempts to by-pass both of these problems for the construction industry professional seeking information through the Internet.

HOW TO USE THIS BOOK

The book may be used in several ways. It may be read straight through to gain some idea of the development of the Internet and the different tools and construction industry information sources that are available but a more usual use would be as a reference text to check the use of specific Internet navigation tools or find specific resource references. Recognising this, each section of the book is as self-contained as possible (and where this has proved impossible contains cross-references to the relevant parts of other chapters). The sections on the Navigator Tools are relatively technical and may be hard going on first reading. The reader may, therefore, wish to look over these chapters and try accessing some of the resources listed in the later sections; this should help place the technical information in context.

THE ORGANIZATION OF THE BOOK

The first part of the book introduces the basic tools required to navigate the Internet. These tools each address different aspects of the Internet, as summarised in Table 0.1.

Table 0.1 Internet tools

Tool	Application	Use
Electronic Mail (e-mail)	Personal communication	Inexpensive communication with other individuals
Usenet	Public discussion	Discussion groups organised by topic. Openly available.
Mailing Lists	email discussion groups	Focused discussion on specific topics. Available by 'subscription'
FTP	File transfer	To download text files or software
Archie	File search	To find files for FTP
Gopher	Information access	Text-based information retrieval system
WWW (World Wide Web)	Information access	Multimedia information retrieval system

The rest of the book then provides a collection of information sources. Chapter 4 describes the World Wide Web 'search engines' that will help locate specific information. Some 'web-masters' have set up sites that provide pointers to large numbers of related information sources: the most important of the construction industry related 'index sites' are listed in Chapter 4.1. Many journals are now published electronically: these are described in Chapter 5 together with Usenet newsgroups, mailing lists and traditional publishers' sites. The rest of the book is then a compendium of information sources organised under broad subject headings. These subject headings broadly follow the subject categories used in the RIBA List of Recommended Books, compiled by the RIBA Professional Literature Committee. This list is incorporated in *The Architect's Reference Annual 1994-95*, compiled and edited by Peter Adderley (RIBA Publications 1994).

CONVENTIONS IN THE TEXT

Some basic conventions have been followed in the text:

- the names of facilities have been highlighted by the use of **bold** fonts;
- addresses of resources are written in Helvetica typeface;
- specific commands for retrieving information are shown in Century Schoolbook.

HOW THE BOOK WAS COMPILED

The information contained in the book was assembled over a period of around eighteen months (although not as a full-time activity). All of the resources listed have been checked.

The book was largely written on an Apple Macintosh PowerBook 540 using Microsoft Word. The Internet access was through a desktop Macintosh connected to the University of Strathclyde server. The cataloguing and description of the various resources was greatly facilitated by the use of ForeFront Technology Inc's Webwhacker and Grabnet software for downloading and organizing World Wide Web sites.

THANKS AND ACKNOWLEDGEMENTS

Several classes of students at the University of Strathclyde in Glasgow and the Technical University Delft have assisted in the collection and checking of the information sources. I am particularly indebted to Charles Brown, Dimitrios Charitos and Peter Rutherford at the University of Strathclyde for checking the technical accuracy of Chapters 2 and 3.

The illustrations of web pages in the text are reproduced by permission of the various authors. Figures 2.6 and 2.7 are reproduced by permission of InterNIC Directory and Database Services. Figure 3.1 by permission of QUALCOMM; Eudora® is a registered trademark of the University of Illinois Board of Trustees, licensed to QUALCOMM Incorporated. Figure 3.4 by permission of Dartmouth College. Figures 3.6–3.8 by permission of the University of Minnesota. Figures 3.10 and 3.11 by permission of

Thanks and acknowledgements

Netscape Communications Corporation. Figure. 4.1 by permission of Yellow Pages ©
British Telecommunications plc. Figure 4.2 by permission of Georgia Institute of
Technology; all copyrights remain with the individual and/or organisation maintaining
the URL. Figure 4.3 by permission of Tradewave Galaxy; Tradewave Galaxy is
copyright 1993, 1994, 1995, 1996 Enterprise Integration Corporation (Tradewave). All
rights reserved. Tradewave is a trademark of Tradewave Inc. Figure 4.4 by permission
of Jeanne M. Brown. Figure 4.5 by permission of Dan Tasman. Figures 4.6 and 4.7 by
permission of Build.com. Figure 4.8 by permission of the Building Research
Establishment, © Crown copyright. Figures 4.9 and 4.10 by permission of James M.
Shilstone, Jr. on behalf of The Shilstone Companies, Inc. (jay.shilstone@
shilstone.com). Figure 4.11 by permission of Inova Communications. Figure 4.12 by
permission of Larsgöran Strandberg, Information Scientist, Environmental Technology
and Work Science, Royal Institute of Technology, Stockholm, Sweden.

Where links to other sites appear in illustrations all copyrights remain with the
individual and/or organisation maintaining those URLs.

Inevitably, with a subject evolving as rapidly as the Internet, there will be omissions
and errors in the text. Comments, corrections, information I have missed, etc. can be
sent to me at a.h.bridges@strath.ac.uk, and updates will be posted on the Spon
Webserver at: http://www.chaphall.com/chaphall/arch/spon.html.

1

Introduction

The purpose in publishing this book is to provide the construction industry professional with a toehold in the world of the Internet. The Internet has a population of several million people, interacting by means of a global network, yet the Internet is also a completely new, hitherto unknown phenomenon. What is the Internet exactly? What can it be used for? And what will be the effects of such a radical revolution in the way we handle the world of information?

By the word 'Internet' we refer to the international system of digital communication, emerging from the agglomeration of thousands of networks that interact through a number of common protocols world-wide. It cannot be physically perceived, or meaningfully located in space and time, over and above the set of interacting networks that constitute it. It is a collaborative initiative of services and resources, each network being accountable only for its own proper functioning. Thus, nobody is ultimately responsible for it as a single enterprise. Chapter 2 provides a brief history of the Internet and some background on how these networks operate.

It is not easy to determine what the Internet can be used for. It isn't that we don't know how to use the system, but that the variety of things that one can do via Internet increases literally every single day. Chapter 3 defines four categories of communication: basic services such as email and file transfer; news sources such as mailing lists, discussion groups, and electronic journals; finding information through text-based systems; and multimedia access to data in all possible forms – software, bibliographic records, electronic texts, images, video clips, musical sounds, whole data banks on an enormous variety of subjects.

The most dramatic effect of the Internet however, is the way it is already transforming some of our most fundamental conceptions and habits. The Internet is fostering the growth of knowledge, yet at the same time it is generating unprecedented forms of ignorance. As always in the history of technology, whenever a radical change occurs, some individuals are left behind while the new technology makes those who do master it suddenly aware of other domains still to be explored. The new model of 'spineless textuality' represented by hypertext, the virtual ubiquity of documents, the appearance of on-line services and electronic sources that need to be catalogued, have radically changed the discipline of librarianship. Even the library itself may disappear: no longer a building, a storehouse of knowledge physically recorded on paper, the new 'consulting' library will be a node in the virtual space of the digital encyclopaedia, providing access to electronic information on the network. Instead of an object-oriented culture, producing multiple copies of physical books for each user, we will become a time-and-information culture, providing services charged per period of use. Even the way we think may be affected. Relational and associative reasoning is nowadays becoming as important as linear and inferential analysis, while visual thinking is at least as vital as symbolic processing. As the skill of remembering vast amounts of facts is gradually replaced by the capacity for retrieving information and discerning logical patterns in masses of data, the Renaissance conception of erudition is merging with the modern methods of information management. Entire sectors of activity such as communicating, writing, publishing and editing, advertising and selling, shopping and banking, teaching and learning are all being deeply affected.

There is also the problem of 'infoglut', as BYTE magazine has called it. Throughout past history there was always a shortage of data, which led to a voracious attitude towards information. Today, we face the opposite risk of being overwhelmed by an unrestrained, and sometimes superfluous, profusion of data. No longer is 'the more the better'. If knowledge is food for the mind, then for the individual mind to survive in an intellectual environment where the exposure to knowledge is greater than ever before, for the first time in the history of thought we desperately need to learn how to balance our diet.

As the Internet is a free space where anybody can post anything, organised knowledge may be easily corrupted, lost in a sea of junk data. In the book age, the relation between writer and reader was (and is still) clear and mediated by cultural and economic filters. On the Internet, the relation between producer and consumer of information is direct, so nothing protects the latter from corrupt information.

The Internet has been described as a library where there is no catalogue, books on the shelves keep moving, and new books are constantly arriving. Unless it is properly structured and constantly monitored, the positive feature of radical decentralisation of knowledge will degenerate into a medieval fragmentation of the body of knowledge, which in turn means a virtual loss of information. Already it is no longer possible to rely on the speed of our networked tools to browse the whole space of knowledge and collect our information in a reasonably short time.

Chapters 4 to 11 attempt to map the net as an information resource for the construction industry. The subject categories are intentionally broad, but are arranged in a consistent pattern moving from the general to the particular. Chapter 4 describes the general search tools which are available and which may be used to try and find specific information. However, the trade off between a quick search time on a few key words (risking thousands of irrelevant citations) and a long wait for a few citations on a heavily constrained search is a difficult one to make. Given the fact that the data may be able to be classified as belonging in a recognizable subject area it may be better to consult a structured information source – section 4.2 describes these so-called 'Index sites'. A still more specific source of information is those on-line catalogues of information sources compiled by various individuals: section 4.3 discusses the 'Construction Industry Lists'. Even these sizeable lists do not include all sites of interest. Chapters 5 to 11 apply the same organizational procedure to specific areas of the industry. In each chapter the general sources are listed first (each of which may include large numbers of further references), followed by a number of more specific site references.

2

What is the Internet?

2.1 A BRIEF HISTORY OF THE INTERNET

In the same way that a detailed knowledge of the internal combustion engine is not necessary in order to drive a car, an in-depth knowledge of computer networks is not required before using the Internet. However, some knowledge of how Internet works (and a slightly deeper knowledge of how some of the Navigator tools operate) will help in making more effective use of the Internet.

The Internet has developed out of a U.S. Advanced Research Projects Agency (ARPA) project to investigate exchanging files between remote computers via long-distance leased telephone lines. This network became known as the ARPAnet and, in late 1969, the first four sites – University of California at Los Angeles, Stanford Research Institute, University of California at Santa Barbara and the University of Utah – were successfully exchanging data with each other.

The network grew slowly to begin with but then developed rapidly. Over the first ten years the network grew at an average rate of one new connection every twenty days. During the 1980s more networks were developed and linked to the system. The U.S. military Defense Advanced Research Projects Agency (DARPA) quickly realised the importance of the network. Education and research associations outside of the original ARPAnet charter formed their own networks: CSNET (Computer and Science Network) and BITNET ('Because It's Time' Network) being the most important. These two later merged to form the Corporation for Research and Educational Networking (CREN) but BITNET is still an active educational network and has also provided a number of unique services to its users (e.g., LISTSERV).

2.2 INTERNETWORKING

The development of these alternative networks and their connection together lead to the concept of internetworking. The network of networks thus became known as the Internet and has evolved into the system we have today. The biggest change has been in the development of 'commercial internets'. The original ARPAnet was restricted to organizations working on U.S. research and defence projects. This access was widened in 1987 when the National Science Foundation became involved and allowed general 'education and research' traffic. Links were made with European networks with 'regional' support for the Internet provided by various consortium networks and 'local' support being provided through research and educational institutions. During the course of its evolution, particularly after 1989, the Internet system began to integrate support for other protocol suites into its basic networking fabric. The present emphasis in the system is on multiprotocol internetworking, and in particular with the integration of the Open Systems Interconnection (OSI) protocols into the architecture.

Meanwhile, other organizations, realizing the commercial benefits of such networks, had developed the concept of 'Commercial Internets' or 'IP (Internet Protocol) Commercials', offering an Internet connection to anyone willing to pay. In 1991, a group of these organizations established a common interconnection point, named the Commercial Internet Exchange (CIX) which enabled them to link together. Thus the final piece of the jigsaw was put in place. After this development was rapid: Figure 2.1 shows the growth in Internet hosts.

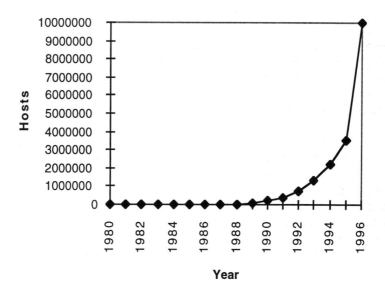

Figure 2.1 Internet host counts, 1980–1996

The Internet has developed as a collaboration among cooperating parties. Certain key functions have been critical for its operation, not least of which is the specification of the protocols by which the components of the system operate. These were originally developed in the DARPA research programme, but more recently this work has been undertaken on a wider basis with support from Government agencies in many countries, industry and the academic community. The Internet Activities Board (IAB) was created in 1983 to guide the evolution of the TCP/IP Protocol Suite and to provide research advice to the Internet community.

What is the Internet? **5**

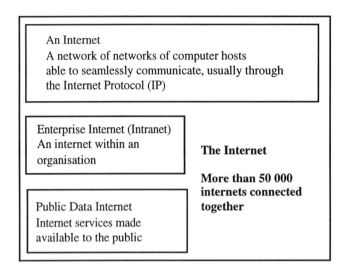

Figure 2.2 Internetworking

2.3 THE DEVELOPMENT OF THE COMMERCIAL INTERNET

During the course of its existence, the IAB has been reorganized several times. It now has two primary components: the Internet Engineering Task Force and the Internet Research Task Force. The former has primary responsibility for further evolution of the TCP/IP protocol suite, its standardization with the concurrence of the IAB, and the integration of other protocols into Internet operation (e.g. the Open Systems Interconnection protocols). The Internet Research Task Force continues to organize and explore advanced concepts in networking under the guidance of the Internet Activities Board and with support from various government agencies.

Two other functions are critical to IAB operation: publication of documents describing the Internet and the assignment and recording of the various identifiers needed for protocol operation. Throughout the development of the Internet, its protocols and other aspects of its operation have been documented, first in a series of documents called Internet Experiment Notes and, later, in a series of documents called Requests for Comment (RFCs). The latter were used initially to document the protocols of the first packet switching network developed by DARPA, the ARPANET, beginning in 1969, and have become the principal archive of information about the Internet. At present, the publication function is provided by an RFC editor. Details of how to access these notes and the use of this editor are discussed in section 2.7: Further Information.

The recording of identifiers is carried out by the Internet Assigned Numbers Authority (IANA) which has delegated part of this responsibility to an Internet Registry. The

Table 2.1 Internet evolution

Year	Event
1969	ARPANET commissioned by DoD to begin research into networking
1971	15 nodes (23 hosts) on experimental network
1972	IWG established
1973	First international connections to ARPANET established (England and Norway)
1974	Vint Cerf and Bob Kahn publish *A Protocol for Packet Network Internetworking* which specified the design of a Transmission Control Program (TCP)
1979	Usenet established
1981	BITNET created
1982	ARPA establishes TCP/IP
1983	Name server established at University of Wisconsin
1984	Number of Internet hosts passes 1000
	JANET (Joint Academic NETwork) established in U.K.
	DNS created
1986	NSFNet created
	NNTP developed to improve Usenet performance over TCP/IP
1987	Number of Internet hosts passes 10 000
1989	Number of Internet hosts passes 100 000
	First public commercial Internets created
	CREN formed by merger of CSNET and BITNET
1990	ARPANet ends
	EFF founded by Mitch Kapor
	Archie released by Peter Deutsch, Alan Emtage and Bill Heelan
1991	WAIS developed by Brewster Kahle
	Gopher released by Paul Lindner and Mark McCahill
1992	Internet Society created
	WWW released by CERN
	Number of Internet hosts passes 1 000 000
1993	InterNIC created by NSF
	With the release of Mosaic the WWW grows at 341 634% p.a.
1994	U.K. Government provides WWW servers
1995	NSFNet ends, the Commercial Internet is established
	Number of Internet hosts passes 10 000 000

Internet Registry acts as a central repository for Internet information and provides the central allocation of network and autonomous system identifiers, in some cases to subsidiary registries located in various countries. The Internet Registry (IR) also provides central maintenance of the Domain Name System (DNS) root database which points to subsidiary distributed DNS servers replicated throughout the Internet. The

DNS distributed database is used, inter alia, to associate host and network names with their Internet addresses and is critical to the operation of the higher level TCP/IP protocols including electronic mail.

There are a number of Network Information Centers (NICs) located throughout the Internet to provide users with documentation, guidance, advice and assistance. The InterNIC was established in January 1993 as part of the commercialisation of the NSF Internet structure. As the Internet continues to grow internationally, the need for high quality NIC functions increases; the initial community of users of the Internet tended to be computer scientists and engineers and were largely computer-literate and self-reliant, whereas Internet users now cover a wide range of disciplines in the sciences, arts, letters, business, military and government administration. InterNIC is a single official reference point which attempts to bring together information about the Internet. Details of how to access this information is provided in section 2.7 below.

The Internet has now been transformed into a 'free-market' system. Colleges and other institutions that were using the NSFNet were advised to find alternate feeds; these are primarily MCI, Sprintnet and ANS, which actually ran the NSFNet backbone as a joint effort between MCI and IBM before selling most of its operations to America Online (AOL) in 1995.

The final stages began on April 25 1995, when the routing tables for NSFNet – essentially, the subway maps for packets on the Internet – were removed. Some problems occurred and part of the routing was re-established. On April 30 1995, NSFNet was turned off. This history of development is summarised in Table 2.1.

2.4 THE INTERNET TODAY

The Internet Monthly Report of October 1995 reported the unanimous passing of a resolution by the Federal Networking Council (FNC) on 24 October 1995 supporting the following definition of 'Internet'.

'Internet' refers to the global information system that:

1. is logically linked together by a globally unique address space based on the Internet Protocol (IP) or its subsequent extensions/follow-ons;
2. is able to support communications using the Transmission Control Protocol/Internet Protocol (TCP/IP) suite or its subsequent extensions/follow-ons, and/or other IP-compatible protocols; and
3. provides, uses or makes accessible, either publicly or privately, high level services layered on the communications and related infrastructure described herein.

There are three primary components in the new NSFNET architecture:

1. The vBNS (very high speed Backbone Network Services), funded by NSF and provided by MCI.
2. The four NSF-awarded Network Access Points (NAPs), provided by Ameritech, PacBell, Sprint and MFS Datanet. An additional interconnection point, known as MAE-West, is supported by MFS Datanet on the West Coast.
3. The NSF-funded Routing Arbiter (RA) project, which provides routing coordination in the new environment. The RA project is a partnership between Merit Network, Inc.; the University of Southern California Information Sciences Institute (ISI); IBM Corporation, as a subcontractor to ISI; and the University of Michigan ROC, as a subcontractor to Merit.

This development and commercialization of the Internet has radically transformed ideas about communication. The 'Old World' was ordered around the highly structured worlds of the broadcasting and telecommunication companies. Information was moved in a 'top-down' fashion, controlled by these corporations and governed by a plethora of regulations and standards. The advent of internetworking and digital technology in broadcasting and telecommunication has revolutionized this old order. The 'New World' is built on distributed network management and applications. The combination of cheap personal computers, Local Area Networks and the Transmission Control Protocol/Internet Protocol has produced a massive 'bottom-up' infrastructure essentially uncontrolled by any single organization.

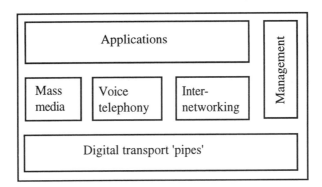

Figure 2.3 The electronic networking universe

This change in world order is also reflected in the growth of the Internet from its early beginnings on the West coast of the U.S. to becoming a major international communication system. Figure 2.4 shows the international connectivity, based on data from the Internet Society.

What is the Internet?

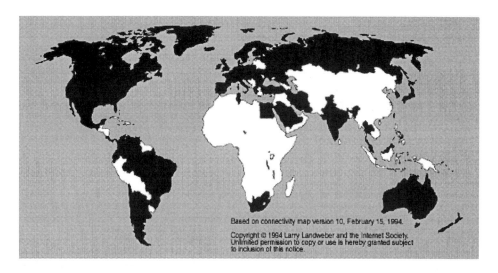

Figure 2.4 Internet connectivity map

2.5 THE DIVERSITY OF THE INTERNET

A rather diferent view of the Internet is provided by *The Internet Index* (inspired by *Harper's Index*, a registered trademark of Harper's Magazine Foundation) and compiled by Win Treese (treese@OpenMarket.com). Some recent facts and figures are shown in Table 2.2.

Table 2.2 Internet index

Number of people over 16 in US and Canada with access to the Internet	37 million
Number of former Venezuelan presidents using the Internet while under house arrest	1
Number of US business listings in the Central Source Yellow Pages	>10 million
Number of business listings of web sites in the Commercial Sites Index	15,379
Number of web sites organising the web using the Dewey Decimal system	1
Number of airlines with web sites	42
Average number of sites added to the Commercial Sites Index, per day	73
Number of daily newspapers in Iran with web sites	2
Percentage of public libraries (serving populations of 100 000 or more) offering Internet access	25
Number of Internet mailing lists known to the Indiana University Support Center	12,850
Number of Internet service providers, worldwide	>14,000

Past issues and citations to sources can be found at:
http://www.openmarket.com/info/internet-index/.
To subscribe to future issues of the Internet Index, send a message with 'subscribe internet-index' in the body to:
internet-index-request@OpenMarket.com.

2.6 INTERNET ADDRESSES

This book does not include lists of Internet Access Providers offering Internet accounts and access but assumes an already existing account and access to the Internet. If that is not the case, six things are needed to join the wired world: a computer with communications software, a modem and telephone line, an Internet address and a book. Several books about the Internet are now available which include CD-ROMs containing all the necessary software and special introductory offers from Service Providers. The Internet book is essentially to help make the initial connection but once on the Net the best sources of up-to-date information are found through the Net itself. This book is a guide to finding that information. Nowadays anyone with access to virtually any PC, together with a modem and telephone line can connect to the Internet. If these basic facilities are lacking it is possible to go to a 'Cybercafé' and, for a small fee, use the equipment there.

Every user with an account on an Internet-connected system has a user-name and an e-mail address. Every computer directly attached to the Internet has an Internet name and address. Every resource reachable through the Internet has an Internet name and address. Every network port on each computer can be identified and reached by an address. An understanding of these addresses will help considerably in tracking down information.

2.6.1 Domain names and IP addresses

Within the Internet there are two major identification systems, the Domain Name system which is made up of ordinary names and specifies addresses (such as 'Strathclyde University') and the Internet Protocol (IP) address which is numerically based and acts as a 'logical' address (in this form Strathclyde University is 130.159.248.4). Whilst each has its uses, most of the references cited in this book use the more understandable Domain names, although most users may well have come across (and had to struggle with) IP addresses in making their original Internet connection.

The Domain Name System (DNS) was developed in 1984 by Paul Mockapetris to identify networks, organizations and individual computer systems by means of English-like names. The main advantage this system has over IP addresses is its readability – it is often possible to guess a DNS address from a knowledge of a company's name, its type of business and its location, whereas an IP address remains totally impenetrable.

Under the Domain Naming System all names are organized into a hierarchical tree structure similar to the directories, subdirectories and file hierarchy within a PC filing system (or folders and files in a Macintosh system). The top level of the DNS consists of the domains.

2.6.2 The structure of domain names

A domain name consists of two or more alphanumeric fields, separated by a period (pronounced 'dot'). Thus Strathclyde University would be strath.ac.uk. Domain names are case-insensitive, that is to say it should not matter if letters are typed in upper or lower case. However, this is not the case when we come to the addresses used in the World Wide Web which are, superficially, very similar to DNS addresses. The rightmost field is the top-level domain the name-owner belongs to. The other fields may specify one or more levels of subdomain and the computer and/or organization name. The complete address thus takes the form: machine.subdomain.organization.domain

2.6.3 Top-level domains

The top-level domains are types of organization and countries. The main organizational domains are:

1. COM – Commercial organizations. For example, companies such as Apple (Apple.com), IBM (IBM.com), etc.
2. EDU – Educational organizations such as M.I.T. (MIT.edu), Harvard (Harvard.edu), etc.
3. AC – Academic organizations. This is the (largely) non-U.S. equivalent of the EDU domain (e.g. Strathclyde.ac).
4. GOV – Government organizations, e.g. Treasury.gov
5. NET – Network operations and service centres (however, many commercial access providers operate in the '.com' domain).
6. ORG – Not for Profit Organizations such as BBC.org and the Construction Industry Computing Association (CICA.org).

The growth in the various domain sectors is shown in Figure 2.5, the biggest change being in the expansion of the non-academic sectors, particularly non-U.S.A. commercial hosts, which, proportionately, almost doubled during that period.

What is the Internet?

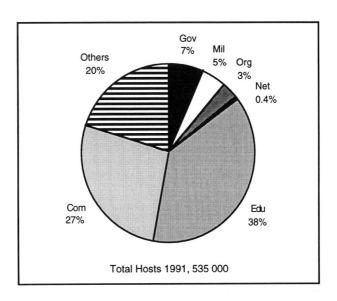

Figure 2.5a Hosts by sector, 1991

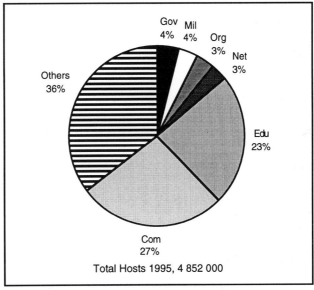

Due to the method of data collection, most sector hosts are
USA based, whilst 'others' represent non-USA hosts

Figure 2.5b Hosts by sector, 1995

2.6.4 Geographic domains

The geographically oriented codes are based on International Standard ISO 3166 names, with each country identified by a two letter code. In the same way that the U.K. postage stamps do not show any country identification, there is no '.US' code, but individual cities and states (e.g. sf.ca for San Francisco, California) may be part of Fully Qualified Domain Names. A Fully Qualified Domain Name (FQDN) is an Internet address which provides all the higher-level fields, including a top-level domain, needed to uniquely identify something. Table 2.3 gives a list of countries with full Internet services as of the end of 1995.

Further (and up-to-date) information on country codes can be found through the World Wide Web at:

http://www.ee.ic.ac.uk/misc/country-codes.html

or by way of clickable international maps at:

http://www.ee.ic.ac.uk/misc/bymap/world.html

Details of how to access information through the World Wide Web are provided in section 3.11 (page 42).

Table 2.3 ISO country codes

Code	Country	Code	Country
AE	United Arab Emirates	CN	China
AG	Antigua and Barbuda	CO	Colombia
AI	Anguilla	CR	Costa Rica
AM	Armenia	CY	Cyprus
AR	Argentina	CZ	Czech Republic
AT	Austria	DE	Germany
AU	Australia	DK	Denmark
AZ	Azerbaijan	DO	Dominican Republic
BA	Bosnia-Herzegovina	DZ	Algeria
BB	Barbados	EC	Ecuador
BD	Bangladesh	EE	Estonia
BE	Belgium	EG	Egypt
BG	Bulgaria	ES	Spain
BH	Bahrain	ET	Ethiopia
BM	Bermuda	FI	Finland
BN	Brunei	FJ	Fiji
BO	Bolivia	FO	Faroe Islands
BR	Brazil	FR	France
BS	Bahamas	GE	Georgia
BY	Belarus	GL	Greenland
CA	Canada	GR	Greece
CH	Switzerland	HK	Hong Kong
CL	Chile	HR	Croatia

Table 2.3 (continued) ISO country codes

Code	Country	Code	Country
HU	Hungary	NO	Norway
ID	Indonesia	NP	Nepal
IE	Ireland	NZ	New Zealand
IL	Israel	PA	Panama
IN	India	PE	Peru
IR	Iran	PH	Philippines
IS	Iceland	PK	Pakistan
IT	Italy	PL	Poland
JM	Jamaica	PR	Puerto Rico
JP	Japan	PT	Portugal
KE	Kenya	RE	Reunion
KR	Korea (South)	RO	Romania
KW	Kuwait	RU	Russian Federation
KY	Cayman Islands	SA	Saudi Arabia
KZ	Kazakhstan	SE	Sweden
LB	Lebanon	SG	Singapore
LC	Saint Lucia	SI	Slovenia
LI	Liechtenstein	SK	Slovak Republic
LK	Sri Lanka	SM	San Marino
LT	Lithuania	SR	Suriname
LU	Luxembourg	TH	Thailand
LV	Latvia	TN	Tunisia
MA	Morocco	TR	Turkey
MC	Monaco	TT	Trinidad and Tobago
MD	Moldova	TW	Taiwan
MK	Macedonia	UA	Ukraine
MO	Macau	UK	United Kingdom
MT	Malta	UY	Uruguay
MX	Mexico	UZ	Uzbekistan
MY	Malaysia	VA	Vatican
MZ	Mozambique	VE	Venezuela
NA	Namibia	ZA	South Africa
NG	Nigeria	ZM	Zambia
NI	Nicaragua	ZW	Zimbabwe
NL	Netherlands		

What is the Internet?

2.6.5 Things to bear in mind

When an Internet application encounters a Domain Name the program will automatically translate it into the corresponding Internet IP address using a facility called a Domain Name Service or DNS. The advantage of this is that users may continue to use the same DNS name even if, due to the development of the host system or the network, the IP address changes. Thus the user is shielded to some extent from the vagaries of the developing network. However, the cost of this flexibility is that a geographic domain may not refer to the actual location of the organization. A large company with several offices may have its location in one country and use that DNS in its address but route messages through IP addresses to its branches throughout the world. Similarly, if an organization moves, there is no need to alter the Domain Name; simply changing the IP address that the domain name refers to is sufficient for the DNS system to find the new location.

2.7 FURTHER INFORMATION

The references to further information given here all refer to material available through the Internet. Chapter 3 gives detailed explanations of the techniques required to access the information.

2.7.1 InterNIC

The InterNIC (Internet Information Centre) service comprises three distinct component parts: a Directory, a Database and a Registration Service, each provided by a different company, but all accessible through a common interface. All of the InterNIC services are available through the WWW at:
http://www.internic.net.
Alternatively, there is a mail-server program which will send information by e-mail. For instructions on how to use this, send e-mail to:
mailserv@is.internic.net
Leave the Subject line blank, and turn off any signature file. Then simply send the basic message:
SEND HELP
Retrieving information by e-mail is discussed further in section 3.3.

The main menu items available through the web page are: About the Internet; Getting Connected to the Internet; and Beginners Start Here. This last contains links to on-line tutorials, glossaries and definitions, and all of the 984 Usenet Frequently Asked Questions. These information services are run by General Atomics.

The InterNIC Directory and Database Services are provided by AT&T. These services help find resources on the Internet. The Directory of Directories provides references to information sources associated with the Internet, such as network providers, library catalogues and so on. The main way of using the Directory is by means of WAIS (Wide Area Information Server, see section 3.11) searches, although it may also be accessed by ftp (ftp:ds.internic.net) or gopher (gopher:ds.internic.net). Explanations of ftp and gopher may be found in sections 3.6 and 3.8. The Database Service contains all the key background documents defining Internet standards, such as the Request For Comments (RFCs are the proposals for Internet Standards), For Your Information (FYIs are explanations of subjects to do with the Internet), and Standards (STDs are the RFCs that have been adopted).

Directory and Database Services

 About InterNIC Directory and Database Services

Directory of Directories

InterNIC Directory Services ("White Pages")

InterNIC Database Services (Public Databases)

Additional Internet Resource Information

Figure 2.6 InterNIC Directory and Database Services

The third element of InterNIC, the InterNIC Registration Service, is provided by Network Solutions. Although intended mainly for those involved in the running of the various networks that make up the Internet, information about the number of addresses allocated, or the Electronic White Pages of organizations that have been registered, may be of wider interest. The Registration Services can be accessed via gopher and WAIS at rs.internic.net or by mail server by sending e-mail to listserv@rs.internic.net with HELP in the body of the message.

It is also possible to subscribe by e-mail to a number of newsletters published by InterNIC. The Internet Scout Report is published weekly and gives details of new resources and other Internet news. The Net-Happenings daily newsletter includes network announcements, publications and information on network resources. To subscribe send e-mail to majordomo@is.internic.net with SUBSCRIBE SCOUT-REPORT NAME or to listserv@is.internic.net with SUBSCRIBE NET-HAPPENINGS NAME in the body of the message.

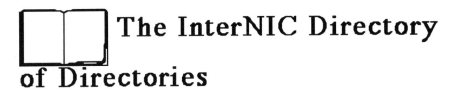 The InterNIC Directory of Directories

The InterNIC Directory of Directories is an index of pointers to resources, products and services accessible through the Internet These pointers provide descriptions of resources available to the Internet community. The Directory of Directories is compiled by the InterNIC Directory and Database Services (admin@ds.internic.net) at AT&T from contributions by members of the Internet community. This work is supported by an agreement with the National Science Foundation (NSF). The editors have made reasonable efforts to provide correct information, but neither AT&T nor the NSF is responsible for the accuracy of the listings in this directory.

 More Information about the Directory of Directories

Figure 2.7 Directory of Directories home page

A more specialized (and technical) newsletter is the bi-monthly NSF Network News, available by e-mail from newsletter-request@is.internic.net, with the message SUB NSF-NETWORK-NEWS.
The Newsletter is also available on the WWW at:
http://www.internic.net/newsletter
The Request For Comments (and other Internet archive material such as Internet Monthly Reports (IMR) and For Your Information (FYI) notes) are also obtainable from the RFC-Info service. This is an e-mail based service which will locate and retrieve documents. The documents requested are then e-mailed back to the enquirer. To use the service simply send e-mail to RFC-INFO@ISI.EDU with the request(s) as the body of

the message. Leave the 'Subject' blank and make sure that 'Signature' is turned off (or else the system will attempt to interpret the signature file as a further request). The body of the message is processed with case-independence. To get started it is worth requesting the 'Help' file. To do this simply send the message: Help:Help. This one page Help file should be sufficient to operate the system with, but more detailed help is available. Help:Manual will retrieve the long (approximately 30 pages) manual. To obtain a list of the 'For Your Information' notes, send: List:FYI. For a list of the 'Request For Comments': List:RFC.

Table 2.4 For Your Information documents

FYI no.	Title and subject	Author	RFC no.
0001	F.Y.I. on F.Y.I Introduction to the F.Y.I. notes	G.S. Malkin	1150
0003	Where to Start A bibliography of Internetworking Information	K.L. Bowers	1175
0004	Answers to Commonly Asked 'New Internet User' Questions	G.S. Malkin and A. Marine	1325
0007	Answers to Commonly Asked 'Experienced Internet User' Questions	G.S. Malkin	1207
0010	There's Gold in them thar Networks! Searching for Treasure in all the Wrong Places	J. Martin	1402
0018	Internet Users' Glossary	G.S. MAlkin and T. LaQuey Parker (eds)	1392
0019	Introducing the Internet - A Short Bibliography of Introductory Internetworking Reading for the Network Novice	E. Hoffman and L. Jackson	1463
0020	What is the Internet?	E. Krol and E. Hoffman	1462
0023	Guide to Network Resource Tools	EARN Staff	1580
0024	How to Use Anonymous FTP	P. Deutsch, A. Emtage and A. Marine	1635
0028	Netiquette Guidelines	S. Hambridge	1855

Having retrieved the list of FYIs and RFCs it is then possible to retrieve specific documents. For example, to retrieve For Your Information 4, send:
Retrieve:FYI
Doc-ID:FYI0004
Note that in this system all document IDs contain four digits. Therefore, to retrieve Request For Comment 822, send:
Retrieve:RFC

What is the Internet?

Doc-ID:RFC0822
When retrieving the Internet Monthly Reports the four digit ID refers to the year and month of publication (YYMM). So, to retrieve the May 1992 IMR, send:
Retrieve:IMR
Doc-ID:IMR9205
Useful 'For Your Information' documents are listed in Table 2.4 (note that the FYI documents also appear in the RFC series).

2.7.2 Other Internet information sources

An informal list of books about the Internet is maintained as the 'Unofficial Internet Book List' at:
ftp:rtfm.mit.edu:/pub/usenet/news.answers/internet-services/booklist
  'Internet Basics' is available by FTP at:
nnsc.nsf.net/nsfnet/internet-basics.eric-digest
  The Internet Services FAQ is posted weekly in the newsgroup alt.internet.services and is downloadable by FTP from:
rtfm.mit.edu/pub/usenet/news.answers/internet-services/faq
or send an email message to mail-server@rtfm.mit.edu with a line in the body of the message reading:
send usenet/news.answers/internet-services/faq
  Several Internet books are available on-line. One of the less serious is *Aether Madness: an Offbeat Guide to the Online World* by Gary Wolf and Michael Stein. It is published in a dead-tree version by Peachpit Press, and is online at:
http://www.aether.com/Aether/
  'Roadmap' provides a good introduction to the Internet in a series of 27 'lessons'. The Roadmap was put together by Patrick Crispin at the University of Alabama at Tuscaloosa.The WWW version is available at:
http://www.eng.auburn.edu/network/help/roadmap/
Alternatively, the lessons may be retrieved from:
LISTSERV@UA1VM.UA.EDU
with the command GET FILENAME FILETYPE F=MAIL in the body of the mail, replacing the words FILENAME and FILETYPE with the actual filename and filetype of the particular lesson it is wished to receive. For example, the first lesson has the filename MAP01 and the filetype LESSON, so the actual command sent would be:
GET MAP01 LESSON F=MAIL
The complete list of lessons are as shown in Table 2.5. These lessons were originally issued in six weekly packages. The easiest way to retrieve the whole course is, therefore, to use the command:
GET WEEK# PACKAGE F=MAIL

replacing # with a number from 1 to 6. To avoid overloading the University of Alabama's ListServ Roadmap students are requested to only retrieve one week's lessons at a time.

Table 2.5 Internet Roadmap lessons

Filename	Filetype	Description
MAP01	LESSON	Welcome
MAP02	LESSON	Listserv commands
MAP03	LESSON	Internet connectivity
MAP04	LESSON	E-mail
MAP05	LESSON	Listservs
MAP06	LESSON	Other mail servers
MAP07	LESSON	Netiquette
MAP08	LESSON	Usenet
MAP09	LESSON	Spamming
MAP10	LESSON	Internet security
MAP11	LESSON	Telnet (part 1)
MAP12	LESSON	Telnet (part 2)
MAP13	LESSON	FTP (part 1)
MAP14	LESSON	FTP (part 2)
MAP15	LESSON	FTP mail
MAP16	LESSON	FTP file compression
QUIZ1Q	LESSON	Pop quiz
MAP17	LESSON	Archie
MAP17B	LESSON	FTP sites
QUIZ1A	LESSON	Pop quiz answers
MAP18	LESSON	Gopher (part 1)
MAP19	LESSON	Gopher (part 2)
MAP20	LESSON	Bookmarks
MAP21	LESSON	Veronica
MAP22	LESSON	Gophermail
MAP23	LESSON	WWW (part 1)
MAP24	LESSON	WWW (part 2)
QUIZ2Q	LESSON	Pop quiz
MAP25	LESSON	Addresses search
NEAT	LESSON	Neat stuff to check out
ADVERT	LESSON	Commercial stuff
MAP26	LESSON	IRC/MUDs/MOOs
SMITH	LESSON	Guest lecture
QUIZ2A	LESSON	Pop quiz answers
MAP27	LESSON	The future

Another general guide to the Internet is Odd de Presno's Online Guide:
http://login.eunet.no/~presno/index.html
or via Listserv@VM1.NODAK.EDU, GET TOW WHERE
The handbook's mission is to provide updates on important developments, with pointers for resources and more information. Covers Internet, Usenet, BITNET, Fidonet, Echo, CompuServe, DIMDI, NIFTY-Serve and others. Automatic information is available by email from presno@login.eunet.no

The Electronic Frontier Foundation is one of the main sources of information on the Internet and probably the fiercest defender of civil liberties on the net. The EFF's Guide to the Internet is available at:
http://www.eff.org/pub/Net_info/Guidebooks/EFF_NET_Guide/netguide.eff
Apart from the Guide it is worth staying in touch through *Everybody's Guide to the Internet* which is a monthly newsletter issued by the EFF and is an on-going primer on the Internet. Check the main 'Everybody's Guide' section before moving on to the updates.
http://www.eff.org/pub/Net_info/Guidebooks/Everybodys_Guide/Updates/
'Everybody's Guide to the Internet' is also available through Gopher and FTP. Gopher to: gopher.eff.org then Net Info, then EFF's Guide to the Internet then Updates.
FTP to ftp.eff.org in the directory:
/pub/Net_info/Guidebooks/Everybodys_Guide/Updates
The Global Network Navigator Help Desk is another good place to look for clear and concise information about the Internet. The site also contains many links to other help sites: http://nearnet.gnn.com/gnn/helpdesk/index.html
CharmNet's Learning Page contains lots of links to 'help centres' explaining Internet access and protocols: http://www.charm.net/learning.html
John December's 'Internet-cmc list' lists pointers to information describing the Internet, computer networks, and issues related to computer-mediated communication. It points to Internet documents for new users, comprehensive Internet guides, specialized and technical information (for instance, Internet growth studies, maps and statistics) together with electronic journals and much else. It is available via anonymous FTP as: ftp.rpi.edu:/pub/communications/internet-cmc
To connect via WWW, use the URL:
ftp://ftp.rpi.edu/pub/communications/internet-cmc.html
The information is also available in Postscript, 80-column text, Tex,
dvi, and .html formats – for more information, read:
ftp.rpi.edu:/pub/communications/internet-cmc.readme
The Internet is, increasingly, being recognized as an important educational resource. Several Internet guides are, therefore, being published by educational institutions. A good basic guide is the U.K. National Council for Educational Technology's *Highways for Learning: an Introduction to the Internet for Schools and Colleges*. This is accessible at the NCET site at:
http://ncet.csv.warwick.ac.uk/WWW/randd/highways/index.html

Steve Franklin (franklin@ug.cs.dal.ca) has written an introduction to the Internet, which, whilst designed for new users also covers advanced Unix and WWW topics. It was written for a preliminary computer science class and gives a thorough description of Internet capabilities. It is at: http://ug.cs.dal.ca:3400/franklin.html

2.7.3 Sorry about the jargon!

Whilst this book attempts to be a straightforward introduction to the Internet and its resources there has been an unavoidable amount of jargon already. If the glossary at the end of the book is inadequate, check out some of the on-line dictionaries:

- Glossary of Internet Terms
  http://www.matisse.net/files/glossary.html
- Dictionary of Computing
  http://wombat.doc.ic.ac.uk/
- BABEL: a glossary of computer oriented abbreviations and acronyms:
  http://www.access.digex.net/~ikind/babel95b.html
  or via anonymous FTP at ftp.temple.edu in cd/pub/info/help-net/babel95b.txt
  or gopher to gopher.temple.edu and select Temple University Computer Resources and Information, then Internet and Bitnet Information (Help-Net), then Glossary of (BABEL95B.TXT)
  or via ListServ by sending e-mail to listserv@vm.temple.edu with the message GET BABEL95B TXT HELPNET.

3

Internet tools

3.1 ACCESSING NETWORK RESOURCES

As the networks expand and more resources and services are made available the task of accessing this data becomes more and more difficult. However, a number of tools are available to facilitate the task of locating and retrieving network resources, so that users anywhere can utilise texts, data, software and information for public access. Facilities to explore public domain software repositories, to consult mailing list archives and databases, to retrieve directory information and to participate in global group discussions are made freely available to all through the Internet itself.

The key to exploiting these resources is a server – special software on a computer somewhere in the network which accepts requests (or queries or commands) and sends a response automatically. The requester does not have to be working on the same computer (or even in the same part of the world) in order to use the server. Many servers accept requests via electronic mail, so that often the requester need not even be on the same computer network as the server. In many cases, servers are interconnected so that once contact is established with one server, it is a simple matter to communicate with other servers as well. In this way the load on any one individual server is minimized.

3.2 THE CLIENT–SERVER CONCEPT

Most tools have two ends – typically a 'working' end and a handle. In computing the same approach is adopted, with the 'working' end doing technical things such as retrieving data from remote sites or looking up IP addresses and the 'handle' being the more user-friendly part that the user interacts with. In computer jargon the software that the user interacts with is known as the client and the program the client interacts with is the server. A number of key Internet tools such as FTP (File Transfer Protocol/Program), HTTP (Hyper-Text Transport Protocol, used by the World Wide Web), archie, gopher and WAIS (various information retrieval systems) adopt this approach. They each consist of client programs (in most cases there is more than one option available) which the user interacts with, and corresponding server programs and databases which their clients work with. For example, when a user sends e-mail or reads a Usenet newsgroup, a client program provides the interface enabling the user to send and receive messages, with server programs responsible for moving those messages around the network.

The benefits of this approach are that the user is separated from the technical aspects of running the server software directly; separate client programs can be developed for different computing environments so that, for example, a Macintosh user may use a graphical point-and-click interface to access the same server software a Unix user would access through typing commands at a keyboard. These machine specific client programs may usually be downloaded from public access software databases. Information about them is obtainable through the Internet by checking the appropriate FAQs (Frequently Asked Questions) and reading articles in the corresponding Usenet Newsgroups. John December's 'Internet-tools List' is a good general guide which contains information about a variety of network tools and information resources (such as Archie, Gopher, Netfind, WWW and so on.) It is available at:

ftp.rpi.edu/pub/communications/internet-tools

To connect via WWW, use the URL:

ftp://ftp.rpi.edu/pub/communications/internet-tools.html

This document is also available in various text formats – for more information, read:

ftp.rpi.edu/pub/communications/internet-tools.readme

Using client programs as the front-end to Internet facilities also reduces the load on the network as the use of client programs places a degree of processing work in the local machine and ensures that the data sent over the network is correctly formatted.

This chapter reviews the basic tools needed to use the Internet. The tools may be considered under basic headings as shown in Table 3.1

Table 3.1 Basic Internet tool functions

Service	*Net tools*
Basic services	E-mail, FTP, Telnet
News feeds	Mailing Lists and Bulletin Boards
Browsing	WWW, Gopher, WAIS
Finding information	Archie, Veronica

3.3 ELECTRONIC MAIL

Electronic mail, or e-mail, is one of the basic tools of the Internet. It may be the first tool most users make use of and often remains the most frequently used. Once links are established, e-mail usually becomes the preferred mode of communication given its speed, convenience and cost. Companies such as Apple, Microsoft, Sun and others make extensive use of e-mail in their internal communications.

Apart from the obvious use in sending and receiving messages between individuals or groups of people, e-mail is of importance here as it may be used to retrieve files and documents and query remote databases. It is also possible to send queries to Usenet newsgroups and receive newsgroup postings.

E-mail systems work by exchanging messages. The message may be created and read using a client e-mail program. The mail transfer is carried out by one or more mail agent server programs. Every e-mail message consists of three parts: a header, a body, and an end of message marker.

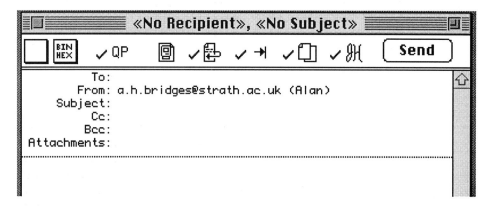

Figure 3.1 The Eudora e-mail client

The header contains a mixture of information, some created by the sender of the message, the rest by the e-mail servers on the various computers the message passed through on the way to the recipient. The section most relevant to the ordinary user is the user provided information. Fields such as 'From', 'Date', 'CC' (copied to), 'BCC' (blind copies to) are self-evident and follow ordinary typing office conventions, but some aspects of two other fields are worth looking at.

The 'To' field must contain at least one name, but the 'name' may refer to:

- an individual (e.g., a.h.bridges@strath.ac.uk)
- a program that accepts e-mail (e.g., mailbase@mailbase.ac.uk)
- an 'alias' (a previously created 'nickname' which can be used instead of having to remember – or type – the full name)
- a mailing list (e.g. listserv@psuvm.psu.edu)

Some client programs allow further options (e.g., reference to a file containing lists of names) beyond those mentioned above.

The 'Subject' field describes what the sender considers the message to be about. Whilst the choice of appropriately descriptive subject lines is important when communicating with newsgroups or individuals, when a message is sent to another program (e.g., ListServ or Archie) the subject field may have to contain a specific keyword or be left blank.

The 'Message Body' contains the actual message. Many users also include standard information such as their full name, postal address, phone and fax number etc., at the end of the message. Rather than type this information every time a message is sent, most client e-mail programs allow the creation of 'signature' files which automatically append this information. When accessing other programs only specific keywords are allowed in the message body and the signature file should be omitted.

Finding someone's e-mail address is not particularly straightforward. The usual advice is that if that person's phone number is known, phone them up and ask them their e-mail address. There is a 'FAQ' (Frequently Asked Question) on the subject, compiled by Jonathan I. Kamens which can be obtained by e-mail. Send a message to 'mail-server@pit-manager.mit.edu', leave the Subject field blank and enter the following in the message body: send usenet/news.answers/finding-addresses. Omit the signature file. This FAQ is also posted to the Usenet Newsgroups news.answers and comp.mail.misc.

Several 'search-engines' for tracing e-mail addresses are available on the World Wide Web. One of the best is Four11, which holds a database of more than two million e-mail addresses and can be found at http://www.Four11.com/. Four11 is a free service, but the condition required before being allowed to search the database is the registration of your own address. After completing the registration it is then possible to search the database immediately, although your own address will take a day or two to be entered. At that time Four11 will e-mail you with a personal Four11 password, giving a URL which uses that password and allows direct access to the database. An alternative search engine is Netfind:

http://alpha.acast.nova.edu/netfind.html

Queries are entered in the format: name key(s), where name is the last name of the person, and the key words are hints at the location to search. Netfind will return a list of possible locations based on the key words. Select one. Netfind will then look for information on the person at that location.

There are three common mistakes to be aware of in using e-mail. The most common cause for non-delivery of a message is a misspelled address. More embarrassingly, replying to a mailing list instead of an individual: broadcasting what might be a private message to possibly thousands of other people is best avoided. Slightly less embarrassing is sending a message to a mailing list rather than its moderator.

One further problem occurs when attempting to send e-mail to people on other networks. Different networks use different addressing conventions and some special forms of address are required for inter-network mailing. John J. Chew has put together an 'Inter-network mail guide' which may be obtained by e-mail from mail-server@pit-manager.mit.edu with 'send inter-network-mail-guide' in the message body. It is also posted monthly to the Usenet newsgroups comp.mail.misc and alt.internet.services and available by FTP from:

csd4.csd.uwm.edu/pub/internetwork-mail-guide

The best guide to using e-mail to access Internet resources is Bob Rankin's 'Accessing the Internet by e-mail'. This is freely available from a number of automated mail-servers. To obtain a copy in Europe send e-mail to mailbase@mailbase.ac.uk with the message 'send lis-iis e-access-inet.txt' in the body of the message. The guide is available by anonymous FTP from the same site (mailbase.ac.uk), get the file pub/lists/lis-iis/files/e-access-inet.txt.

3.4 USENET

Usenet is a message sharing system that exchanges messages electronically around the world in a standard format. Messages exchanged on Usenet are arranged by topic into categories called newsgroups. The messages may contain both plain text and encoded binary information (which may be images or software). The messages also contain header lines that define who the message came from, when the message was posted, where it was posted, where it has passed, and other administrative information. Through Usenet millions of computer users are able to share information, find advice and conduct multi-person debates on anything from technical aspects of computer graphics to what is the best fish restaurant in Boston. The Usenet is a source for downloading software or documents and many Usenet newsgroups provide detailed pointers to wider resources on the Internet.

Usenet was originally organized in seven main groups. These are:

- **comp** dealing with computer, network and information science issues. For a source of free technical advice participation in appropriate sections of this group could, on its own, justify access to the Internet.
- **misc** literally the miscellaneous subjects which did not seem to fit anywhere else.
- **news** news that is, about the Usenet, including administrative issues, announcements, general information and so on.
- **rec** the recreation section is one of the largest and ranges across almost anything that people could do in their spare time.
- **sci** the hierarchy for engineering and sciences other than computer science.
- **soc** societies seeking to convert the masses to their cause
- **talk** debating groups arguing over hundreds of topics

In addition to these seven original categories an **alt** hierarchy was added. This is where the esoterica of the Usenet is collected and it is possible that not all of it will be available from any particular service provider.

The major categories are further broken down into more than 1200 newsgroups on different subjects which range from education for the disabled to Star Trek and from environmental science to politics in the former Soviet Union. The quality of the discussion in newsgroups is not guaranteed to be high. Some newsgroups have a moderator who scans the messages for the group before they are distributed and decides which ones are appropriate for distribution.

3.4.1 Using Usenet

If the service provider is a Usenet site then Usenet access follows automatically. To read and post to Usenet groups a client program known as a 'Newsreader' is required. Usenet newsreader programs are widely available for most kinds of computer and may be downloaded at no cost via Internet file-retrieval services (anonymous FTP, e-mail, gopher, etc.). The Usenet newsgroup news.software.readers is dedicated to newsreader software. More detailed information about participating in newsgroups is contained in the newsgroup news.announce.newusers. Other Usenet information of importance to all users (not just new users) is posted in the newsgroup news.announce.important, which should be checked regularly. Another general information group is the alt.internet.services group which contains postings of what is available on the Internet.

Most, if not all, of the news readers provide the same basic abilities:

- Subscribing to newsgroups: The news reader will make these user-selected groups immediately accessible, thus enabling easy access (rather than searching through the complete list of groups every time).
- Unsubscribing from newsgroups: Removing groups from the easy access list.
- Reading newsgroup postings: The news reader presents postings for reading and keeps track of which postings have and have not been read.
- Discussion threads: Enables the reader to follow groups of postings that deal with the same subject.
- Posting to news groups: Enables participation in group discussions.
- Responding to a posting: To send a response to the newsgroup (often called follow-up) or to the author of a posting (often called reply).

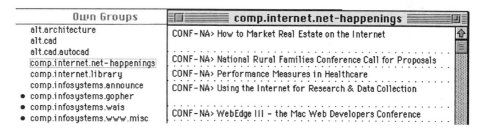

Figure 3.2 Own Groups window with postings for selected group

3.4.2 Required reading for new Usenet users

There are several articles written by Usenet gurus which are considered to be required reading for all new users of Usenet. Several groups do not take kindly to new users posting requests for information which is published in 'FAQs' or other easily available sources. Most articles of interest to new users may be found in the news.answers newsgroup. Some worth looking at are:

- What is Usenet?
- A Primer on How to Work With the Usenet Community
- Rules for Posting to Usenet
- Answers to FAQs About Usenet
- Emily Postnews Answers Your Questions on Netiquette
- Hints on Writing Style for Usenet
- Introduction to the news.answers Newsgroup

3.5 LISTSERV

ListServ is an e-mail based distribution list management package. By sending messages to a ListServ program the user can automatically retrieve information. It allows groups of computer users with a common interest to communicate among themselves, whilst making efficient use of computer and network resources. ListServ lists are international and eclectic, containing lists in every imaginable field, for every audience, in many different countries and in many different languages. See the description of the List command in the section Using ListServ for instructions on getting an up-to-date list of lists. Anyone who can send electronic mail to an EARN/Bitnet address can participate in a mailing list and access other ListServ facilities, as long as the e-mail format is valid (according to the RFC822 standard) and has a usable return address.

3.5.1 Basic rules for using ListServ

To use ListServ facilities, send electronic mail with the required ListServ commands to: LISTSERV@host-id where host-id is the host computer's Internet domain name.

More than one command can be sent to ListServ in the same mail message, but each command must be on a separate line. ListServ will ignore the 'Subject' line of the mail header, so ensure that the commands are in the body of the e-mail. Do not include any text in the message body apart from the ListServ commands. This means no 'Hi', 'Please', 'Thank you' or 'signature' as the ListServ program will attempt to interpret all text as ListServ commands. For the same reason do not use any punctuation marks: separate commands must be on separate lines. In commands that ask for 'Your Name' this means 'real name' (e.g. Alan Bridges) rather than the e-mail name.

3.5.2. Some basic commands for LISTS

The primary function of ListServ is to operate mailing lists (sometimes referred to as distribution lists). Mailing lists are used to distribute the e-mail sent to them to a list of recipients. They provide the means for a group of users to establish an e-mail forum on any topic or area of common interest. This service provides an extremely convenient means for the exchange of ideas and information between list members since ListServ (and not the mail sender) manages the distribution of e-mail to all of its final recipients. Users need only to remember one list address to which they send their mail in order to communicate with a potentially large number of users. Due to the efficiency with which ListServ distributes e-mail to list members, discussions or debates with a world-wide audience may be conducted.

The following commands are designed for use with ListServ mailing lists. They enable such things as finding the names and addresses of lists, signing on to or off lists, reviewing lists or changing options for the way in which the list material is received.

Commands are presented in a particular format: CAPITAL letters indicate acceptable abbreviation, angle brackets (<>) indicate an optional parameter, and vertical bar (l) indicates a choice of parameters. All parameters are fully explained in each command description.

- Help: gets a brief list of ListServ commands
- Info <options>

  Gets further information about ListServ. The basic choices for the options parameter are:

  ? (i.e. Info ?) will return a list of ListServ information guides

  pr (Info pr) retrieves the document 'Presentation of ListServ for New Users'.
- List <options>

  Use the List command to get a listing of available mailing lists at a ListServ server. The options parameter may be any of the following:

  Short

  This option displays a summary of all the lists managed by a ListServ in a brief, one line description. This is the default.

  Long

  The Long (or Detailed) option will send a file (called node-name LISTS) that contains a comprehensive description of the lists managed by a ListServ server.

  Global <pattern>

  This option gives a complete list of all known ListServ mailing lists at all servers at the time the command is issued. A file (called LISTSERV LISTS) will be sent containing the names, titles and e-mail addresses of these lists. This is a very large file (there are some 4000–5000 lists). The optional pattern parameter can be used to match any string in the list name, list title or list address.

- REView list-name <options>

  Use the REView command to receive more information about a mailing list. A file called list-name LIST (or list-name node-name for peered lists) will be sent. A mailing list is made up of two parts: a control section and a subscription section. The control section holds the definition parameters for a list which includes information such as who is authorized to review or join a list and whether or not it is archived. The subscription section holds the e-mail addresses and names of all list members. The REView command allows a listing of either or both of these sections (the default is both) for any list, provided the requester is authorized to do so. (At the discretion of the list owner(s), the REView command can be restricted in use to list members only and individual list members can restrict the appearance of their e-mail address and name in response to a REView command if they have set the CONCEAL mailing list option). The list-name parameter is the name of the ListServ list it is wished to review. The important options are:

  Short

  This option restricts the information received to the control section of a list (giving its definition parameters) and does not return the subscription section of a list (giving the list members).

  Countries

  Returns a list of members by the nationality given in their e-mail address.

  LOCal

  If the list is peered (that is, it is linked to other mailing lists of the same name but on different ListServ servers), listings of all of these mailing lists are sent in response to a REView command. The LOCal option can be used to suppress the propagation of the REView command to the ListServ servers hosting these peered mailing lists.

- SUBscribe list-name <full-name>

  Use the SUBscribe command to join a mailing list. The list-name parameter is the name of the list to which a subscription is required. The optional full-name parameter allows the subscriber to give the name by which they wish to be known on the mailing list. If specified, it should be the full, real name (at least first name and last name) and not an e-mail address. A request to join a mailing list can be processed in three ways: subscription to a list may be OPEN, CLOSED or BY-OWNER. If it is OPEN, the subscriber will be automatically added to the list and sent notification. If it is CLOSED, it is not possible to join the list, and ListServ will send a message telling the potential subscriber that the request has been rejected. If it is BY-OWNER, the subscription request will be forwarded to the list owner(s), who will decide whether or not to allow admission to the list (ListServ will inform the subscriber to whom the request has been forwarded). To see what kind of subscription a list has, use the REView command.

- UNSubscribe list-name * <(NETWIDE>

  Use the UNSubscribe command to leave a mailing list. The listname parameter is the name of a mailing list from which the subscription should be removed. It is possible for a subscriber to UNSubscribe from membership of all lists at any particular ListServ site by using the '*' (asterisk) character in place of a list name. To UNSubscribe from all ListServ servers on the network, include the (NETWIDE option.

- Query list-name | *

Upon joining a mailing list, a subscriber is assigned a default set of list options that control such things as the way mail is delivered when it is distributed and the type of notification ListServ will give when it distributes mail sent by a subscriber to a list. These are the personal list options that may be set by each subscriber on every mailing list to which they are subscribed. See the SET command for a complete descriptions of these options. The Query command can be used to review the personal list options in effect at any mailing list. The listname parameter is the name of the list concerned; if an '*' (asterisk) character is used instead of a list name, information is returned about the subscribers personal options for all lists to which they are subscribed at the particular ListServ server to which the command was sent.

- SET list-name | * options

Use the SET command to change the personal options for a mailing list. These options will remain in effect until they are explicitly changed. The list-name parameter is the name of the mailing list for which the options are to be changed. To effect the changes for all the lists subscribed to at a particular ListServ use the '*' (asterisk) character in place of a list name. After processing the SET command, ListServ will send confirmation of the successful alteration of the mailing list options via e-mail. The important options are:

Mail | DIGests | INDex | NOMail

These options of the SET command alter the way in which information is sent from a mailing list. The Mail option means that ListServ mail postings will be distributed as ordinary e-mail. This is the default. The DIGests and INDex options are available only if a list has had these features enabled by its owner(s). Digests hold all the mail messages sent to a list over a certain period of time. Instead of receiving each mail individually as it is distributed to list members, the mail in Digest form is sent in one batch for a given day, week or month. Note that mail is not edited with the DIGests option, it is simply distributed in batches. The INDex option will send only the date, time, subject, number of lines and the sender's name and address for all mail messages sent to a list. The text of the mail message will not be included. Subscribers may then select and retrieve any mail of interest from the list archive. Both the DIGests and INDex options provide a means of listening in to discussions on mailing lists without having to deal with large quantities of incoming mail messages. The NOMail option stops mail distribution from the list and is useful to prevent mail piling up during periods of absence. Upon return the SET command with the Mail option will restore the mail service.

SHORThdr | FULLhdr

All mail messages are comprised of header and body sections. The header section provides details such as the recipients, the original sender and the date and time a mail message was sent. The mail body section contains the text of a mail message. These options of the SET command indicate the type of mail headers used in the mail distributed from a mailing list. SHORThdr means that the mail header will include only the essential informational headers (for instance the Date:, To:, From:, Subject:, Sender: and Reply-to: headers). This is the default and may be changed to FULLhdr, which means that all (including non-essential) mail headers will be present in e-mail.

CONCEAL | NOCONCEAL

Indicates whether or not a subscriber's name and mail address will appear in the display of list members which is given in response to a REView command. The default is NOCONCEAL. Note that a complete list of members is always given to list owners and ListServ administrators regardless of this option.

• CONFIRM list-name

The CONFIRM command is used to renew a subscription to a list. Some mailing lists require subscription renewal at regular intervals (usually once a year). A mail message is automatically sent to list members indicating that they must send a CONFIRM command within a given number of days or they will be removed from the list. This command must be sent from the same e-mail address that received the confirmation notice. The list-name parameter is the name of the mailing list to which the subscription is being confirmed. ListServ will send a message confirming that the subscription has been confirmed.

Detailed documentation on ListServ (and related services) is available from the DOC FILELIST at:

LISTSERV@EARNCC.EARN.NET or LISTSERV@EARNCC.BITNET

This includes the ListServ User Guide which is available in both postscript and plain text formats. To obtain a list of available documents use the INDex command (see the section Commands for FILES).

3.6 FTP

FTP stands for File Transfer Protocol and is the tool for moving files from one computer to another across the Internet. If the service provider is connected to the Internet and allows its users to ftp out to other Internet sites, then 'anonymous ftp' access is automatically available. The usual procedure for using anonymous ftp is to type the command 'ftp machine-name', where 'machine-name' is the name of the machine to which a connection is required, and then to use 'anonymous' as the username and 'user@host' (i.e. your e-mail address) as the password when prompted for it by ftp. This will make a connection to the public data area of the host computer system. The term 'anonymous' is used because most individuals logging-in to remote machines will not have their own user account on that machine: instead everyone using FTP uses the generic user account 'anonymous'. To transfer files using anonymous FTP, a client program is used to copy computer files from the host machine. Slightly confusingly, FTP is the name not only of the protocol, but also of the program (File Transfer Program) that the user invokes to execute it.

Usually, when reference is made to a file available for FTP, two pieces of information are provided: the machine name and the path name. The machine name refers to the Internet address of the computer where the file is stored and the pathname is the directory on that machine where the file is located. Many files are 'mirrored' at several sites, that is to say that they are available from more than one host computer. It is worth finding local mirrors where possible.

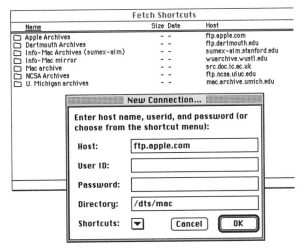

Figure 3.3 The Fetch FTP client

3.7 ARCHIE

'Archie' is a database of anonymous FTP sites and their contents and is supported by Bunyip Information System Inc., Canada. The software for it was written by the Archie Group (Alan Emtage, Peter Deutsch, and Bill Heelan) at McGill University in Montreal, Canada; the name was derived from 'archive with no v'. Archie keeps track of the contents of more than 1000 anonymous ftp sites, and allows a user to search for files on those sites using various different kinds of filename searches. Currently, this database contains more than 2 100 000 file names from anonymous FTP sites. This database is known as the Archie database.

The files made available at anonymous FTP sites range from software packages for various systems (Windows, MS-DOS, Macintosh, Unix, etc.), utilities (such as FTP client programmes, graphics converters, etc.), information or documentation files, through to mailing list or Usenet group discussion archives. At most FTP sites, the resources are organized hierarchically in directories and subdirectories. The database tracks both the directory path and the file names.

The archie database is automatically updated, thereby ensuring that the information is accurate. Using this database, users can easily find the location of files they need without logging onto several machines. Users on any network can access the archie database by electronic mail. Other means of access are available to users on the Internet. The archie database is maintained at the locations shown in Table 3.2.

Table 3.2 Archie database mirrors

Host	Country
archie.au	Australia
archie.edvz.uni-linz.ac.at	Austria
archie.univie.ac.at	Austria
archie.uqam.ca	Canada
archie.funet.fi	Finland
archie.th-darmstadt.de	Germany
archie.doc.ic.ac.uk	Great Britain
archie.ac.il	Israel
archie.unipi.it	Italy
archie.wide.ad.jp	Japan
archie.kyoto-u.ac.jp	Japan
archie.hana.nm.kr	Korea
archie.sogang.ac.kr	Korea
archie.nz	New Zealand
archie.rediris.es	Spain
archie.luth.se	Sweden
archie.switch.ch	Switzerland
archie.ncu.edu.tw	Taiwan
archie.ans.net	USA
archie.internic.net	USA
archie.rutgers.edu	USA
archie.sura.net	USA
archie.unl.edu	USA

Users are requested to respect a few basic rules when requesting information from an archie server:

• avoid connecting during working hours; most of the archie servers are not dedicated machines – they have local functions as well;
• make queries as specific as possible; the response will be quicker and more likely to be relevant;

• use the geographically closest archie server and, in particular, do not overload the transatlantic lines.

3.7.1 Using Archie

There are three ways to access the Archie database: via a local client, interactive Telnet session or electronic mail. Access by e-mail is described in Bob Rankin's *Accessing the Internet by e-mail*. The easiest (and most efficient) way to access Archie is with a local client. Usage of these clients is encouraged since they provide quick and easy non-interactive access to the Archie servers, leading to less load on the servers and better response time for the user.

Public domain clients for accessing Archie servers are available for most computer systems and the appropriate clients are available by anonymous FTP from the Archie sites in the directories /pub/archie/clients or /archie/clients.

When using a graphical interface client, the archie functions are accessed by pressing mouse buttons. The results are displayed with selectable fields for further explorations. Another useful source of anonymous FTP sites (with overviews of their contents) is maintained by Jon Granrose. The list is posted monthly to comp.misc, comp.sources.wanted and alt.sources.wanted.

Figure 3.4 shows the result of a search on the keyword 'architecture' and Figure 3.5 the contents of the first folder/directory returned.

Name	Size	Date	Zone	Machine
Aigen.An_architecture_of_consciousness	-	3/10/95	2	omega.gmd.de
architecture	65k	25/5/94	2	ftp.sunet.se
architecture	-	5/6/94	2	ftp.sunet.se
architecture	-	18/10/95	2	ftp.ibp.fr
architecture	61k	10/4/92	2	info.dkrz.de
architecture	65k	25/5/94	2	ftp.sunet.se
architecture	61k	8/4/92	2	info.dkrz.de
architecture	65k	2/12/92	3	ftp.std.com
architecture	-	27/4/95	3	sw-eng.falls-churc
architecture	65k	23/4/93	3	ftp.std.com
architecture.dvi.Z	24k	6/6/91	2	omega.gmd.de
architecture.ps.gz	24k	7/5/95	2	omega.gmd.de
draft-ietf-idpr-architecture-05.txt.gz	2k	26/7/93	2	ftp.forthnet.gr

Architecture from archie.doc.ic.ac.uk

Figure 3.4 Results of a search on 'Architecture'

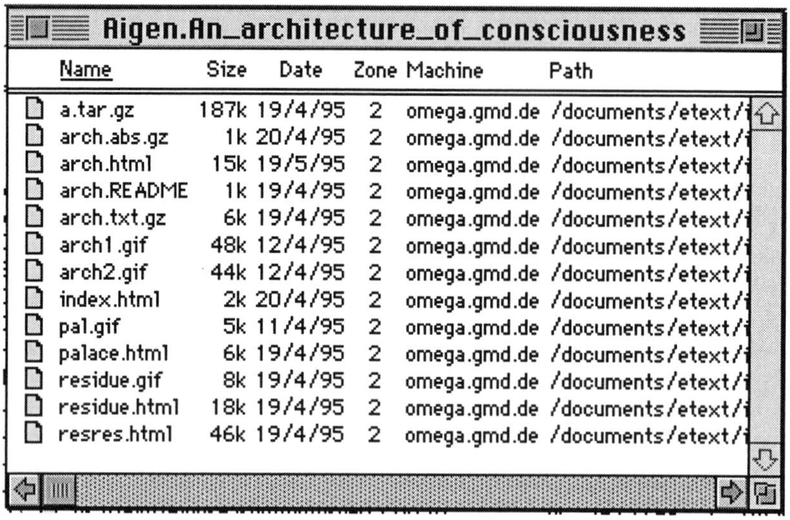

```
╔═════════════════════════════════════════════════════════╗
║ ▦ ▤  Aigen.An_architecture_of_consciousness  ▦ ▣ ║
╟─────────────────────────────────────────────────────────╢
║   Name          Size   Date   Zone Machine      Path      ║
║ ▯ a.tar.gz      187k 19/4/95   2  omega.gmd.de /documents/etext/ ⇧
║ ▯ arch.abs.gz     1k 20/4/95   2  omega.gmd.de /documents/etext/ 
║ ▯ arch.html      15k 19/5/95   2  omega.gmd.de /documents/etext/ 
║ ▯ arch.README     1k 19/4/95   2  omega.gmd.de /documents/etext/ 
║ ▯ arch.txt.gz     6k 19/4/95   2  omega.gmd.de /documents/etext/ 
║ ▯ arch1.gif      48k 12/4/95   2  omega.gmd.de /documents/etext/ 
║ ▯ arch2.gif      44k 12/4/95   2  omega.gmd.de /documents/etext/ 
║ ▯ index.html      2k 20/4/95   2  omega.gmd.de /documents/etext/ 
║ ▯ pal.gif         5k 11/4/95   2  omega.gmd.de /documents/etext/ 
║ ▯ palace.html     6k 19/4/95   2  omega.gmd.de /documents/etext/ 
║ ▯ residue.gif     8k 19/4/95   2  omega.gmd.de /documents/etext/ 
║ ▯ residue.html   18k 19/4/95   2  omega.gmd.de /documents/etext/ 
║ ▯ resres.html    46k 19/4/95   2  omega.gmd.de /documents/etext/ ⇩
╟─────────────────────────────────────────────────────────╢
║ ⇦ ▥                                              ⇨ ▣ ║
╚═════════════════════════════════════════════════════════╝
```

Figure 3.5 Files from the first source in Fig. 3.4

3.8 GOPHER

The Internet Gopher, usually just known as Gopher, is a distributed document delivery system. It allows users to seamlessly explore, search and retrieve information from various sources and in various formats. Gopher can simplify what might otherwise be a series of separate operations (an Archie search followed by FTP for example) into a sequence of gopher commands. Whilst the name is a pun on 'go for' the software is named after the official animal of the State of Minnesota. This is not really such an obscure derivation as the software was originally developed as a campus information network by the Computer and Information Services group at the University of Minnesota. Gopher presents information to the user as a series of nested menus, similar to the organization of a directory system with many sub-directories and files. However, in Gopher's case, the sub-directories and files may be located either on the local server site or on remote sites served by other Gopher servers, but as far as the user is concerned, all of the menus appear to come from the same place. This 'GopherSpace' includes some 1500 Gopher servers, giving access to over a million files. The information objects that Gopher operates on may be text or binary files, directory information, image or sound. Gopher also offers gateways to other information systems such as VERONICA, WAIS, WWW and Archie, and is able to navigate in FTP directories and download files.

3.8.1 Using Gopher

Gopher uses the client-server model to provide access to the Gopher web and a full Internet connection is required to access Gopher. Public domain clients for accessing a Gopher server are available by anonymous FTP from many sites, including the 'home' Gopher at Minnesota (boombox.micro.umn.edu in the directory /pub/gopher).

Most Gopher clients allow the creation of 'bookmarks'. A bookmark keeps track of the exact location of a Gopher item, regardless of where it resides. Thus it is possible to directly reach frequently used services which are otherwise located far from the top-level menu. The bookmarks thus act as a form of customized Gopher menu.

Some capabilities of a local Gopher client are linked to resources in the host computer. For the interpretation of sound and graphics files, the Gopher client looks for appropriate software on the host computer and passes the file to that software. When the task is completed, control is returned to the Gopher client.

More information on Gopher is to be found in the Gopher FAQ which is posted in the Usenet newsgroup comp.infosystems.gopher. The file is also obtainable by anonymous FTP from:
pit-manager.mit.edu:/pub/usenet/news.answers/gopher-faq.

Figure 3.6 shows a typical Gopher menu and Figure 3.7 the result of a selecting 'Gophers by Subject' and then 'Architecture'.

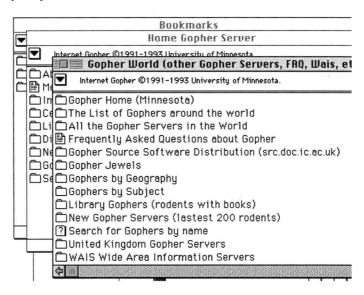

Figure 3.6 Gopher menu

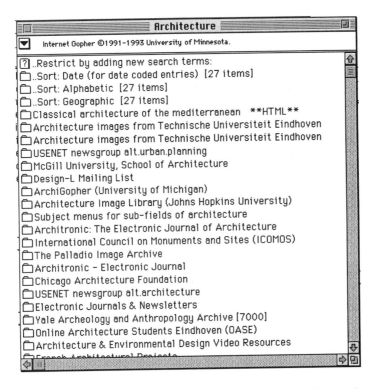

Figure 3.7 The result of following 'Gophers by Subject' then 'Architecture'

3.9 VERONICA

VERONICA is the 'Archie companion' for Gopher. It was designed as a solution to the problem of resource finding in the rapidly expanding GopherSpace. Each individual server maintained searchable indexes, but there was no overall index covering all of the Gopher servers. Steven Foster and Fred Barrie of the University of Nevada, Reno developed the 'Very Easy Rodent Oriented Net-wide Index to Computerised Archives' to overcome this problem. The VERONICA index contains over 10 million items from more than 6 000 gopher servers.

VERONICA is accessible from most top-level Gopher menus. VERONICA operates on a keyword search, returning a menu composed of items whose titles match the keyword specification. These are directly accessible as Gopher selections or for saving as bookmarks. A comprehensive description of VERONICA search methods is available from the VERONICA menus.

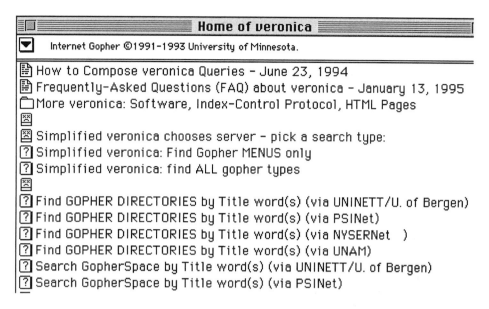

Figure 3.8 VERONICA menu

3.10 TELNET

Telnet is a facility which allows computer users to log-in remotely from one computer to another. When telnet is run the local system:

- opens a connection to the specified remote system;
- interacts with the remote system as though it was a terminal rather than a computer;
- operates to the local user as a 'terminal emulator';
- forwards the user's input as its output to the remote computer which treats it as terminal input;
- forwards the remote system's output to the local user.

Telnet clients are available for most computer systems and the details of their operation varies considerably. The use of these clients is, however, essentially the same. To use telnet the target system's Internet name or IP address must be known. When a telnet connection to that system has been established the user is prompted for a password. In the context of the uses of telnet required to access the services described in this book it is usually sufficient to simply hit 'Return' in response to the password prompt or provide your e-mail name and address. This is known as 'anonymous telnet' and is similar to anonymous ftp. Sometimes the host system log-in prompt will provide details of what user identification and/or password is required.

3.11 WORLD WIDE WEB

The World Wide Web (usually abbreviated to 'the web', WWW or W3) is an information system based on 'hypertext'. Hypertext documents are linked to each other through a selected set of words, thus enabling the user to move from document to document (usually called 'navigate') within a network of information. The World Wide Web was developed by Tim Berners-Lee and others at CERN, the European Particle Physics Laboratory in Geneva, as a way of organizing information for their researchers. The hypertext system allows seamless links to all information sources – Gopher menus, WAIS databases, FTP directories, Usenet newsgroups as well as documents prepared specially for the WWW. WWW presents the user with documents and links. A link will lead to another document, which, in turn contains further links. Some documents may be indexes, containing links to many other documents. Individual documents may be held on different computer systems anywhere in the world.

The web is the fastest growing section of the Internet. In the second half of 1993, the web doubled in size in under 3 months, and even today the doubling period is only around 5 months. Additionally, the percentage of commercial web sites has increased dramatically. The numbers below show the percentage growth in the .com domain, which excludes foreign commercial sites (such as the .co.uk domain, etc.).

Table 3.3 WWW growth (data from Matthew Gray of net.Genesis)

Month	No. of web sites	% .com sites	Hosts per web server
June '93	130	1.5	13 000
Dec. '93	623	4.6	3 475
June '94	2 738	13.5	1 095
Dec. '94	10 022	18.3	451
June '95	23 500	31.3	270

The growth of the web has been remarkable even when compared to the Internet at large, as shown by the number of hosts per web server. In June of 1995, even with the phenomenal growth of the Internet, the number of web servers soared to a point where one in every 270 machines on the Internet is a web server. (Figure 3.9).

3.11.1 How the links are made

The key to the organization of the WWW is the URL or Uniform Resource Locator. This 'code' is a unique descriptor which can identify any document, graphic, Gopher menu or item, Usenet article, computer or file directory anywhere on the Internet. As the format for specifying a URL is standardized across all services it is worth spending

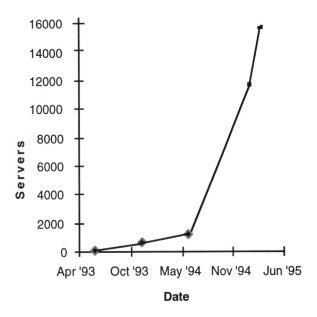

Figure 3. 9 WWW server growth

some time to understand it. In many respects it is like an e-mail address, but with a few extra pieces of information added. In general terms a URL is composed of the following elements:

service://hostname:port/directorypath

Not all of these elements necessarily appear in all URLs, but the basic structure is important. For example:

http://www.strath.ac.uk/home.html

In this URL the service is defined as being 'http' – that is HyperText Transport Protocol (the standard method of moving web documents across the Internet). The http immediately indicates to the client program being used the way in which it will need to connect to the document. The computer that holds the document is **www.strath.ac.uk**. Here all of the component parts are familiar from e-mail addresses: the computer ('web server') is called www and is at strath, an academic institution in the U.K. No port is specified as this server uses the default setting (80) and thus does not require the explicit specification in the URL. After the slash, home.html specifies the required file. The html indicates that the file is formatted in HyperText Markup Language, the native format of the WWW. In several places in the reference sections of this book files are referenced as .htm. This is not a misprint but an allowable alternative which, if used, must be followed. Unlike e-mail addresses, all URLs are case-sensitive

The following example shows the version of URL used for FTP:

ftp://info.cern.ch/pub/www/src

This URL identifies a file archive at CERN. The service identifier specifies ftp (File Transfer Protocol); the server is info at cern in Switzerland (ch). Upon connection to that server the URL specifies that the browser should move through the pub directory to the subdirectory www and then to the sub-subdirectory src and display the files it finds there.

Gopher URLs are slightly more complicated. A basic gopher connection takes the form: gopher://gopher.nrel.gon:70. By default, specifying a host within Gopher makes a connection to the top-level menu of the host. Gopher menu items consist of files or other menus, and selecting an item either retrieves the file or moves the user to the selected directory. This difference between files and directories is reflected in the construction of the URL. Within a gopher URL, the prefix 0 denotes a file and 1 indicates a directory.

One further example shows a differently constructed URL:

news:comp.infosystems.www

This URL specifies that the browser is to read the Newsgroup comp.infosystems.www. The service identifier news is clearly specified but no hostname appears. This is because, in configuring the browser program, the user will have had to specify a Usenet host; this is usually the news server at the Internet provider being used. The URL thus has the host information already and simply requires the newsgroup name.

3.11.2 Interpreting URLs

As URLs have to specify exactly both the format and location of different types of files they have strict regulations regarding their construction. The most important to be aware of are that they cannot contain spaces and that they are case-sensitive. Uppercase and lowercase letters must be typed exactly as specified (even on otherwise case insensitive systems).

Given these restrictions on their use, however, it is possible to manipulate URLs, given a basic understanding of their structure. A URL that gives access to the main CERN WWW page is:

http://info.cern.ch/hypertext/WWW/TheProject.html

However, there could well be other items of interest in the hypertext or WWW directories that are passed through to retrieve the specified file. To examine the WWW file the URL may be abbreviated to:

http://info.cern.ch/hypertext/WWW/

and a list of resources at that higher level will be retrieved. This approach may be used with most of the URLs in the reference section of this book.

3.11.3 Accessing the WWW

A client program (known as a 'browser') is required to access the WWW. A graphics oriented browser is preferable, and public domain software, documentation and installation instructions are available via anonymous FTP from a number of sources, including CERN itself (info.cern.ch in the directory /pub/www/src). A list of WWW clients is at:

http://info.cern.ch/hypertext/WWW/Clients.html

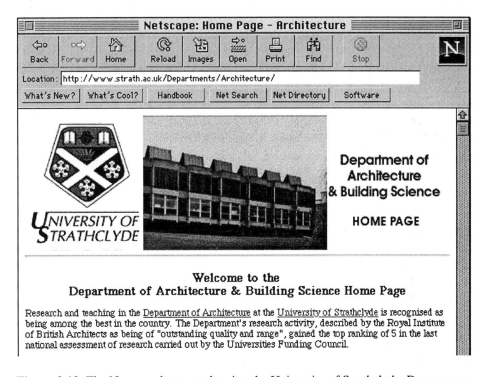

Figure 3.10 The Netscape browser showing the University of Strathclyde, Department of Architecture and Building Science home page

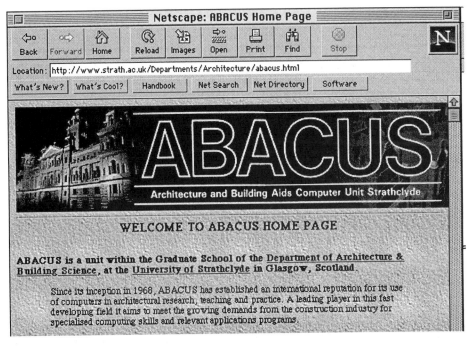

Figure 3.11 Following a link on the Architecture home page brings up the ABACUS page.

3.11.4 Further information on WWW

As the web is the fastest growing section of the Internet the only up-to-date source of information is the web itself. Places to look for information include:

- The main CERN WWW page:
  http://info.cern.ch/hypertext/WWW/TheProject.html
- General information on WWW is at:
  http://www.bsdi.com/server/doc/web-info.html
- WWW FAQ file: a set of answers to introductory WWW questions:
  http://sunsite.unc.edu/boutell/faq/index.html
- Usenet newsgroups
  For general discussion: comp.infosystems.www
  A list of other web related newsgroups can be found at:
  http://info.cern.ch/hypertext/WWW/Newsgroups.html
- An on-line guide to the WWW is provided by Kevin Hughes' *Entering the World-Wide-Web : A Guide to Cyberspace* which can be found at:
  http://www.eit.com/web/www.guide

- *Surfing the Internet*, a guide to Web sources, is available at:
  nysernet.org:/pub/guides/surfing.2.0.3.txt
- A 15-lesson training guide and tutorial for new Internet users with software and educational links for all areas of the Internet (also including hundreds of not-so-serious, strange, bizarre and funny links all over the Web) is at:
  http://www.geopages.com/TheTropics/1945/index1.htm
- Heriot Watt University produces a newsletter about WWW resources at:
  http://www.hw.ac.uk/libWWW/irn/irn.html
- WWW Software
  http://www.steview.com
  This site is dedicated to the sharing of information about WWW software, including WWW Programming, HTML, Graphics, Security, Server Setup/Maintenance, Internet Connections, Free Software, and Frequently Asked Questions. There is also a News Forum where questions, problems, statements and follow-ups on anything related to WWW software may be posted. Most of these areas also include tutorials, examples and links to other relevant sites.

3.12 WAIS

Whilst Archie and VERONICA provide ways of searching archived files by keyword searches based on document titles, WAIS (the Wide Area Information Server) is designed to find information using natural language queries on document contents. The result of a WAIS search is a set of documents that contain the words of the query.

WAIS uses the client-server model to provide access to the databases. The WAIS project was begun at Thinking Machines Corporation under the leadership of Brewster Kahle who later set up a new company, WAIS Inc., to sell customized, fully-supported commercial client software for WAIS searching. However, client software for WAIS is freely available by anonymous FTP from a variety of sources. WAIS information is available in the Usenet newsgroup comp.infosystems.wais and software and documents on using WAIS are available by anonymous FTP from ftp.wais.com, quake.think.com and ftp.cnidr.org. A bibliography of WAIS information is maintained by Barbara Lincoln Brooks of WAIS Inc. (barbara@wais.com) and is available from ftp.wais.com in the directory /pub/wais-inc-doc along with many other WAIS documents.

3.12.1 Using WAIS

The client interface differs slightly on various platforms, however, the queries are performed in the same way, whatever the interface.

1. The user selects a set of databases to be searched from the list of available databases (Figure 3.12).

Figure 3.12 WAIS databases

2. The user formulates a query by giving keywords to be searched for (Figure 3.13).
3. When the query is run, WAIS asks for information from each selected database.
4. Headlines of documents satisfying the query are displayed. The selected documents contain the requested words and phrases. Selected documents are ranked according to the number of matches (Figure 3.14).

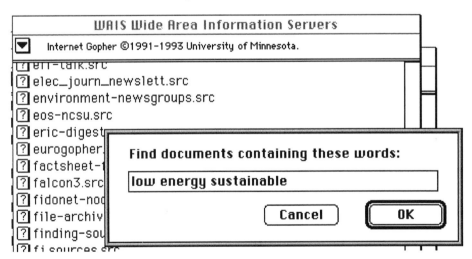

Figure 3.13 Specifying the keywords for the search

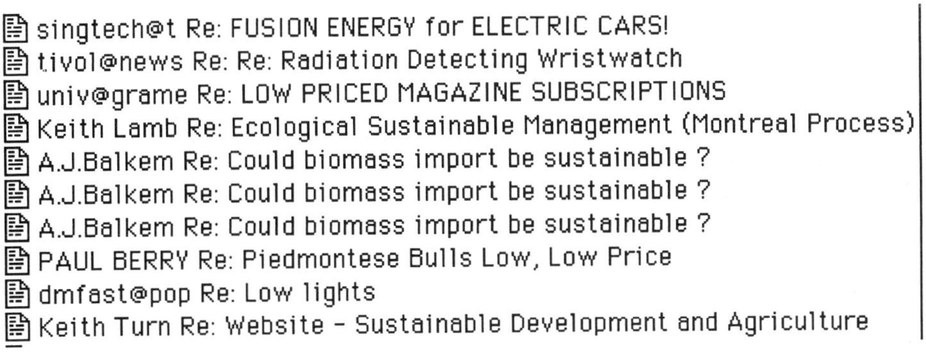

📄 singtech@t Re: FUSION ENERGY for ELECTRIC CARS!
📄 tivol@news Re: Re: Radiation Detecting Wristwatch
📄 univ@grame Re: LOW PRICED MAGAZINE SUBSCRIPTIONS
📄 Keith Lamb Re: Ecological Sustainable Management (Montreal Process)
📄 A.J.Balkem Re: Could biomass import be sustainable ?
📄 A.J.Balkem Re: Could biomass import be sustainable ?
📄 A.J.Balkem Re: Could biomass import be sustainable ?
📄 PAUL BERRY Re: Piedmontese Bulls Low, Low Price
📄 dmfast@pop Re: Low lights
📄 Keith Turn Re: Website – Sustainable Development and Agriculture

Figure 3.14 Part of the document list returned

5. To retrieve a document, the user simply selects it from the resulting list.
6. If the response is incomplete, the user can state the question differently or feed back to the system any one or more of the selected documents found relevant.
7. When the search is run again, the results will be updated to include documents which are similar to the ones selected, meaning documents which share a large number of common words.
8 Note that the document list contains files which are not of direct interest, the keyword 'low' having triggered 'low price' in several cases.

4

General information sources

This chapter discusses the three main ways of searching for information on the Internet. The first is to use a 'search-engine' which will search a database of sites to find matches against specified keywords. The second is to use a general 'index site' which holds a collection of site references organized by subject. The last is to go to a specific construction industry index site.

4.1 SEARCH ENGINES

4.1.1 WWW Search Engines

As the web grows so do the number of 'search engines' that attempt to index the ever-increasing number of sites. This list of places to go to to look for directions was effective at the end of 1995, but no guide could possibly hope to list everything that is out there, and there can be no guarantee that addresses given will still be operational at any time in the future. Unfortunately, the fastest and most comprehensive search engines tend to be the newest.

A good place to start searching is with the reference pages of the main browser programs. These pages all offer links to several search engines and other search related pages on the web. Using these pages is straightforward but a forms capable web browser such as Netscape or Mosaic is required to enter the search criteria. The Netscape search page is directly accessible at:

http://home.mcom.com/home/internet-search.html

At the time of writing, the current 'hot' search engine was Alta Vista. It is both large – over 16 million web pages and 13 000 Usenet newsgroups indexed – and fast. It is at:

http://www.altavista.digital.com

Alta Vista offers a number of notable features, including:

- boolean searching with AND, OR, NOT and NEAR operators;
- case-sensitive and quoted string searching;
- ability to search on portions of a URL.

OpenText Corporation
http://www.opentext.com
OpenText Web Index
http://opentext.uunet.ca:8081/intro.html
http://opentext.uunet.ca:8080/omw.html
The OpenText Web Index is another relatively new search engine: it builds its indexes on full text (rather than just page titles) and is updated each night in an effort to track the web as closely as possible. It has currently indexed about half a million pages (http, gopher, ftp), and intends, in the near future, to index over 2 million pages and over 1 billion words of text.

Lycos
http://www.lycos.com/
Robot catalogue of web, gopher and ftp sites. Even though Lycos has now signed a non-exclusive agreement with Microsoft to be carried on the new MicroSoft Network, Lycos' Dr. Mauldin has emphasized the point that Lycos will remain free to all users.

Yahoo (Yet Another Hierarchically Officious Oracle)
Home page: http://www.yahoo.com
General search engine: http://www.yahoo.com/search.html
Architecture links: http://www.yahoo.com/art/architecture
Civil Engineering links:
http://www.yahoo.com/science/engineering/civil_engineering/
Construction links:
http://www.yahoo.com/science/engineering/civil_engineering/construction
The index is searchable by web page title and keyword. Once the search is completed a list of sites is presented that the user can automatically link to. This Home page is one of the most popular in the WWW and may be busy or slow. The search index is free.

W3 Search Engines Page
http://cuiwww.unige.ch/meta-index.html
The W3 page offers multiple searches to be initiated from the same page using several different search engines and criteria. The results of the search are then presented onscreen with an option to save the results page and download for future reference. The University of Geneva also supports a WWW catalogue that may be downloaded and run directly from the user's own system:
http://cuiwww.unige.ch/w3catalog/

Internet Search Engines
http://www.netins.net/showcase/nwc-iowa/
Collection of Internet search engines available for public use.

Search Tools Page
http://galaxy.einet.net/search-other.html
Connections to some thirty search tools and indexes.

4.1.2 U.K. based search engines

UK Index
http://www.ukindex.co.uk/
Fully searchable index using both free text and category combinations. Also provides:
UK Index Quick Reference, The Beginner's Guide to the Net, The Data Protection Act
and The Net, Sites new to the UK Index this week.

Yell
http://www.yell.co.uk
The U.K.'s 'Internet Yellow Pages'. A comprehensive guide to what's on the web in the
U.K. (Figure 4.1).

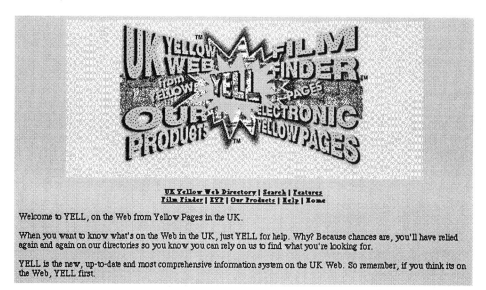

Figure 4.1 YELL home page

Searching the Internet
http://www.shef.ac.uk/uni/academic/I-M/is/search.html

JumpStation II
http://www.stir.ac.uk/jsbin/jsii
Robot search engine for locating sites and documents on the Web.

Global On-line Directory
http://www.cityscape.co.uk/gold/search2.html

4.1.3 Information on WWW robots

Virtually all of the data in the search engines' databases are collected automatically. This is done by 'Web Robots' – special programs that search out keywords in URLs and, sometimes, documents themselves. It is possible to utilize similar tools directly.

4.1.3.1 General information about web robots
List of Robots
http://asearch.mccmedia.com/embed.html

WWW Robots, Wanderers and Spiders
http://web.nexor.co.uk/mak/doc/robots/robots.html
A general reference for information on web robots.

Information on web search tools
http://cuiwww.unige.ch/meta-index.html

MOMspider WWW94 paper
http://www.ics.uci.edu/WebSoft/MOMspider/WWW94/paper.html
Roy Fielding's description of MOMspider and how other web robots work.

Intelligent Software Agents Resources and Information
http://retriever.cs.umbc.edu:80/agents/

MIT Media Lab's Autonomous Agents Group
http://agents.www.media.mit.edu/groups/agents/

4.1.3.2 Searching Robots
SG-Scout home page
http://www-swiss.ai.mit.edu:80/~ptbb/SG-Scout/SG-Scout.html
A Web cataloguing robot which is run every few months to update its data.

World Wide Web Wanderer Index
http://www.netgen.com/cgi/wandex
A searchable index of over 28 000 documents from over 14 000 sites.

The WebCrawler
http://webcrawler.com

General information sources

53

The WebCrawler II
http://webcrawler.cs.washington.edu/WebCrawler/WebQuery.htm

The WWW Worm
http://wwww.cs.colorado.edu/wwww

GNN Home page
http://gnn.com/gnn/gnn.html
Has a huge list of home pages from around the web.

SavvySearch
http://guaraldi.cs.colostate.edu:2000/
http://www.cs.colostate.edu/~dreiling/smartform.html
A search system designed to query multiple Internet search engines simultaneously. It includes e-mail addresses, Usenet, FTP sites, gopher and web space.

4.1.3.3 Other Useful Robots
CheckWeb
http://www.stuff.com/~bcutter/home/programs/checkweb.html
A robot that checks web documents for dead links.

WWW growth-bot
http://www.netgen.com/info/growth.html
A robot that measures the size of the Web.

4.1.4 Other (non-WWW) search tools

Archie Request Form
http://hoohoo.ncsa.uiuc.edu/archie.html

Veronica
gopher://veronica.scs.unr.edu/11/veronica

WAIS WAISGate
http://www.wais.com/newhomepages/directory-or-servers.html
http://www.wais.com/newhomepages/waisgate.html

Discussion Groups
http://alpha.acast.nova.edu/cgi-bin/lists
http://alpha.acast.nova.edu/listserv.html

Find Newsgroups
http://www.cen.uiuc.edu/cgi-bin/find-news

Usenet Groups Search Page
http://sunsite.unc.edu/usenet-i/
The 'Official' description reads: 'Welcome to the Usenet Info Center, your source for Usenet Information. This service contains pointers to many useful Usenet FAQs and the Newsgroups Info Center – what the project is really about. The Newsgroups Info Center is your source for info on Usenet's newsgroups. It contains a heritage browsable list of the newsgroups and a way to search for a group of interest. The Newsgroups Info Center is one of the first big attempts to gather all the useful information on a group in one location; including a long description.'

Stanford University Electronic Library
http://sift.stanford.edu
Enables the monitoring of Usenet newsgroups by keyword entry.

Who is on Usenet?
email to: mail-server@rtfm.mit.edu
Subject: send usenet-addresses/UserName
(note that there is no space between addresses/Username)
This is a search service available using email. The subject line is the command line that requests a search on the user name specified. This will return everyone matching that name who has ever posted to Usenet.

Gopher Searchable Look-up site
gopher://boombox.micro.umn.edu
University of Minnesota 'Home' gopher. The 'mother of all gophers' still maintains an impressive site which has become an Internet standard in the world of gophering.

Gopher Searchable Look-up site
gopher://liberty.uc.wlu.edu
Washington and Lee University in Virginia, U.S., provides an alternative to 'boombox'. Includes a WAIS-indexed database and provides a list of new gophers updated daily.

Gopher Jewels
gopher://cwis.usc.edu
then select /Other Gophers and Information Resources/Gopher-Jewels
Or use the URL:
gopher://cwis.usc.edu:70/11/Other_Gophers_and_Information_Resources/
Gopher-Jewels

Probably, in terms of links, the best single gopher URL available. Apart from the quantity of information directly available at this site it also provides pointers and gopher links to elsewhere and includes search engines to navigate around gopher-space.

Yanoff Internet List
gopher://gopher.uwm.edu
then select /Remote Information Servers/Special Internet Connections
A selection of sites for gopher clients, arranged in subjects.

Internet People search services
gopher://yaleinfo.yale.edu:7700/11/Internet-People
Lots of links to gopher, whois and telnet sites that can search for netusers. Also searches for Usenet posts to provide a similar service to the e-mail 'Who is on Usenet?'.

4.2 GENERAL INDEX SITES

Yanoff Internet List WWW URLs
Yanoff special internet connections
http://www.uwm.edu/Mirror/inet.services.html
http://www.w3.org/hyper-text/DataSources/Yanoff.html
These are the best known general index sites.

BigSurf Netguide
http://www.capman.com.au/bigsurf/
A large listing of web sites with special sections for Macintosh computer users.

CUI W3 Catalog
http://cuiwww.unige.ch/w3catalog
Huge linked searchable catalogue of web sites.

Point
http://www.pointcom.com
A new web service that plans to have 1 000 new reviews compiled each month.

Industry.Net
http://www.industry.com
A business related web search guide which includes an online yellow page listing and product information on all types of products and vendors. The database is searchable.

The Keepers of Lists
http://www.dtd.com/cgi-bin/topall
A 'list of lists', updated daily. Publishes a 'Top Ten' of most visited sites.

The Whole Internet Catalog
http://nearnet.gnn.com/wic/newrescat.toc.html
The electronic version of the 'Whole Earth Catalog'.

O'Reilly's Global Network Navigator and Catalog
http://nearnet.gnn.com
http://nearnet.gnn.com/gnn/wic/alpha.toc.html
Index of net resources. Travel information, financial, weather and a host of other links and data.

Planet Earth Home Page Virtual Library
http://godric.nosc.mil/planet_earth/info.html
Includes a lot of science related and Earth environment links.

Listserv of Top-Ten URLs
Send e-mail to: listserv@clark.net with:
Subject line: Subscribe top-ten
Message body: subscribe top-ten <your email address>
In return the keepers of the listserv will send updates and new URLs that they deem as worthy of top-ten status.

McKinley Internet Directory
http://www.mckinley.com
A 'yellow pages' directory of over 80 000 URLs and one of the largest directory listings available on the web to date. Sites are reviewed and rated by the McKinley Group's staff.

Internet White pages
http://home.mcom.com/home/internet_white_pages.html
Links and pointers to listings and searchers that can find individuals on the Internet. Includes e–mail addresses and web URLs. This site is operated by Netscape Communications.

Internet Yellow Pages directory and the Four11 listings
http://yellow.com/
http://www.four11.com
The Internet 'phone books' which contain listings of both personal and business addresses.

NetPages
http://www.aldea.com/wwwindex.html

General index sites

A combined white pages and yellow pages directory of the Internet offering a searchable database.

4.2.1 On-line libraries

The WWW Virtual Library
http://www.stars.com/Vlib/
http://www.w3.org/hypertext/DataSources/bySubject/Overview.html
One of the main information sources on the web. The various sections of the 'catalogue' are maintained at different locations and these URLs provide the index links.
The Virtual Library (Architecture) is at:
http://www.clr.toronto.edu:1080/VIRTUALLIB/arch.html
Virtual Library (Civil Engineering) (Figure 4.2)
http://www.ce.gatech.edu/WWW-CE/home.html
Virtual Library (Engineering)
http://epims1.gsfc.nasa.gov/engineering/engineering.html
Virtual Library (Landscape):
http://www.clr.toronto.edu:1080/VIRTUALLIB/larch.html
Virtual Library (Computing)
http://www.utexas.edu.computer/vcl

Figure 4.2 WWW Virtual Library: Civil Engineering
(http://www.ce.gatech.edu/WWW-CE/home.html)

Einet Subject Pages
http://galaxy.einet.net/galaxy/Arts-and-Humanities/Architecture.html
http:///galaxy/Engineering-and-Technology/Civil-and-Construction-Engineering.html (Figure 4.3)
http://galaxy.einet.net/galaxy/Humanities/Arts/Architecture/Interior-Design.html
http://galaxy.einet.net/galaxy/Humanities/Arts/Architecture/Landscape-Architecture.html

Architectural Engineering - *Civil and Construction Engineering* - *Engineering and Technology*

See also

- Architecture - Humanities
- Architecture - General Products and Services

New Items - *less than 7 days old*

- California Contractors State License Board - Information Services

Articles

- Electrical Hazards - Aluminum Wiring

Directories

- AECNET-The Electronic Resource Network of Architecture, Engineering and
- ICARIS Research Network for Civil Engineering and Architecture (Slovenia)
- Marshalls Plc. Home Page
- Univ at Buffalo PAIRC, Planning & Architecture Internet Resource Center

Figure 4.3 Tradewave Galaxy Einet Architecture and Engineering index (http:///galaxy/Engineering-and-Technology/Civil-and-Construction-Engineering.html)

Reader's Guide to Periodical Literature
Telnet to: lib.uwstout.edu
Log-in as 'library'. Exit by Control+D twice.
An often overlooked information source which can be used to perform comprehensive searches through hundreds (thousands?) of magazines published in the US. Search by author, subject, title or keyword to find the resources or articles. The search results are then printed to screen and include a small abstract of the source article and information about the publication it is in.

On-Line Complete Ready Reference
gopher://sol1.solinet.net
Once connected choose the On-Line Ready Reference menu item
This site contains such things as the Periodic Table of Elements, Webster's Dictionary, Roget's Thesaurus, US telephone area codes, Zip Code directories, Amtrak train schedules, US State Department Travel advisories and more.

Online Computer Library Center (OCLC)
http://www.oclc.org
A not-for-profit government funded project that is attempting to catalogue many of the Internet resources into a large organized 'virtual' library.

The WELLgopher
gopher://gopher.well.com
This gopher site houses a huge library organized under subject headings. It is an especially good source of information on the development of the Internet and issues related to the use of the Internet.

CIA Web server
http://www.ic.gov
Global facts galore. Extensive information on virtually every country in the world.

Web Site for Educators, Students, Scientists and Engineers
http://www.thomson.com
gopher://gopher.thomson.com
FTP to: ftp.thomson.com (contains the file archives only)
This site includes a searchable database of more than 20 000 education, reference, scholarly, scientific, technical and business products, as well as discipline-specific Resource Centres, electronic discussion and newsletter lists, and on-line supplements to products. The number of products will continually increase to an estimated 50 000 within the next twelve months. On-line order forms enable users to place orders for texts, journals and electronic products (video, software and CD-ROM).

4.3 CONSTRUCTION INDUSTRY LISTS

4.3.1 Architectural Lists

Jeanne Brown's List
http://www.unlv.edu/library/ARCH/index.html
The original annotated list of Architectural web sites, compiled by Jeanne M. Brown, Architecture Studies Librarian at the University of Nevada, Las Vegas (Figure 4.4). The list is mirrored at LAVA which may give a better response for European users:
http://www.tue.nl/lava/other/brown/

Section 1:

WEB AND GOPHER SITES

Section 1.1: ARCHITECTURE AND COMPUTING

1.1.1

artNtec (Architecture and Technology) [http://uxa.cso.uiuc.edu/~phoebec/]
Created and maintained by Phoebe Jacobson, this site is an innovative presentation and exploration of handling information. Using four design interfaces (outline, hypertext, icon, and floor plan), artNtec provides "a series of world-wide web documents pointing to on-line resources for architectural CAD. The purpose of artNtec is to provide a world-wide network environment for CAD users to interact with information and extend their learning resources."

Figure 4.4 The first section of Jeanne Brown's List

LAVA

http://www.tue.nl/lava/

The Lab voor Architectuur provides links to related information sources, reviews, discussions and examples of student work from the University of Eindhoven.

PAIRC

http://www.arch.buffalo.edu/pairc/

The Planning and Architecture Internet Resource Center (Figure 4.5); Dan Tasman's list of planning and architecture related Internet pointers. Categories include: architecture and planning firms and services; architecture exhibits and images; building and construction technology resources; CAD and GIS resources; census information and demographic resources; conferences and design competitions; economic development agencies and resources; environmental resources; government agencies and services; historic preservation resources; housing resources; international planning resources; journals and publications; mailing lists; miscellaneous planning and architecture resources; municipal governments and local information; organizations; schools and academic departments; text files; transportation resources; and usenet newsgroups.

Matiu Carr's Architecture Internet Resources

http://archpropplan.auckland.ac.nz/misc/sources1.html

Annotated listing covering the following areas: schools, journals, planning, property, libraries, galleries and miscellaneous.

ArchWeb

http://cidoc.iuav.unive.it/architettura/archweb.ope/homenuova.html

Substantial set of links in five broad categories: worldwide architecture, degree programs, resources on the net, architectural history, and landscape and environment.

The lists look similar to those on the WWW Virtual Library for Architecture (see section 4.2.1).

PAIRC now contains over **1,500** links to Web, Gopher and FTP sites with urban planning, architecture and landscape architecture related information. Most links have annotated descriptions. PAIRC also contains information about 110 architecture and planning related mailing lists.

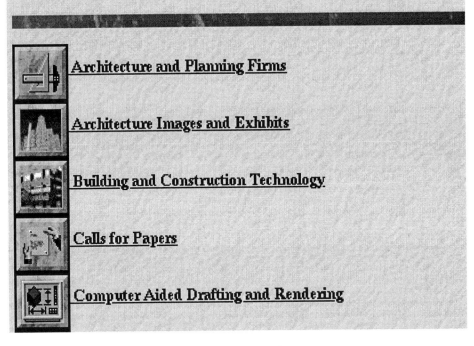

Architecture and Planning Firms

Architecture Images and Exhibits

Building and Construction Technology

Calls for Papers

Computer Aided Drafting and Rendering

Figure 4.5 The first part of the PAIRC index

ArchiWeb
http://www.archiweb.com/
ArchiWeb is an information exchange relating to architecture on the Internet with particular reference to Japanese architecture. The Digital Library section is extensive (500 links, some to general sites). The Virtual Lab is for students or studios and the Architecture Yellow Pages is for companies. A section on Japanese Traditional architecture has been posted.

De Architectura
http://www.dea.polimi.it/dea/dea.htm
This site promises to become an 'on-line European information bookshelf' with information ranging 'from EC news to technical handbooks and data sheets, research results and papers'. Currently just a few links, but ambitious goals.

4.3.2 Construction lists

AEC Net
http://www.aecnet.com
The Electronic Resource Network of Architecture, Engineering and Construction. AECNet provides World Wide Web services, Internet access, and an Internet based bulletin board service for professionals in the architecture, engineering and commercial construction industry. The BBS software is free and can be had via anonymous FTP to ftp.aecnet.com in the /pub/aecnet/ directory (both Windows and Mac available).

The AEC InfoCenter provides a keyword search engine to retrieve a variety of data. It holds a database of over six thousand building product manufacturers organized using the Masterformat system from the Construction Specifications Institute. The code directory includes contact information for every code and regulatory agency in every state in the US, and will include synopses of the code and regulatory structure for each state as well. The site has also been enhanced by the addition of the full text of the New York State Uniform Building Code, the New York State Energy Conservation Code for Construction and the complete Americans With Disabilities Act Accessibility Guidelines, complete with illustrations.

Building Industry Exchange
http://www.building.org/

The Building and Home Improvement Products Network (Figures 4.6 and 4.7)
http://www.build.com/

Figure 4.6 Build.com home page

Construction industry lists

Builder Sites

Real Estate & Builder Connection
AEC InfoCenter
The Home Front - The internet reference guide for the Professional Home Builder.
The Home Builders Utopia - A consumers guide to Professional Home Builders on the Internet
BouwWeb - a link to the Building Industry in the Netherlands
Home & Design Online - a global information resource and communications network for the housing industry
Log Homes on the Internet - featuring a log home company each month and a discussion group.
BuildingOnline A Building Products Search Engine
TrussPros Information headquarters for building components.

Construction Sites

AECNET: Architecture, Engineering, and Construction
Building Industry Exchange (BIX) - Global Center for Building Industry Businesses, Resources, & Communication, including Education, Career, News, Library, Chat Forums, Newsgroups, Classified Advertising, and a Virtual Industrial Park for architecture, engineering, construction, real estate development, government agencies, universities, environmental protection services, health & safety services, manufacturers, distributors, planners, designers, consultants, attorneys and related businesses.
Index - Explorer Software - World Wide Web heavy construction server
Galaxy Construction
The Construction Site
The Construction Web
TC&I Electronic Highway - an online service for the Transportation, Construction and Industrial industries.
InterPRO Resources, Inc. - Serving the Construction Industry on the WWW - Welcome to the PSLD System
AEDILE - located in Italy, AEDILE contains the web sites of 3 International Trade Shows of the Building Industry plus web sites of leading ceramic tile manufacturers.

Figure 4.7 Some of the linked sites at Build.com

The Construction Information Gateway (Figure 4.8)
http://cig.bre.co.uk/

Welcome to the Construction Information Gateway. This system is host to a variety of construction services and is of importance to all involved in the building industry. The icons below illustrate some of the more general sections of this site. There is also a "free text" search engine if you know what you're looking for but are unsure where to find it.

Figure 4.8 Construction Information Gateway home page

4.3.3 Civil engineering lists

Civlist

http://rampages.onramp.net/~shilston/shilston.html

A comprehensive list maintained by Jay Shilstone (Figures 4.9 and 4.10). In fact, due to the increasing number of civil engineering sites coming online, Jay is considering restricting the list to his own speciality area of concrete.

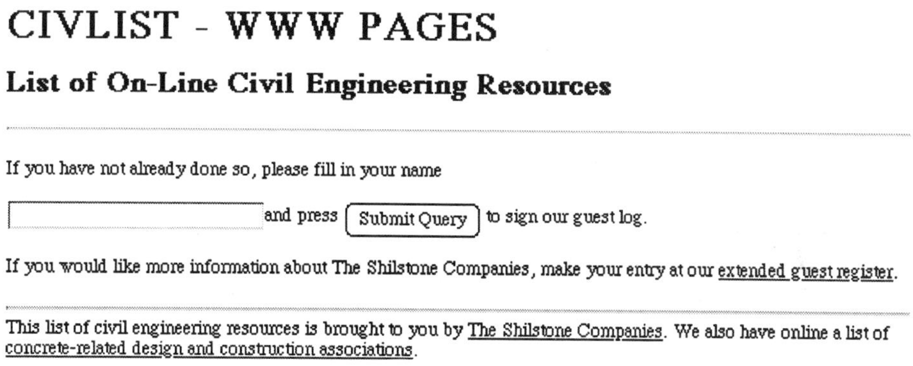

CIVLIST - WWW PAGES

List of On-Line Civil Engineering Resources

If you have not already done so, please fill in your name

[   ] and press [Submit Query] to sign our guest log.

If you would like more information about The Shilstone Companies, make your entry at our extended guest register.

This list of civil engineering resources is brought to you by The Shilstone Companies. We also have online a list of concrete-related design and construction associations.

Figure 4.9 Civlist home page

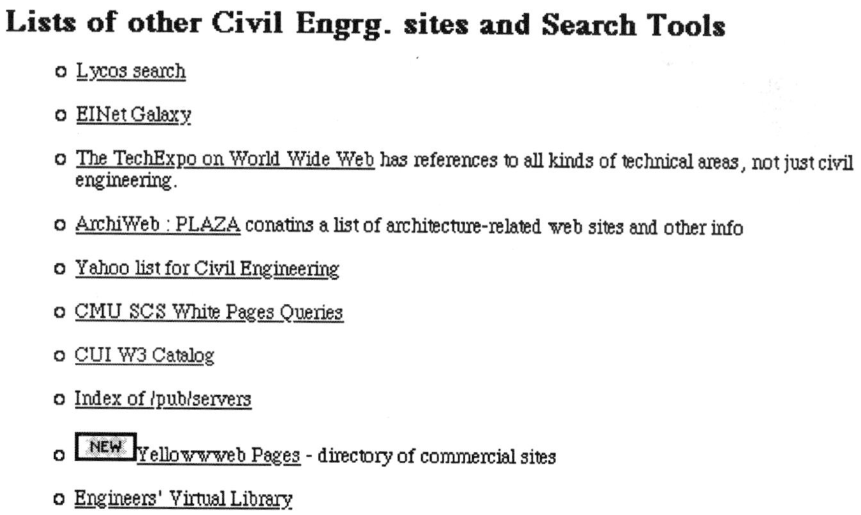

Lists of other Civil Engrg. sites and Search Tools

- o Lycos search

- o EINet Galaxy

- o The TechExpo on World Wide Web has references to all kinds of technical areas, not just civil engineering.

- o ArchiWeb : PLAZA conatins a list of architecture-related web sites and other info

- o Yahoo list for Civil Engineering

- o CMU SCS White Pages Queries

- o CUI W3 Catalog

- o Index of /pub/servers

- o [NEW] Yellowwweb Pages - directory of commercial sites

- o Engineers' Virtual Library

Figure 4.10 Some of the linked sites at CivList

General information sources

Construction industry lists

Proconet
http://www.cityscape.co.uk/users/fa08/menu.htm
A U.K. based site maintained by chartered surveyor Mark Wilderspin

Welcome To PROCONET!

To access the main PROCONET menu please click here

PROCONET is the first major new one-stop junction on the Information Superhighway for the UK Property and Construction industry. Launched in July 1995, PROCONET has been designed to provide easy access to a wide variety of relevant information and services as well as acting as a primary gateway to other global property and construction web sites.

Figure 4.11 Proconet home page

4.3.4 Environmental Engineering

Environmental Sites on the Internet
http://www.lib.kth.se/~lg/envsite.htm
An extraordinarily comprehensive list of links compiled and maintained by Larsgöran Strandberg (Figure 4.12).

Mike Donn's Building Science Educators' Useful Addresses
http://brick.arch.vuw.ac.nz:85/interesting_addresses.html
Very extensive listing. Categories of links include: associations, schools of architecture, journals, data sources, energy, environment, design, building science, lighting, acoustics, cad/graphics and radiance references.

4.3.5 Planning and landscape architecture

Planning resources on the Internet
http://www.lib.berkeley.edu/ENVI/cityweb.html
The University of California at Berkeley Library website for planning replaces and improves upon the UCB planning gopher site. Although several items relate specifically to California there is a more general index of electronic discussion lists for planning.

ENVIRONMENTAL SITES ON THE INTERNET

(developed by Larsgöran Strandberg, Royal Institute of Technology Library and Center for Environmental Science at KTH - Royal Institute of Technology - Stockholm, Sweden)

Figure 4.12 Part of Larsgöran Strandberg's home page
(http://www.lib.kth.se/~lg/envsite.htm)

WWW Virtual Library: Landscape Architecture
http://www.clr.toronto.edu:1080/VIRTUALLIB/larch.html
Categories similar to the Web Virtual Library: Architecture; again managed by Rodney Hoinkes.

Landscape Architecture Web
http://tdg.uoguelph.ca/nav/LA_startingpoints.html
Includes links to environmental servers and landscape images. Categories: pages to start on, servers with lots of stuff, text and image archives. Site managed by Paul Graham.

4.3.6 Gopher sites

List of Art and Architecture Gopher Sites
http://www.uky.edu/Artsource/gophers.html

Construction industry lists

Michigan ArchiGopher
gopher://libra.arch.umich.edu/
Includes Palladio image archives, student CAD models, lunar architecture, scenes of
Ann Arbor Michigan, and images of Hellenic and Byzantine architecture. The author of
this archive, Wassim Jabi, has now developed a web server:
http://libra.caup.umich.edu/ArchiGopher
The Palladio archive may be accessed directly at:
http://libra.caup.umich.edu/ArchiGopher/Palladio/Palladio.html

Berkeley Architecture Database
gopher://library.berkeley.edu
Then select 'Research Databases' and 'Architecture'.

Academic Lists – Art, Architecture and Urban Design
gopher://nisp.ncl.ac.uk:70/0Other/kovacs/acadlist.art

Academic Lists – Ecology and Environmental Studies
gopher://nisp.ncl.ac.uk:70/0Other/kovacs/acadlist.environ

Academic Lists – Internet Tools and Resources
gopher://nisp.ncl.ac.uk:70/0Other/kovacs/acadlist.internet

5

Electronic journals, mailing lists and newsgroups

5.1 CONSTRUCTION RELATED JOURNALS

Archaeology Magazine
http://www.he.net/~archaeol/index.html
Published by the Archaeological Institute of America, *Archaeology Magazine* reports all the latest archaeological discoveries. The net version includes the cover, table of contents, newsbriefs, subscription information, and links to other relevant web sites.

Architronic
http://www.saed.kent.edu/Architronic/
gopher gopher.saed.kent.edu 70
Architronic attempts to ensure the timely and inexpensive exchange of scholarly and critical ideas about architecture. It aims to gather and disseminate articles not only of occasional but also of permanent interest. It is a platform for both presenting and reviewing research as a journal, while providing a forum for stimulating dialogue on emerging ideas. The journal appears three times per year, with irregular supplements. The most recent issue and the full archive are maintained at the Kent State web site. It is indexed by the Avery Index to Architectural Periodicals. The vol.4 no.3 (1995) edition, edited by Elwin C. Robison, Ph.D. contained the following articles:
v4n3.01 Title, Contents and General Information.
v4n3.02 Jack Kremers, Guest Editor
        Defining Sustainable Architecture
v4n3.03 Terry Meyer Boake
        In Support of a New Sustainable Vernacular
v4n3.04 Terry Meyer Boake
        A Survey of Sustainability Curriculum
v4n3.05 Kirk Martini
        Beyond Competence
v4n3.06 Kevin Harrington
        The Arts Club, 1948 - 1951
v4n3.07 Reviews

Construction related journals

In the table of contents above, the filenames appear in the left-hand column. All Architronic issues are also archived and can be downloaded through the FTP process:

1. ftp ZEUS.KENT.EDU
2. LOGIN: architecture
3. PASSWD: archives
4. ls
5. get <filename>
6. bye

Responses, inquiries, and submissions can be sent to:
Architronic, School of Architecture and Environmental Design, Kent State University, P.O.Box 5190, Kent, Ohio 44242-0001.
Telephone: 216/672-2869. Fax: 216/672-4706
email: ARCITRON@KENTVM.KENT.EDU
Subscriptions: The Architronic listserv is used to inform subscribers when new issues of Architronic are released. It is also used to relay information and requests by other subscribers.
To subscribe, send an e-mail message to LISTSERV@KENTVM.KENT.EDU
devoid of all information except the following line:
SUBSCRIBE ARCITRON FIRSTNAME LASTNAME

BauArt
http://www.nextroom.at/nr/KIOSK/BauArt/
A German/English architectural magazine published in Austria.

Center for American Architecture and Urbanism
http://mirror.syr.edu/american.html
Defines itself as an electronic journal for 'the analysis, research and dissemination of ideas and issues associated with the American urban, sub-urban, and rural existential conditions. CAAU is conceived as a laboratory-platform for the exploration of theoretical and practical concerns of built media i.e. architecture, landscape architecture, urban planning.'

CinC
Culture in Cyberspace is a weekly newsletter that covers events associated with the intersection of culture and information technology.
email to: wlefurgy@radix.net
message: SUBSCRIBE CinC firstname lastname <e-mail address>

Complexity International
http://life.anu.edu.au/ci/ci.html

A new hyper-textual publication from the Australian National University.

CORE
http://www.iastate.edu/~stu_org/CORE/
The Iowa State University Student Journal of Architecture.

CyberSight (Published by Internet Marketing, Inc.)
http://cybersight.com
A true hypermedia publication that links to other hypermedia from around the world. Includes articles and links from underground artists.

CyberWire Dispatch
http://cyberwerks.com
High quality coverage of the Internet and cyberspace. Also incorporated in HotWIRED.
e-mail to: majordomo@cyberwerks.com
Subject: Ignored
Body: subscribe cwd-l
Usenet: comp.society.privacy
Gopher: cyberwerks.com

Design Architecture Electronic Journal
http://www.netaxis.com/design/Design_Architecture.html
'This web site presents the recent work of various architects in still photographs, audio, video and animation. All media is produced for this page.' Produced by Cornish Productions, Dan Cornish.

Dxfout
http://info.cardiff.ac.uk/uwcc/archi/jonesmd/dxf/index.html
'The E-zine for Cyber Architecture.' A relatively new initiative, the site has instructions on how to contribute and a table of contents for issue one.

EFFector
The Electronic Frontier Foundation's membership newsletter.
e-mail to: listserv@eff.org
Subject: Ignored
Body: subscribe your@address effector-online
Usenet: comp.org.eff
Gopher: gopher.eff.org
FTP: ftp.eff.org

Electronic Green Journal
http://gopher.uidaho.edu/1/UI_gopher/library/egj/
Published by the University of Idaho Library.

Electronic Journal of Information Technology in Construction (ITcon)
http://itcon.fagg.uni-lj.si/~itcon/
Edited by Prof. Bo-Christer Björk (Royal Institute of Technology, Stockholm, Sweden) the publication is the de facto journal of the CIB-78 working commission. The journal aims to cover the following topics:

- IT strategies within organizations and groups, ranging from the level of the individual firm to a consortium of firms to national construction industries.
- Construction process and enterprise modelling.
- Reengineering of the construction process using IT as an enabling technology.
- Methods of concurrent engineering.
- IT-supported communication across or within disciplines and life cycle stages (hypermedia, Internet, videoconferencing etc.).
- Databases, translation methodologies, remote communication between programs, shared object libraries and other computing techniques for data exchange and sharing.
- Technologies and standards for the digital representation of buildings (building product models).
- Standards for structuring and exchanging data in the construction process (building classification systems, EDI messages, CAD-layering, document management, representation of building regulations, component libraries).
- The use of IT-based techniques for problem solving in construction (expert systems and AI, case-based reasoning, simulation, neural networks, genetic algorithms etc.).
- Technologies for the electronic representation of building codes and standards.

An ITcon.announce mailing list has been set up to distribute news, announcements, calls for papers and abstracts of published papers. The list is not public – no discussion may take place in the list and only the editors are allowed to write into it so it should really be a low volume high content information source. To subscribe send email:

to: maiser@fagg.uni-lj.si
Body: sub itcon.announce
        end

FineArt Online
http://www.msstate.edu/Fineart_Online/home.html -
Online information for Fine Art.
ftp://ftp.msstate.edu/pub/archives/fineart_online

Gardening Resources
http://www.olympus.net/gardens/welcome.html
gopher to: gopherleviathan.tamu.edu
contains the Master Gardener archives and Q&A.

GreenClips
http:solstice.crest.org/environment/greenclips
gopher://gopher.igc.apc.org:70/11/pubs/greenclips
Subscribe to greenclips@aol.com.
'GreenClips is a summary of recent articles in the media on environmental news. It has a special focus on sustainable design for buildings (green architecture) and related government and business issues. The one-page digital summary is published every two weeks.'

Habitat
http://ctiweb.cf.ac.uk/Habitat/Contents.html
The newsletter of the CTI Centre for the Built Environment

Home Energy Magazine
http://www.eren.doe.gov/ee-cgi-bin/hem.pl
Issues from 1993 and 1994 online, with plans to add them back to volume 1, 1984.

HotWired
http://www.hotwired.com
The digital version of *Wired* magazine.

Image Soup Magazine
http://www.emedia.net/imagesoup
Image Soup Magazine is a quarterly periodical designed for users of Adobe Photoshop, Macromedia Director, Fractal Design Painter, KPT Bryce, etc. Packed with useful tips, techniques, articles, and a downloadable gallery in Acrobat file format, Image Soup is an ongoing collective design project for the good of all artists surfing the World Wide Web.

Journal of Computer-Mediated Communication (JCMC)
http://www.usc.edu/dept/annenberg/announce.html
The current issue of Computer-Mediated Communication (CMC) Magazine is posted at:
http://www.december.com/cmc/mag/current/toc.html
CMC Magazine reports on people, events, applications, and study related to computer-mediated communication. It draws on an interdisciplinary mix of perspectives from communication, technology, journalism and other disciplines.

LBL Center for Building Science News
http://eande.lbl.gov/CBS/NEWSLETTER/CBSNEWS.html
Full-text of the 1994 and 1995 issues of the Lawrence Berkeley Lab newsletter on energy.

Construction related journals

Leonardo Electronic Almanac
http://www.mitpress.mit.edu/Leonardo/home.html
Anonymous FTP to: mitpress.mit.edu
Leonardo is the leading journal in the cross-over area of arts/technology/computing.

The New Environmentalist
http://198.69.129.152/
The journal of sustainability.

PLAN
http://sap.mit.edu/plan/plan.html
Newsletter of the MIT school of Architecture and Planning.

Planning Commissioners Journal Citizen Planners Resource Center
http://www.webcom.com/~pcj/welcome.html
A cross between a newsletter, a topical site and a link collection.

Portfolio IV
http://www.arc.cmu.edu/portfolio/
Student publication of the Carnegie Mellon Department of Architecture.

Post-modern Culture
http://jefferson.village.virginia.edu/pmc/contents.594.html
Original material written in hypermedia format.

rachitecture
http://www.gold.net/ellipsis/rachitecture/index.html
Issued monthly since March 1995, 'Charlie Cannon's view of architecture on the Internet', is well worth the exploration. Of particular interest is the one on sustainability, including cohousing, but each provides unique perspectives and presentation. Other issues are on 'cyberspace, e-zines, cyberpunk, net communities', and 'real architecture, light', Also available through subscription from webworks@sirius.com.

Recycling World Magazine
http://www.tecweb.com/recycle/rwcont.htm
Europe's best magazine for commercial recyclers and for anyone interested in the environment, updated regularly, contains latest news and special features.

SITES Online
http://www.arch.carleton.ca/SITES/CONTENTS/Contents.html
'An architecture and design e-publication presenting the work of emerging and established architects and designers as well as critics and writers.' Graphics-capable

browser needed. Electronic departments do or will include 'texts, images, projects, news, conferences, reviews, video, BBS mail, SITES Store and tools.'

SPEED
http://www.arts.ucsb.edu/~speed

SPEED, the Electronic Journal of Technology, Media and Society, is a web-based journal that brings together artists, theorists and technicians in critical debate over the appropriate and possible roles for technology and media in society.

Student Solar Information Network Newsletter
http://lesowww.epfl.ch/ssin/ssin.html

'Comes out every two months and contains information on solar developments, issues and academic resources, both on and off- line.' To subscribe send a message to: ssin@tfc-bham.demon.co.uk.

Studio
http://www.p-pub.com

Published in Portable Document Format (PDF) contains information on CAD, building products, electronic journals, furniture design, VRML, etc.

Technology and Human Responsibility for the Future
http://www.ora.com/staff/stevet/netfuture/

What degrees of freedom do we have with respect to the dominant technologies, and how can we begin to take fuller responsibility for the role of technology in our society? Read this unusual newsletter and think about the issues. For e–mail access: send a 'subscribe netfuture Your Name' message to:
listproc@online.ora.com

Technology Online
http://www.tol.mmb.com

The Technology CyberMagazine is the focal point on the Internet for information regarding computers and technology, and their relationship with businesses. Includes links to major computer vendors and the latest press releases from High Tech Companies. Specifically includes: TechNews; Search from the 'Industry Index and Corporate Showcase' pages; and Register for free products, catalogues, software and subscription offers.

The Technology Reporter
http://www.albany.net/~twood/index.html

The Technology Reporter is for those interested in computers, technology, the internet, and telecommunications. Daily news feeds, editorials, weekly market summaries and more are available.

Technology Review
http://www.mit.edu:8001/afs/athena/org/t/techreview/www/tr.html
Technology Review 'addresses the practical implications of of science, as opposed to laboratory breakthroughs and theoretical and conceptual abstractions that have no bearing on practicality.' The 'zine incorporates hypertext links that can take the reader to other places related to an article such as a link to the EPA gopher while reading an article on ways to produce environmentally safe products. Although the entire hardcopy version of the magazine is not on the web most of the articles and features are and it is one of the best science publications on the web.

Urban Desires
http://desires.com/
Put out every two months, this e-zine deals with 'metropolitan passions' and contains many links.

Vitruvius Online
http://www.inforamp.net/~vitruv/
Vitruvius Online is a topical magazine featuring design theory, politics of the constructed environment and innovation in construction technology. The magazine seeks to increase communication of new design ideas and encourage border crossings at all levels. The publishers are soliciting articles in three areas: design theory, economic politics in the production of built work and new technologies.
Transcripts or comments may be forwarded by e-mail to either:
vitruv@inforamp.net or zoomarch@inforamp.net

To find electronic journals in related areas, gopher to gopher.cic.net (URL:gopher://gopher.cic.net). Journals are organized in various ways, including subject. Art is a subject; the subject 'Science' includes engineering, environment, and other topics of interest.

5.2 GENERAL BOOKS AND REFERENCES

Bibliobytes
http://bb.com/

Book Links
http://freenet.vcu.edu/education/literature/bklink.html

Booknews for new books in science, technology and medicine
http://www.aladdin.co.uk/booknews

Bookstores and Publishers
http://agent2.lycos.com:8001/bookstores/

Carnegie Mellon On-line Books Page
http://www.cs.cmu.edu:8001/Web/books.html

Electronic Books on WWW
http://gopher.lib.utk.edu:70/1/Electronic-Books

Electronic Texts
http://www.lysator.liu.se:7500/etexts.html

Enchanted E-Books
http://www.e-books.com

Ejournal SiteGuide : a MetaSource
http://unixg.ubc.ca:7001/0/providers/hss/zjj/ejhome.html
A comprehensive net journal site.

Feedback
Feedback is an e–mail–based newsletter organized by Ron Hogan, intended to keep its subscribers informed of new and interesting books, dealing with issues that effect contemporary society. To subscribe send the following command in the body of your e–mail: subscribe feedback youremail@address and mail to:
majordomo@primenet.com

Hyperjournal
Hyperjournal is a discussion list devoted exclusively to electronic journals, especially those which publish on the World Wide Web. It is concerned with all aspects of the production and publication of electronic journals, particularly those managed by academics themselves.
Send an email message as follows:
To: Mailbase@mailbase.ac.uk
Subject: Join hyperjournal-forum Firstname Lastname

Hypertext Fiction on the WWW
http://is.rice.edu/~riddle/hyperfiction.html

Hypertext Webster Dictionary
http://c.gp.cs.cmu.edu:5103/prog/webster

InfoSurf at The University of California, Santa Barbara
http://www.library.ucsb.edu

InfoSurf includes a variety of information about the UCSB Library, links to full-text sources online and an extensive collection of e-journals. The heart of the system is a collection of Internet resources.

International Booksearch Service
http://www.henge.com/~abrabks/welcome.html

Internet Book Information Center
http://sunsite.unc.edu/ibic/IBIC-homepage.html

Literature
http://www.arts.cuhk.hk/Lit.html

MacMillan General Reference
http://www.mgr.com

No Dead Trees
http://www.acy.digex.net/~dobenson/NDT.html

Que Publishing
http://www.mcp.com/que

The University of Pennsylvania Guide to Electronic Journals and Newspapers
http://www.library.upenn.edu/resources/ej/
An academic journals index. Newspapers are listed by language and country.

5.3 INTERNET RELATED JOURNALS

Everybody's Internet Update
http://www.eff.org/pub/Net_info/Guidebooks/Everybodys_Guide/Updates/
Monthly newsletter from the Electronic Frontier Foundation aimed at picking up where the EFF's Guide to the Internet (formerly the Big Dummy's Guide) left off. Available by e-mail from: listserv@eff.org
Subject: Ignored
Body: add net-guide-update
By FTP from: ftp.eff.org: /pub/Net_info/Guidebooks/Everybodys_Guide/Updates
Gopher: gopher.eff.org: /Net Info/EFF's Guide to the Internet/Updates
Usenet: comp.org.eff.talk, alt.internet.services
Information on Internet and Information Highways
http://www.itworks.be/
The new issue of I.T. Works' guide.

The Internet Press
A guide to electronic journals about the Internet by Kevin M. Savetz (savetz@northcoast.com) and John M. Higgins (higgins@dorsai.dorsai.org)
To get 'The Internet Press' once send e-mail to: ipress-request@northcoast.com
Subject: archive
Body: send ipress
To get periodic updates to 'The Internet Press' send the message:
Subject: subscribe
Body: ignored

Internet Resources Newsletter
http://www.hw.ac.uk/libWWW/irn/irn.html
A WWW newsletter produced by Heriot-Watt University Library.

The Online World
http://login.eunet.no/~presno/index.html
Odd de Presno (Author, Publisher, Norwegian)
The handbook's mission is to provide updates on important developments, with pointers for resources and more information. Offerings outside North America are emphasized. Examples range from databases to entertainment to special services for professionals and organizations. Sample articles in hypertext from The Online World Monitor newsletter are available at
http://login.eunet.no/~presno/monitor.html
The newsletter is a bi-monthly, ASCII online product that focuses on the changes in the online world, trends and important new developments around the world.

Weekly Bookmark
http://www.webcom.com/weekly/thisweek.html
The 'Weekly Bookmark' is a weekly newsletter that reviews and highlights new sites on the World Wide Web. Past issues are available at:
http://www.webcom.com/weekly/archives.html
To Subscribe/UnSubscribe, use the form at:
http://www.webcom.com/weekly/weekly-mail.html
Or to Subscribe, send the following command in the subject of mail to: weekly@webcom.com: Subscribe WeeklyB

5.4 PUBLISHERS AND BOOKSELLERS

Addison-Wesley
http://www.aw.com/devpress/
The computer books division.

Art/Architecture Titles from Princeton University Press
gopher://aaup.pupress.princeton.edu:70/11/books/presses/princeton/subject/art
Path: gopher gopher.pupress.princeton.edu
/Princeton University Press/Browse by Subject/ Art and Architecture

The Atlantic Monthly
http://www.TheAtlantic.com
The magazine devoted to politics, society, the arts, and culture since 1857, especially notable here as the journal in which Ted Nelson's vision of what became 'hypertext' was first mooted.

Blackwell's Bookshops
http://www.blackwell.co.uk/bookshops/

Books, E-Text, articles
http://www.amug.org/~a165/
Large lists of links to many e–text items.

CadCam Online
http://www.emap.com/cadcam/
The Internet companion to *CadCam* magazine.

Center for Architecture and Urban Planning Research (CAUPR), University of Wisconsin-Milwaukee
http://129.89.71.35/HTML/SARUP6/CAUPR/publist/publist.html
Publications catalogue of their 'series of monographs based on the results of research on such subjects as Children's Environments, Aging and Environment, Educational Facilities, Environment-Behavior Studies, Planning, Aero Space Architecture, Housing, Law, Urban Design, Cultural Facilities, Adaptive Reuse and Women and Architecture.'

Chapman & Hall
http://www.thomson.com
Science, technology, medecine and business publishers. A U.K. server is also available at: http://hermes.chaphall.co.uk/

Complete List of Electronic 'Zines
Gopher to: gopher.cic.net
Then select 'Electronic Serials'
A complete list of all available digitally distributed magazines and other electronic publications.

The Construction Site
http://www.emap.com/construct/
The Architects' Journal, Construction News and *New Civil Engineer* on-line.

Dillons Bookshops
http://www.Dillons.co.uk/

Electronic Frontier Foundation
EFF ftp site: ftp.eff.org
Contains e-zines together with articles relating to freedom of speech and censorship of online data.

The Electronic Newsstand
http://www.enews.com
Excerpts and sample articles from over 250 newspapers and publications from across the US. It is an incentive ploy for users to eventually subscribe to the magazines and publications but to the Internetter it is a free way to get lots of information as the articles are changed daily.

Electric Postcard
http://postcards.www.media.mit.edu/Postcards/
Not quite architecture but a nice idea all the same. Pick a postcard out of 35 designs from MIT Media Lab's version of the postcard rack and send them to friends by typing in their email address and then typing in your message on the virtual 'postcard'. Then add your name and address, hit 'Send' and away it goes. Colour and monochrome postcards are available. The recipient will get a claim number and e–mail notification that their postcard is ready and waiting at the site's pick-up address. If the recipient does not have a graphical web browser they can still see the text of the postcard – but will not be able to view the graphics.

Hayden Books
http://www.mcp.com/
Lists and excerpts from books published by one of the largest computing publishers.

The Internet Bookshop
http://tolstoy.bookshop.co.uk

The List of Free Computer-Related Publications
http://www.soci.niu.edu/~huguelet/TLOFCRP/
The List of Free Computer-Related Publications is a list of print magazines, newspapers, and journals related to computing which can be subscribed to free of charge.

MIT Press

http://www-mitpress.mit.edu

Links to interesting pages such as Leonardo and the on-line version of Bill Mitchell's *City of Bits.*

http://www-mitpress,mit.edu/City_of_Bits/welcome.html

William J. Mitchell, Professor of Architecture and Media Arts and Sciences, Dean of the School of Architecture and Planning at MIT, and author of *City of Bits: Space, Place, and the Infobahn,* the first book published simultaneously in hardcover and on the World Wide Web.

The MIT Press Bookstore

http://www-mitpress.mit.edu/bookstore.html

Massachusetts Institute of Technology

292 Main Street

Cambridge MA 02142

'Outside of a dog, a book is a (hu)man's best friend.

Inside of a dog, it's too dark to read.' – Groucho Marx.

New Scientist

http://www.newscientist.com

New York Times Online (TimesFax)

http://www.nytimesfax.com

This news service is available for downloading and reading using Adobe Acrobat Reader. Each day at midnight the NY Times puts out its online version which is a compilation of the day's most important news stories, news briefs and the crossword puzzle.

Van Nostrand Reinhold Architecture and Design Titles

http://www.vnr.com/vnr/adhome.html

A browseable new title list and a searchable catalogue.

Project Gutenberg

http://jg.cso.uiuc.edu/pg/lists/list.html

Project Gutenburg now has over 150 out of copyright full texts available. A list of files may be obtained by sending the message 'send gutenberg catalog' to almanac@oes.orst.edu. Texts may be retrieved by anonymous ftp from: mrcnext.cso.uiuc.edu in the etext directory, or by e-mail. Further details of the project are available by subscribing to the Gutnberg (with no 'e' between t and n) list server. Mail the message 'sub gutnberg yourname' to listserv@vmd.cso.uiuc.edu, leaving the subject line blank.

Rosalind Resnick's Web Page of Electronic Publication reviews
http://www.gate.net/~rosalind
Contains some 50 reviews of major electronic publications and other information relating to e-zines and publishing on the net.

Routledge
http://www.routledge.com/routledge.html
Professional and business publishers.

Science Search
http://www.control.com.au/search
A monthly publication featuring news and commentary on scientific issues of public interest, including health/medicine, the environment, information technology, science policy, agriculture etc.

William Stout Architectural Books has an e–mail distribution list. Contact Hans Phillips (hansl@ix.netcom.com) to be added to the distribution list. They promise a web site soon.

Tables of Contents of Computer related Magazines
http://www.mag-browse.com
Front covers and content listings for 43 leading computing magazines. (More are being added.)

The Telegraph
http://www.telegraph.co.uk
The first of the U.K. press to go on-line (on November 15, 1994).

UnCover Home Page
http://www.carl.org/uncover/unchome.html
The UnCover Company has now made its UnCover database and other services available via a home page on the World Wide Web. UnCover provides table of contents indexing from nearly 17 000 journals worldwide. In addition to database access, UnCover's home page provides information about services, pricing and a copy of the current UnCover Update newsletter as well as back issues. A list of all UnCover titles is also there and will be updated on a monthly basis.

Weekly Science News Hotlist
http://sln.fi.edu/tfi/hotlists/sciencenews.html

Yahoo
http://www.yahoo.com/Business_and_Economy/Companies/Books/
Some 400 bookshop and book-related links.

ZDnet (Ziff-Davis Interactive)
http://www.ziff.com
This site includes all of Ziff-Davis' publications online, downloadable software, computer industry news and analysis, story updates, special articles that are not to be found in printed editions and more. The publications included are: *MacUser, MacWEEK, PCWeek, PCMagazine, ComputerLife, PC Computing, InterActive Week, Computer Gaming World* and other informative links.

5.5 MAILING LISTS

5.5.1 Finding mailing lists

Finding ListServ lists via WWW
http://tile.net/listserv/
This WWW site for finding ListServ lists is being developed as part of the tile.net project. Tile.net is a searchable index of information available to the Internet community. The index to ListServ lists is a hierarchically organized database, grouped by name, topic, settings, etc., with a free-text search ability. Tile.net also has indices to all Usenet groups, FTP sites, and computer products vendors.
Tile.net is available at: htpp://tile.net/
List of Lists: http://www.tile.net/tile/listserv/index.html

Stephanie DaSilva's List of Lists
ftp to: rtfm.mit.edu
located in: /pub/usenet/news.answers/mail/mailing-lists
Complete set of lists along with descriptions for each list. The site also includes directions on how to join each mailing list or ListServ.

Finding Mailing Lists and Newsgroup Lists
gopher://cs1.presby.edu/11/net-resources/mailing-lists
gopher://cs1.presby.edu/11/net-resources/newsgroup-lists

Interest Groups Finder
http://www.nova.edu/Inter-Links/cgi-bin/news-lists.pl

Archives of mailbase lists
gopher://nisp.ncl.ac.uk:70
Lists are in sections, alphabetically by list name.

The Directory of Scholarly Electronic Conferences by Diane Kovacs
http://www.mid.net/KOVACS
This is the standard source of information about ListServs in various disciplines. The directory is searchable by keyword, subject, discussion name, topic, and contact address. The list is also available alphabetically or by subject. The section of the Kovacs list on Art and Architecture is compiled by Kara Robinson. That section is posted separately at the University of Michigan Clearinghouse for Subject-Oriented Internet Resource Guides:
gopher://una.hh.lib.umich.edu:70/00/inetdirsstacks/artarch:robinson.

Lists of Lists – MIT
http://www.NeoSoft.com:80/internet/paml/

Liszt: Searchable Directory of e-Mail Discussion Groups
http://www.liszt.com/
Searchable information on (at the last count) 22 346 listserv, Majordomo, listproc and other mailing lists.

Mailing List Info and News Groups
http://www.users.interport.net/~ednorman/listserv.html

Thousands of Mailing Lists
http://ancho.ucs.indiana.edu/mlarchive
A web page provided by the Indiana University Support Center with a searchable list of more than 11 000 mailing lists.

5.5.2 Construction related lists

AASL-L
A discussion group for architectural librarians sponsored by the Association of Architecture School Librarians. (See also ARLIS)
Subscribe to: listserv@unllib.unl.edu

AAT-L
AAT-L is a list for current and future users of the *Art and Architecture Thesaurus*. The purpose of this list is to facilitate timely discussion of matters of mutual interest between subscribers and to provide a more expeditious route of communication between the AAT office and AAT users.
Subscribe to: listserv@uicvm.cc.uic.edu

AE

The Alternative Energy Discussion List is intended to provide a forum to discuss the current state of the art and future direction alternative energy sources that are renewable and sustainable.

Subscribe to: listserv@sjsuvm1.sjsu.edu

Submission Address: AE@SJSUVMI.SJSU.EDU

AMART-L

AMART-L is a moderated electronic discussion list devoted to scholarly and intellectual discussions of topics of specific interest to historians and scholars of American art. Covers American art, artifacts, architecture and related topics from the colonial period to the present.

Subscribe to: listserv@cunyvm.cuny.edu

Architects and Construction Conferences on CIX

CIX (Compulink Information eXchange) is one of the best known online conferencing systems in the U.K. CIX conferences are similar to Internet's Usenet but are only accessible by fellow CIXen. This means they tend to be rather more focused and applicable to U.K. circumstances. Two conferences of interest are:

Architects: Moderator Christopher Shaw (cshaw@cix.compulink.co.uk)

Construction: Moderator Richard Morris (rhmorris@cix.compulink.co.uk)

General information on CIX: http://www.compulink.co.uk/

ARCO

ARCO is an open, unmoderated, discussion list. The aim of the 'ARt and COmmunication' list is to discuss themes and questions about the importance of art and its relationships with literature, psychology, techniques and sciences of communication. Archives of ARCO mail items are kept in monthly files. They may be obtained by sending the command: INDEX ARCO in the body of e-mail to LISTSERV@SJUVM.STJOHNS.EDU

To subscribe, send the following command in the body of mail:

SUB ARCO yourfirstname yourlastname

ARLIS-L

Architecture librarians have several discussion groups. In the United States one list is sponsored by the Art Libraries Society of North America (ARLIS/NA). ARLIS-L has substantially more postings than AASL-L but has many postings not related to architecture.

Subscribe to: listserv@ukcc.uky.edu

Australia/New Zealand ARLIS has its own list, ARLISANZ-L (send a message to majordomo@info.anu.edu.au).

ARQUITECTURA-L
ARQUITECTURA-L is the only specifically 'architecture' discussion group which is open. It originates in Venezuela and is published in Spanish. To subscribe, send a message to listserv@conicit.ve

ART-SUPPORT
Art-Support exists as a forum for the discussion of art related matters. Potential members include artists, art administrators, writers, theorists, students, teachers and others with an interest in art. The focus of the e-conference is intended to be the UK art community.
Subscribe to: mailbase@mailbase.ac.uk

ARTNET
ARTNET provides a forum for the discussion of art that is concerned with: network, installation, project communication, temporary ad-hoc transient, mobile, time-based, formless, de-centred. All projects involve some aspect of lack of enclosure: the promotion of action without centre. Peripatetic art tends towards the transient, the time based, the mobile. Peripatetology is as much about receiving the action, the project, as it is about initiating it.
Subscribe to: mailbase@mailbase.ac.uk
Submission Address: ARTNET@mailbase.ac.uk

ARTNEWS
Art News Headlines (ARTNEWS) is a synopsis of the print media's coverage of the art world. Covers collectors, museums, artists, art and government.
Subscribe to: artnews-request@arttrak.metronet.com

AUTOCAD
Subscribe to: AUTOCAD@jhuvm.hcf.jhu.edu

BEPAC (Building Environmental Performance Analysis Club)
Subscribe to: mailbase@mailbase.ac.uk.
JOIN BEPAC First Name Last Name

BIOSPH-L
Discusses anything related to the biosphere, pollution, CO_2 effect, ecology, habitats, and climate, etc.
Subscribe to: listserv@ubvm.cc.buffalo.edu
Submission Address: BIOSPH-L@ubvm.cc.buffalo.edu

BUILT-ENVIRONMENT

An open, unmoderated discussion of all aspects relating to the built environment including Architecture, Building, Surveying, Civil-, Mechanical-, Services-Engineering, Construction Computing, etc.

Subscribe to: mailbase@mailbase.ac.uk

Submission Address: BUILT-ENVIRONMENT@mailbase.ac.uk

CAAH

Art History Forum – Consortium of Art and Architectural Historians. This is a restricted list. To apply send a subscribe message to

Subscribe to: listserv@pucc.princeton.edu

Further instructions will be sent by e–mail.

Submission Address: CAAH@pucc.princeton.edu

C-ARTS, C-ARTSdb

C-ARTS is a moderated forum to announce, describe and evaluate arts-related resources available on the Internet. Its companion list, C-ARTSdb, functions as a database for these resources. Archives are kept on C-ARTSdb. C-ARTS itself is not archived. Files are kept on C-ARTSdb. You may obtain lists of these files by sending the following commands:

INDEX C-ARTSdb

GET INDEX C-ARTS C-ARTSdb

to LISTSERV@UNB.CA in the body of e-mail.

To subscribe, send the following command in the body of mail:

LISTSERV@LISTSERV.UNB.CA

SUB C-ARTS firstname lastname

Archived files for C-ARTSdb include instructions and ListServ templates for searching C-ARTSdb's database. For initial information send the command:

GET C-ARTSdb FAQ

in the body of e-mail to LISTSERV@UNB.CA

Note: You cannot subscribe to C-ARTSdb; you can only search and retrieve from its database. C-ARTS is a joint project of Industry Canada's Community Access initiative and the Canadian Society for Education Through Art. The lists are housed at the University of New Brunswick.

CNBR-L

Cooperative Network for Building Researchers

To join, send a message to edwards@rmit.edu.au with your name, department, institution, e–mail, fax, phone and postal addresses and indicate your main teaching and research areas. Not a discussion group, this list's mission is to circulate research enquiries and distribute information of common interest. Gopher to the Daedalus gopher (daedalus.edc.rmit.edu.au) for a list of members. The member list is also available for ftp from fedcdos.edc.rmit.edu.au.

CPLFYI-L
The Council of Planning Librarians list.
Subscribe to: listserv@asuvm.inre.asu.edu

CTI-Built Environment
The CTI Centre for the Built Environment maintains four lists, CTI-ARCH-L, CTI-PLAN-L, CTI-CONSTR-L and CTI-PROPMAN-L, for Architecture, Planning, Building Construction and Property Management.
Subscribe to: majordomo@cardiff.ac.uk
With the message: subscribe <listname>, where <listname> is CTI-ARCH-L or one of the other listnames above.

CTI-Engineering
The discussion group of the CTI Centre for Engineering.
Subscribe to: mailbase@mailbase.ac.uk
With the message: join cti-engineering yourname

DESIGN-L
This discussion group interprets 'design' broadly to include arts, architecture, industrial design, etc. The list owner pulls many postings from other discussion groups (like ARTCRIT) and newsgroups (like alt.architecture).
Subscribe to: listserv@psuvm.psu.edu
Submission Address: DESIGN-L@psuvm.psu.edu

Drive-ins
Drive-in Movies. The discussions on this list will concern drive-in movie theatres and classic indoor bijous across the U.S. and even around the world. We'll focus on those that are still in operation but would love to hear tales, too, of gone-but-not-forgotten ones. We will also discuss drive-in movies from the golden era of drive-ins, which I define as roughly 1950-1970. If a movie contains a giant insect or lizard, juvenile delinquents, rock'n'roll music, flying saucers, then it is worthy of discussion on this list.
Subscribe to: listproc@echonyc.com
with the body of the e–mail: SUBSCRIBE DRIVE-INS firstname lastname

ECDM
Environment is addressed in a different context by the Environmentally Conscious Design and Manufacture list. Topics include design for disassembly, life-cycle analysis, design for product reuse and design for repair/rework.
Subscribe to: listserv@pdomain.uwindsor.ca

ECIXFILES

The Energy and Climate Information Exchange (ECIX) is a project of EcoNet aimed at educating the environmental community and the general public on the potential of energy efficiency and renewable energy to reduce the use of fossil fuels and their contribution to climate change. ECIX now offers as a public service the distribution of files pertaining to energy and climate change. We accept files electronically submitted by those who wish to share information, advertise the existence of the files and electronically mail files to those who request them. ECIX is an EcoNet project funded by a grant from the Joyce Mertz-Gilmore Foundation with added support from the Energy Foundation.
Subscribe to: ecixfiles@igc.org
Submission Address: ECIXFILES@IGC.ORG

ECOCITY

Ecological issues in urban design.
Subscribe to: listserv@searn.sunet.se
(sub listname firstname lastname organization)

ECOCT-A

This is a 'read-only' list for announcements from the organizers of the International ECOCITY Electronic Network.
Subscribe to: listserv@searn.sunet.se
Submission Address: ECOCT-A@searn.sunet.se

ECOL-ECON

It is necessary to have major change in the way we think about economics if we intend to make a credible response to the environmental threats to the planet. The list is to create discussion around alternatives to the prevailing economic paradigms, whether Marxist or neoclassical. This is an invitation to join persons of similar intent for creative intellectual work and to create more rapid change in economic thought. We plan to discuss and build archives around such questions as sustainability, the role of economic growth, free trade and the environment and the role of multilateral economic institutions in the sustainability of the development process.
Subscribe to: listproc@csf.colorado.edu
Archives: ftp://csf.colorado.edu
Submission Address: ECOL-ECON@csf.colorado.edu

ECOLOG-L

This is the discussion list for the Ecological Society of America. Information distributed on this list included grants, jobs and news.
Subscribe to: listserv@umdd.umd.edu
Submission Address: ECOLOG-L@umdd.umd.edu

ECONET
Ecology E-conferencing System (fee-based service) serves organizations and individuals who are working for environmental preservation and sustainability.
Subscribe to: Contact ECONET@IGC.ORG
Submission Address: ECONET@IGC.ORG

ECOSYS-L
List for 'ecosystem theory and modelling'. Discussion in the field of ecosystem theory and modelling.Typically the material will be question-and-answer, where someone wants information on any problem in this field. In addition contributions to build up a list of mathematical models, to build up an address-list of scientists who are engaged in modelling and to standardization of mathematical formulation of ecological processes are welcomed.
Subscribe to: listserv@vm.gmd.de
Submission Address: ECOSYS-L@vm.gmd.de

ECOTHEOL
Academic discussion list for environmental issues from a theological or ethical perspective.
Subscribe to: mailbase@mailbase.ac.uk
Submission Address: ECOTHEOL@mailbase.ac.uk

EDITEC-L
EDITEC-L was 'created to allow the sharing of experiences, documents, etc. concerning the teaching of IT to civil engineering students or practitioners, e.g. how it can be used for automating information processing tasks in construction and for re-engineering the process as a whole'.
Subscribe to: maiser@fagg.uni-lj.si
The web site for Editec is http://www.fagg.uni-lj.si/ICARIS/EDITEC/

ENTREE-L
This list is for discussion and solution of questions regarding the field of Environmental Training in Engineering Education. This list finds its origin in the ENTREE '94 conference in Lyngby, Denmark.
Subscribe to: listserv@nic.surfnet.nl
Submission Address: ENTREE-L@nic.surfnet.nl

ENVBEH-L
The environment, design and human behavior discussion group addresses 'topics concerning the relations of people and their physical environments'. Send a message to rwener@vm.poly.edu if you would like to join the discussion.

ENV-LINK+

Provides free information for environmentalists around the world, for the discussion of matters both profound and mundane, which reflects a shared set of core environmental issues.
Subscribe to: ENV-LINK+FORMS@ANDREW.CMU.EDU
Submission Address: ENV-LINK+@ANDREW.CMU.EDU

ENVENG-L

The ENVENG-L list has been created to serve as a medium of communications for those interested in education, research and professional practice of environmental engineering. Environmental engineering topics will encompass the entire field, including water and wastewater treatment, air pollution control, solid waste management and radioactive waste treatment.
Subscribe to: listserv@vm.temple.edu
Submission Address: ENVENG-L@vm.temple.edu

ENVINF-L

List for Environmental Information.
Subscribe to: listserv@nic.surfnet.nl
Submission Address: ENVINF-L@nic.surfnet.nl

ENVIROLAW

Environmental and natural resource law students throughout the world.
Subscribe to: mailserv@oregon.uoregon.edu
Submission Address: ENVIROLAW@oregon.uoregon.edu

ENVLAWPROFS

International discussion list for professors of environmental law.
Subscribe to: mailserv@oregon.uoregon.edu
Submission Address: ENVLAWPROFS@oregon.uoregon.edu

ENVST-L

The Environmental Studies list discusses undergraduate and graduate environmental studies and environmental science degree programs.
Subscribe to: listserv@brownvm.brown.edu
Submission Address: ENVST-L@brownvm.brown.edu

ENVTECSOC

ENVTECSOC was established at the American Sociological Association meetings in Los Angeles, August 1944, by the Environment and Technology Section of the ASA.
Subscribe to: listproc@csf.colorado.edu
Archives: ftp://csf.colorado.edu
Submission Address: ENVTECSOC@csf.colorado.edu

ENVBEH-L

Environment, Design and Human Behavior provides for discussion on a variety of topics concerning the relations of people and their physical environments. Anyone may contribute comment related to environmental psychology as such issues are studied by groups such as the American Psychological Association, the Environmental Design Research Association, the International Association of People and their Physical Settings, People and Physical Environment Research or the Man-Environment research Association.

Subscribe to: listserv@vm.poly.edu

Submission Address: ENVBEH-L@vm.poly.edu

ENVBUS-L

Environment and Business in Central and Eastern Europe

The ENVBUS-L list is to facilitate discussion among persons and organizations who are interested in business and environmental issues in Central and Eastern Europe (CEE) to include the following countries: Albania, Bulgaria, Croatia, Czech Republic, Hungary, Poland, Romania, Slovak Republic, Slovenia and the Former Yugoslav Republic of Macedonia. The main mission of this list is to promote cooperation among diverse environmental groups and interests in Central and Eastern Europe; to act as a catalyst for developing solutions to environmental problems in this region; and to promote the development of a civil society.

This list is the first attempt by the Regional Environmental Center for Central and Eastern Europe (REC) to encourage businesses to join the dialogue in the CEE. The REC believes that before sustained environmental progress can be achieved in the CEE, it is necessary to promote the development of a strong environmental business sector. Environmental professionals are essential for the practical implementation of environmental policies, regulations and innovative ideas in the industrial and urban settings. With this in mind, this list hopes to encourage dialogue between environmental professionals and organizations in the CEE and from around the world with a focus on CEE environmental problems. Some of the topics that might be discussed on BIS will be related to the CEE and include:

- available environmental services in CEE;
- available technologies for environmental protection in CEE;
- available 'green' products;
- regulations affecting the demand for environmental services or technologies (new national initiatives, EU harmonization, financial instruments for environmental protection);
- available financing for environmental projects in CEE;
- request for partners for consortiums bidding on environmental projects;
- project opportunities or request for bids for environmental services and technologies from government or private sector organizations;

- technology transfer opportunities;
- case studies of good environmental practices in the industrial setting;
- 'ideal' environmental practices (ISO 14000, eco-efficiency, pollution prevention, clean production, sustainable industrial activities);
- conference information for environmental businesses.

The list is currently unmoderated. If conditions warrant a change to a moderated list, we will, with the help and cooperation of involved subscribers, move to a moderated list. To subscribe to ENVBUS-L, send the following command to: listserv@REC.HU
in the body of e-mail: SUBSCRIBE ENVBUS-L yourfirstname yourlastname
Archives of ENVBUS-L mail items are kept in monthly files.These may be retrieved by sending the command: INDEX in the body of e-mail to listserv@REC.HU.

ET-ANN
International conference on Ecotechnology for Sustainable Development.
Subscribe to: listserv@searn.sunet.se
Submission Address: ET-ANN@searn.sunet.se

FACXCH-L
Exchange list for Department of Architecture faculty. The purpose of this list is to help establish faculty exchanges throughout the world. Faculty would exchange both their living accommodations and their educational positions within a given department. A curriculum-vitae must be sent to the listowner prior to being added to the list.
Subscribe to: listserv@psuvm.psu.edu
Submission Address: FACXCH-L@psuvm.psu.edu

H-URBAN
History of urban settlements.
Subscribe to: listserv@uicvm.uic.edu

IBPSA (International Building Performance Simulation Association)
Subscribe to: mailbase@mailbase.ac.uk.
JOIN IBPSA First Name Last Name

ICARIS-L
In addition to its web site and running the CIB WG78 list, ICARIS runs its own discussion group.
Subscribe to: mailserv@fagg.uni-lj.si

IDFORUM
Industrial Design Forum provides a global electronic meeting place for all involved in industrial design. Practising designers, design educators and design students are invited

to subscribe. Subscribers will receive *Voice of Industrial Design* (VOID), a newsletter complied by industrial design students.
Subscribe to: listserv@vm1.yorku.ca
Submission Address: IDFORUM@vm1.yorku.ca

IMAGELIB
Image databases and conversions from non-digital formats to digital are some of the topics of IMAGELIB.
Subscribe to: listserv@listserv.arizona.edu

Infoterra
The Infoterra subscription list is a public list intended for general communications on environmental topics; posing queries to the Infoterra network; requesting information from UNEP (United Nations Environment Programme); etc. Subscription to this list is open. In addition to posing queries, subscribers are encouraged to respond to queries as well, since this list will ultimately be comprised of both sources and users of environmental information on a global basis.
Subscribe to: listproc@pan.cedar.univie.ac.at
Submission Address: infoterra@pan.cedar.univie.ac.at

INGR-EN
Intergraph list.
Subscribe to: mailserv@ccsun.tuke.sk

IRNES
Communication channel for members of the Interdisciplinary Research Network on the Environment and Society. IRNES is open to all those who have an interest in the interplay between the ecosystem and its sub-unit that we call society. The network is made up of young researchers in this field.
Subscribe to: mailbase@mailbase.ac.uk
Submission Address: IRNES@mailbase.ac.uk

IT-RD (Construction Industry Information Technology)
Subscribe to: mailbase@mailbase.ac.uk.
JOIN IT-RD FirstName LastName

JANITORS
For the discussion of 'any topic of interest to those engaged in cleaning Public Buildings'.
Subscribe to: LISTSERV@UKANVM.CC.UKANS.EDU

LARCH-L
The main discussion group for landscape architects.
Subscribe to: listserv@listserv.syr.edu

LARCHNET
Another, but less busy, forum for landscape architecture.
Subscribe to: listserv@vm.uoguelph.ca

LIGHTING
A lighting discussion group, still continues despite the establishment of newsgroup sci.engr.lighting. Join by sending a subscription request to LIGHTING-REQUEST@garnet.nist.gov.

MEGACITIES
Subscribe to: mavisser@megacities.nl (with the text subscribe megacities)

PRA
Participatory Community Development. An e–mail discussion list devoted to the topic of participatory community development. It is not limited to devotees of the PRA approach specifically, but embraces dialogue about any form of intentional change initiated and owned by community members.
Subscribe to: listserv@uoguelph.ca
Submission Address: PRA@uoguelph.ca

RADIANCE-DISCUSS
Discussion group for users of the 'ray-tracing' program RADIANCE.
Subscribe to: radiance-request@hobbes.lbl.gov

RECYCLE
Recycling in practice in academic, commercial and community environments.
Subscribe to: listserv@umab.umd.edu
Submission Address: RECYCLE@umab.umd.edu

Roadside
Roadside attractions. The discussions on the ROADSIDE list will concern great cheezy tourist attractions across the U.S. We'll focus on those that are still in operation but would love to hear tales, too, of gone-but-not-forgotten ones. If you love old-fashioned roadside attractions, if you'd rather visit an alligator ranch than Epcot Center, if you'd drive out of your way to dine in a restaurant shaped like a coffeepot, if you'd opt for Route 66 over I–40 in a heartbeat, if you scour the horizon looking for jackelope while vacationing, this list is for you. It is my intention to eventually create, and make accessible via the Internet, a database of roadside attractions around the USA. Before

traveling, folks will be able to visit the web page or gopher site and discover whether or not any classic attractions exist in the area they're about to visit.
Subscribe to: listproc@echonyc.com with the body of the mail containing
SUBSCRIBE ROADSIDE firstname lastname

SAFETY

E-conference for people interested in the various environmental, health and safety issues and problems on college and university campuses.
Subscribe to: listserv@UVMVM.UVM.EDU
Submission Address: SAFETY@UVMVM.UVM.EDU

SEAC+DISCUSSION

Student Environmental Action Coalition Network.
Subscribe to: listproc@ECOSYS.DRDR.VIRGINIA.EDU
Submission Address: SEAC+DISCUSSION@ECOSYS.DRDR.VIRGINIA.EDU

STUXCH-L

Exchange list for Department of Architecture students. The purpose of this list is to help establish student exchanges throughout the world. A curriculum vitae must be sent to the listowner prior to being added to the list.
Subscribe to: listserv@psuvm.psu.edu
Submission Address: STUXCH-L@psuvm.psu.edu

SUSTAG-PRINCIPLES

A list for discussions of sacred geometry, sacred architecture, religious and Freemasonic iconography in architecture, labyrinths and symbolic landscaping, geomancy, relationships between architecture and music, celestial observatory sites and sacred site tourism. Periodically posts an extensive bibliography on sacred geometry and architecture.
Subscribe to: almanac@ces.ncsu.edu
Submission Address: SUSTAG-PRINCIPLES@ces.ncsu.edu

SUSTAINABLE-DEVELOPMENT

Subscribe to: majordomo@civic.net

UNCEDGEN

Public discussion list about environmental issues.
Subscribe to: listserv@lci.ufrj.br
Submission Address: UNCEDGEN@lci.ufrj.br

Universal Design Information Network
The Universal Design Information Network operates a list as well as a gopher. To subscribe send a message containing the word subscribe and your Internet address to udep-info-request@umbsky.cc.umb.edu.

URBAN-L
E-conference for information exchange, ideas, etc., on the science of Urban Planning.
Subscribe to: listserv@vm3090.ege.edu.tr
Submission Address: URBAN-L@vm3090.ege.edu.tr

URBANET
The urban planning student network.
Subscribe to: listserv@msu.edu

URBAN-REGIONAL-PLANNING
Subscribe to: mailbase@mailbase.ac.uk

URBAN-RESEARCH-L
Subscribe to: majordomo@coombs.anu.edu.au

VRA-L
VRA-List is the electronic bulletin board of the Visual Resources Association, the professional organization of curators of visual resources collections including slides, photographs, etc.
Subscribe to: listserv@uafsysb.uark.edu
Submission Address: VRA-L@uafsysb.uark.edu

VTCAD-L
Computer-Aided-Design discussion sponsored by Virginia Polytechnic University.
Subscribe to: listserv@vtvm1.cc.vt.edu
Submission Address: VTCAD-L@vtvm1.cc.vt.edu

W78
The mailing list for the International Council for Building Research Studies and Documentation (CIB) Working Group 78 (WG78) aims to 'encourage and promote research and development in the application of integrated IT throughout the life-cycle of buildings and related facilities.' To subscribe send the message sub W78.ITCON to maiser@fagg.uni-lj.si. The archive of the list is at:
http://www.fagg.uni-lj.si/ICARIS/w78.

WESTPLAN
Western Planners Network.
Subscribe to: majordomo@csn.org

5.5.3 Internet related newsgroups

ANN-LOTS
ANN-LOTS is meant for announcing subject-oriented meta-lists, catalogues and indices of: bibliographies, 'who-has-more-on...', contact persons, ftp dirs, FYI/FAQs, etc. For listmakers, reference librarians, postmasters and researchers.
Subscribe to: listserv@vm1.nodak.edu
Submission Address: ANN-LOTS@vm1.nodak.edu

GOPHERJEWELS
GopherJewels@EINet.net is a list service for the sharing of interesting gopher finds. This list expects subscribers that are either gopher developers or gopher users.
Subscribe to: listproc@EINET.NET
Archives: ftp://ftp.einet.net/pub/GOPHERJEWELS
Submission Address: GOPHERJEWELS@EINET.NET

GOPHERJEWELS-TALK
The GOPHERJEWELS-TALK@einet.net list is an unmoderated forum for the exchange of questions and answers with regard to 'gopher jewels' and their use.
Subscribe to: listproc@EINET.NET
Archives: ftp://ftp.einet.net/pub/GOPHERJEWELS-TALK
Submission Address: GOPHERJEWELS@EINET.NET

The Internet TourBus
Are you looking for neat stuff on the Internet but have no idea where to start looking? Are you starting to feel like roadkill on the Information Superhighway? TOURBUS is for you! TOURBUS is a bi-weekly e-mail distribution list brought to you by the team of Patrick Douglas Crispen, author of the popular ROADMAP workshop, and 'Doctor Bob' Rankin, columnist for Boardwatch Magazine and author of *Accessing the Internet by E-mail*. To subscribe to TOURBUS, send an e-mail letter to:
LISTSERV@LISTSERV.AOL.COM
with SUBSCRIBE TOURBUS yourfirstname yourlastname
in the body of your e-mail letter.

INTERPEDIA
Interpedia is for discussion of the proposed Internet Encyclopedia. The original idea, due to Rick Gates, was for volunteers to cooperatively write a new encyclopedia, put it in the public domain, and make it available on the Internet. Participants on the mailing-

list have expanded the concept by noting that the bibliography entries and references provided with Interpedia articles could include hypertext links to other resources available on the Internet. Unlike any printed encyclopedia, the Interpedia could be kept completely up-to-date. Indeed, it could include hypertext links to ongoing discussions, and perhaps evolve into a general interface to all resources and activities on the Internet.
Subscribe to: interpedia-request@telerama.lm.com
Usenet: comp.infosystems.interpedia
Submission Address: interpedia@telerama.lm.com

IWATCH
http://www.webcom.com/~cybernet/welcome.html
'Always Watching for the Best on the Internet!'
We search to uncover the entertaining as well as the useful sites, sources and secrets hidden away on the Internet. If you have 50–75 extra hours a week you could do the same! To subscribe to IWatch Disgest, send a 'subscribe' message to:
iwatch-request@webcom.com

NET-HAPPENINGS/NET-RESOURCES
Announcements of new Internet resources and excerpts from various discussions of Internet related events.
Subscribe to: listserv@IS.INTERNIC.NET

NETSCOUT
A forum for the general user of the Internet to discuss and exchange information about Servers, ftp sites, Filelists, lists, tools and any related aspects. Are you trying to find that Wizmo.exec on a forgotten ListServ? Where were those great utilities to transfer files from PC to Mac? Do you want to know the latest ftp directories? Where is the NutWorks list? This is the place to ask.
Subscribe to: listserv@itesmvf1.rzs.itesm.mx
Submission Address: NETSCOUT@itesmvf1.rzs.itesm.mx

NEW-LISTS
When a new list starts on the Mailbase system the details are posted to this list. It is an open moderated list.
Subscribe to: mailbase@mailbase.ac.uk
Submission Address: NEW-LISTS@mailbase.ac.uk

NEWJOUR-L
NewJour-L is the place to announce brand new or revised electronic networked academic, professional, research, scholarly, societal or topical electronic journals or newsletters. It is a place for messages that announce and describe briefly these new ventures in the early planning/announcement stages and/or at a more mature stage of

actual development and availability. It is also the place to announce availability of paper journals and newsletters as they become available on – move into – electronic networks. Scholarly discussion lists which regularly and continuously maintain supporting files of substantive articles or preprints may also be reported, but this is not the outlet for reporting new lists.

Subscribe to: listserv@e-math.ams.org

Submission Address: NEWJOUR-L@e-math.ams.org

NIS

Network Information Services announcements. Nis@cerf.net list will be a group effort (in true Internet style) to concentrate network information services (nis) announcements onto one list for everyone's use. A few dozen individuals around the Internet will each be monitoring a specific source (mailing list, news group, list serve) and sending the information to CERFnet. We will serve as the moderator, forwarding pertinent submissions to the entire readership of the list, omitting duplicates. To volunteer to monitor a source: send mail to nis@cerf.net. Sponsored by CERFnet.

Subscribe to: listserv@CERF.NET

Submission Address: NIS@CERF.NET

ONLINE-NEWS

ONLINE-NEWS is a list on the topic of online newspapers and magazines. It will serve as a forum to discuss the evolution of newspaper and magazine experiments in electronic publishing. ONLINE-NEWS is not a general journalism discussion.

Subscribe to: majordomo@marketplace.com

Submission Address: ONLINE-NEWS@marketplace.com

Web-Support

For the discussion of issues relating to the World Wide Web, web browsers (Mosaic and Cello in particular), web servers (MacHTTP and serweb), the HTML language, HTML documents and editors, across Macintosh, DOS and Unix platforms in particular.

Subscribe to: mailbase@mailbase.ac.uk

5.6 USENET NEWSGROUPS

5.6.1 Finding newsgroups

To obtain a list of the over 12 000 newsgroups with their descriptions, FTP to ftp.uu.net, and get the file /networking/news/config/newsgroups. This file may contain some newsgroups which some sites do not receive, and may omit some local groups. If this is the case ask the local news administrator for details or see the note below on 'missing' newsgroups.

The list is also available by automatic mail server. Send e-mail to:

ftpmail@doc.ic.ac.uk

subject line: request usenet list

body text: send usenet list info

The Master List of Newsgroup Hierarchies is now available on-line in hypertext format. The List is an alphabetical index of several hundred 'hierarchies' of distributed newsgroups (not the names of the newgroups themselves). Each hierarchy is accompanied by a brief explanation of its affiliation, purpose or topic areas. It is located at:

http://www.magmacom.com/~leisen/master_list.html

Alternative sources for finding Mailing Lists and Newsgroup Lists are:

Gopher to: cs1.presby.edu

Look in the 'Internet Resources' submenu.

Alternatively, try the following URLs:

gopher://cs1.presby.edu/11/net-resources/mailing-lists

gopher://cs1.presby.edu/11/net-resources/newsgroup-lists

A new 'Humanities' domain has been started recently and includes the humanities.design.misc newsgroup. Not all news-servers carry the humanities domain yet although it is a fully legitimate global distribution.

Further details at: http://www.dol.com/

Some News Servers do not carry all Newsgroups. Several schemes to access 'missing' groups are detailed in the FAQ 'How to Receive Banned Newsgroups', which may be obtained by sending e-mail as follows:

To: mail-server@rtfm.mit.edu

Subject: (leave blank)

Body: send usenet-by-group/news.answers/usenet/banned-groups-faq

5.6.2 FAQs and where to find them

The Usenet FAQ documents (Frequently Asked Questions) are available from:

ftp to: rtfm.mit.edu

gopher to: rtfm.mit.edu

This site is worth revisiting just to keep in touch with developments. To retrieve specific FAQs FTP to: rtfm.mit.edu/pub/usenet-by-group/*

Insert the name of the specific newsgroup for the *. Otherwise the * is interpreted as a 'wildcard' and all the newsgroups that have FAQs posted (thousands of them) will be downloaded. Alternatively they can be obtained by sending an e-mail message to mail-server@rtfm.mit.edu, with a blank subject line, and with one or more of the following commands in the message body:

send usenet/news.answers/*name_of_newsgroup1*

send usenet/news.answers/*name_of_newsgroup2*
etc.
The automatic mailserver will return the FAQs of the required lists.

  It is also possible to retrieve FAQs by http. Ohio State University maintains a complete archive of all Usenet FAQs. To access the list of Usenet FAQs (complete listing) go to:
http://www.cis.ohio-state.edu:80/hypertext/faq/usenet

  To learn how to start a newsgroup, see the periodic posts in:
news.announce.newusers, especially:
Newsgroups: news.groups,news.announce.newusers,news.answers
Subject: How to Create a New Usenet Newsgroup
Subject: Usenet Newsgroup Creation Companion
Alternatively, get the files 'How_to_Create_a_New_Usenet_Newsgroup' and 'Usenet_Newsgroup_Creation_Companion' by FTP from
FTP to: rtfm.mit.edu in the directory /pub/usenet/news.groups
or FTP to: src.doc.ic.ac.uk in the directory:
/usenet/usenet-by- group/news.announce.newusers

5.6.3 Newsgroups

alt.1d
One-dimensional imaging and the thinking behind it.

alt.3d
Three-dimensional imaging

alt.architecture
Building design / construction and related topics

alt.architecture.alternative
Solar energy, green issues, etc.

alt.architecture.int-design
Interior Design.

alt.cad
CAD in general.

alt.cad.autocad
AutoCAD related topics.

alt.energy.renewable
Renewable energy technology.

Electronic journals, mailing lists and newsgroups **103**

alt.landscape.architecture
Landscape architecture.

alt.planning.urban
Planning issues.

comp.cad.autocad
Hardware issues related to AutoCAD.

comp.graphics
Computer graphics, art, animation, image processing.

comp.home.automation
Home automation.

comp.infosystems.gis
Geographic Information Systems.

comp.society
Impact of technology on society.

news.answers
News.answers is a repository for periodic informational postings (also called 'Frequently Asked Questions' postings, or 'FAQs') from all Usenet newsgroups.
Usenet: news.answers
Archives: ftp://rtfm.mit.edu/pub/usenet/new.answers

news.newusers.questions
Q & A for users new to the Usenet.
Usenet: news.newusers.questions
Archives: ftp://rtfm.mit.edu/news.newusers.questions/

sci.bio.ecology
Discussion of various aspects of ecology.
Usenet: sci.bio.ecology
Archives: ftp://rtfm.mit.edu/sci.bio/

sci.energy
Energy, science and technology.

sci.engr.heat-vent-ac
Heating, ventilation and air–conditioning.

sci.engr.lighting
Lighting science and technology.

sci.environment
Discussion of the environment.
Usenet: sci.environment
Archives: ftp://rtfm.mit.edu/sci.environment/

5.6.4 Internet access to TheArchitectureForum@Compuserve.com

The forum, moderated by Linda Joy Weinstein, AIA, is accessable at:
http://ourworld.compuserve.com/homepages/lindajoy/cis.htm
or http://www.aecnet.com/lindajoy/cis.htm

5.7 LIBRARY CATALOGUES

Archpics, Index to Architectural Illustrations
telnet://library.cmu.edu
Path: telnet library.cmu.edu, login:library (press the esc key and 2 at the same time to change databases and get to archpics).

Arizona State University
telnet://pac.carl.org
Path: telnet pac.carl.org/Other Library Systems/ Carl Corporation Network Libraries – Western US (Menu 1)/ Arizona Libraries
Arizona State University has an architecture collection of about 20 000 volumes, and a specialization in solar and energy efficient design.

Arizona State's Solar Energy Index
telnet://csi.carl.org
Path: telnet csi.carl.org/ Other Library Systems/ Carl Corporation Network Libraries – Western US (Menu 1)/ Arizona Libraries/ Other ASU Libraries Specialized Collections and Databases
Journal articles, patents, technical reports, pamphlets on alternative energy sources.

ArtSource
http://www.uky.edu/Artsource/general.html
Guides and bibliographies from several libraries including Beryl Smith's *Art Bibliographies Modern User Guide*, Jeffrey Weidman's *Researching Your Art Object*, and Shelly Olim's *Subject List of Special Libraries in Washington, D.C.*

Avery Index to Architectural Periodicals

http://www.ahip.getty.edu/ahip/home.html

Access to the most comprehensive index to architectural periodicals is made available by the Getty Art History Information Program research into database retrieval.

University of California Melvyl

telnet://melvyl.ucop.edu

In addition to strong collections in architecture at UCLA (23 000 volumes) and Berkeley (160 000 volumes), the UC Melvyl catalogue is also a gateway to the catalogues of many other impressive collections including Harvard, Princeton, Penn State, and Yale.

Calpoly Library Gopher

gopher://library.calpoly.edu:70/11/Subject_Guide/Architecture

Path: gopher library.calpoly.edu/subject guide to online resources /architecture

The 'Descriptive Guide to the Julia Morgan Collection' provides information on the local collection.

Columbia University Library

telnet://columbianet.columbia.edu (Choose Clio; to exit type q twice)

The Avery is the premier architecture collection; however their online catalogue, named CLIO, dates from 1981 only.

Library of Congress LOCIS

telnet://locis.loc.gov

Environmental Design Library, UC Berkeley

Library guides (e.g. to reference books, book review sources) in three major disciplines:

architecture: gopher://library.berkeley.edu/11/resdbs/arch

landscape architecture: gopher://library.berkeley.edu/11/resdbs/land

planning: gopher://library.berkeley.edu/11/resdbs/plan

Environmental Protection Agency National Catalog Database

telnet://epaibm.rtpnc.epa.gov (Choose Public, then OLS)

Harvard University

telnet://hollis.harvard.edu (Choose HOLLIS; type exit to disconnect)

About 235 000 volumes in architecture. VT100 emulation required.

Iowa State Visual Resources Collection (College of Design)

gopher://isumvs.iastate.edu:70/1~db.SLIDES

Path: gopher isumvs.iastate.edu/ISU Research Information/VRC

Indexes for medium, country, artist, title, style, technique, century, location. Includes architecture.

Kunstbib
gopher://kari.uio.no:7075/71/kunstbib%3f
Path: gopher gopher.ub.uio.no/ English/ Norwegian National Database Services/ Search 'Art bibliography' (Kunstbib)
Index to articles, books, pamphlets, etc. in the field of Norwegian design, including architecture.

Leininger Home Page
http://nimrod.mit.edu/depts/rotch/subjects/architecture/pageone.html
Set up by MIT's Architecture Librarian, Michael Leininger, this site provides guides, some annotated, to standard print library information in architecture and construction, including guides to construction dictionaries, biographical sources, directories, building codes, accessibility information and Boston architecture. The Rotch Library home page is: http://nimrod.mit.edu/depts/rotch/services/rotch.html.

University of Maryland College Park
telnet://victor.umd.edu
Path: telnet victor.umd.edu/ pac/vt 100/ UMS Campus Library Catalogs/ UM College Park
Includes the National Trust Library.

University of Michigan
telnet://hermes.merit.edu (At host? prompt type mirlyn)
VT100 emulation required. About 50 000 volumes in architecture.

Julia Morgan Collection, San Simeon
Calpoly State University, San Luis Obispo
telnet://library.calpoly.edu (Choose Polycat; to exit type x at menu)

National Register of Historic Places
telnet://victor.umd.edu
Path: telnet victor.umd.edu/other databases/NPS
National Register entries include building name, location, date listed and National Register number.

Quakeline
telnet://bison.cc.buffalo.edu (from the menu choose General Indexes, then enter QKLN)
'The database of the National Center for Earthquake Engineering Research (NCEER) contains bibliographic information on the subjects of earthquakes, earthquake

engineering, natural hazards mitigation and related topics.' Primarily 1987 onwards. Includes non-book as well as print materials.

Rensselaer Polytechnic
telnet://infotrax.rotary.its.rpi.edu (Choose Library, then Slides)
About 30 000 volumes in architecture, with a special interest in emerging technologies, and a separate architecture slides database.

Roman Ecclesiastical Architecture
University of Wisconsin Milwaukee
telnet://uwmcat.lib.uwm.edu

Smithsonian Institute
telnet://siris.si.edu

Uncover
telnet://database.carl.org/Uncover or telnet://csi.carl.org
http://www.carl.org/uncover/unchome.html
A table of contents index covering many architecture periodicals (from 1986). Uncover is accessible without charge. To exit type //exit. The web site provides the latest Uncover newsletter, and promises to have instructions on how to search Uncover.

University of Waterloo Library
http://library.uwaterloo.ca/discipline/arch/index.html
Useful guides to finding traditional information sources. 'Quick Facts and Bibliographies in Architecture' includes two bibliographies: Library Reference Materials in Architecture, and Library Resources on Architecture Schools and Practices. 'Doing Research in Architecture' has guides on Architecture: How to Find Journal Articles, as well as other more general guides such as 'How to Find a Book Review'.

Yale University
telnet://umpg.ycc.yale.edu:6520 (To exit type stop or use telnet escape key)
VT100 emulation required. About 75 000 volumes in architecture, with emphasis on theory and research.

6

Government and university information sources

6.1 GOVERNMENT INFORMATION SOURCES

6.1.1 U.K. Government

The British Council
http://www.open.gov.uk/bc/bcchom01.html
The British Council promotes educational, cultural and technical cooperation between Britain and other countries. The site is under development but it is intended to provide comprehensive information about the British Council services worldwide, and will also provide a single point of access to relevant British resources.

Centre for Information Systems
The U.K. is only just starting to make information available on the WWW. The basic URL is: http://www.open.gov.uk
The Centre for Information Systems and HM Treasury have home pages at: http://www.open.gov.uk and http://www.hm-treasury.gov.uk
U.K. Department of the Environment: http://www.open.gon.uk/doe/
HM Inspectorate of Pollution: http://www.open.gov.uk/hmip
Department of Transport: http://www.open.gov.uk/dot/dothome.htm
A more general jumping off point for UK information is:
http://www.city.net/countries/united_kingdom

British Library
gopher://portico.bl.uk
General information about the collections, opening times and so on.

Data Protection Act
http://www.open.gov.uk/dpr/dprhome.html

Foreign and Commonwealth Office
http://www.fco.gov.uk/reference/travel_advice/advice.html
The Travel Advice Notices for 125 destinations from Afghanistan to Zimbabwe.

Foresight Panel Reports
http://www.dcs.ed.ac.uk/foresight/
The full texts of the Foresight Panel Reports, taking a forward look at possible scenarios for key U.K. industries, including construction. Back issues of *Foresight News,* which gives details of projects arising from the panel reports is at:
http://www.open.gov.uk/ost/osthome.htm

The Met on the Net
http://www.meto.gov.uk
Regional weather reports, coverage of inshore waters, shipping forecasts, gale warnings and downloadable satellite images of the U.K. More general meteorological information, with many links to other web sites is available at WeatherNet, run by Michael MacDonald at the University of Michigan:
http://cirrus.sprl.umich.edu/wxnet/

6.1.2 European Union

E.U.
Increasing numbers of EU reports are being published on the web. The Bangemann Report, for example, describes specific measures to be taken by member states for information infrastructures. It is available at:
http://www.earn.net/EC/bangemann.html

International Organisation for Standardisation
http://www.iso.ch/welcome.html
A list of ISO members and technical committees, background information on the ISO and catalogue of ISO standards.

French Embassy Gopher
Gopher:iep.univ-lyon2.fr
select 'l'ambassade de france'
Most of the material here is in English. There are tourism itineraries that give information and advice on travelling in France together with climate and weather data.

FranceWeb
http://www.francenet.fr

FranceWeb is one of the most important web sites in France. 'Our aim is to provide a comprehensive navigational aid, illustrated and commented links (classified by subjects), to our French speaking visitors.'

The URLs for direct access to some of the Resource Pages are:

Directories: http://www.francenet.fr/franceweb/Fra/FraAnn.html

France and Paris: http://www.francenet.fr/franceweb/Fra/FraFrance.html

French culture: http://www.francenet.fr/franceweb/Fra/FraCult.html

French newsgroups: http://www.francenet.fr/franceweb/Fra/FraNews.html

Arts: http://www.francenet.fr/franceweb/Cul/culart.html

Government: http://www.francenet.fr/franceweb/Eco/ecogovernement.html

Netherlands Ministry of Education

http://www.minvrom.nl

Provides link to the Netherlands Government Buildings Office.

6.1.3 United States

The U.S. is developing a policy of placing documents on the Web and there are many gophers linked to U.S. government information. Several government sites, such as the Energy Efficiency and Renewable Energy Network, are listed in the detailed subject listings elsewhere in this book. This is a selection of sites with more general information thought to be of interest to architecture/building. Extensive guides to government sources are found at the University of Michigan Clearinghouse for Subject-Oriented Internet Resource Guides.

Argonne National Laboratory

http://www.mcs.anl.gov

Bureau of Reclamation

http://www.usbr.gov

Contains many links relating to sand and aggregates. The aggregate database is directly accessible at:

http://donews.do.usbr.gov/merl/aggtests.html

Census of Population and Housing

gopher://bigcat.missouri.edu:70/11/reference/census/us

1990 data with comparisons from 1980.

DOE

http://www.eren.doe.gov/

Government information sources

Department of Transportation
http://www.dot.gov:80/

Energy Efficiency and Renewable Energy Network
http://www.eren.doe.gov
Information on EREN and many links to energy related information sources.

Environmental Protection Agency
gopher://gopher.epa.gov:70/11
The EPA gopher includes EPA information locators such as ACCESS EPA (a directory full of information that gives pointers to other sources, to the EPA online library catalogue, and to EPA gophers), EPA standards, rules, etc.

Federal Government
http://www.fedworld.gov
A sorted list of over 100 U.S. government information sources. Documents may also be retrieved by ftp from:
ftp://ftp.fedworld.gov (192.239.92.205)

Federal Information Exchange
gopher://fedix.fie.com:70
On research programs, grants and more.

Federal Web Locator
http://www.law.vill.edu/fed-agency/fedwebloc.html
As a point of entry covers almost all U.S. judicial and legislative topics.

Geological Survey
http://info.er.usgs.gov

Government Documents in the News
http://www.lib.umich.edu/libhome/Documents.center/docnews.html

Government gophers at the UC-Irvine
gopher://peg.cwis.uci.edu:7000/11/gopher.welcome/peg/GOPHERS/gov.
Path: gopher gopher-server.cwis.uci.edu/Library/virtual reference desk / US government gophers.

Government gophers at the University of Missouri at St. Louis
gopher://umslvma.umsl.edu:70/11/library/govdocs
Includes, amongst other material, the U.S. Industrial Outlook (for information on construction and construction materials).

Government Information Sharing Project
http://govinfo.kerr.orst.edu/index.html
U.S. and State census and agricultural economy data, with links to other data sources.

InfoSlug at the University of California Santa Cruz
gopher://scilibx.ucsc.edu:70/11/The Community/
Guide to U.S. state and local government .

Lawrence Berkeley Laboratory
http://www.lbl.gov
Apart from the Library Catalogue and Publications list LBL has a Center for Building Science which has programmes in Building Technologies (particulary windows and daylighting), Energy Analysis and Indoor Air Quality.

Library of Congress
gopher://marvel.loc.gov:70/11/federal
http://www.loc.gov/
http://lcweb.loc.gov/homepage/lchp.html

National Science Foundation
gopher://x.nsf.gov:70
NSF publications, awards, agencies, as well as links to other government gophers.

National Technology Transfer Center
gopher://iron.nttc.edu:70/1
Information on funding and research opportunities, technology available for licensing and contacts in the federal laboratories.

NTIS FedWorld
http://www.fedworld.gov
In addition to NTIS information, this is a major gateway to government information. It is, however, often busy and difficult to access.

National Institute of Standards and Technology
http://www.nist.gov/welcome.html
gopher://zserve.nist.gov:79/1
Information on the laboratory programmes. The Materials Science and Engineering Laboratory and the Building and Fire Research Laboratory are of particular interest. The High Performance Construction Materials and Systems section is at:
http://titan.cbt.nist.gov

National Park Service
http://www.nps.gov

Government information sources

Some information on the National Register, HABS/HAER, and other NPS programs, as well as a cultural landscape bibliography.

National Renewable Energy Laboratory
gopher://gopher.nrel.gov:70
Details of research in progress, NREL publications database, new energy information locator, solar radiation data and maps, wind energy resources maps, etc.

Office of Applied Economics
http://www.bfrl.nist.gov/oae
Projects include economic methods for building standards.

Office of Technology Assessment
http://www.ota.gov

Public Buildings Service
http://www.gsa.gov/pbs.htm
'PBS is responsible for planning, designing, building, restoring, providing landscaping for and leasing government office buildings and facilities.'

State and Local Government on the Net
http://www.piperinfo.com/~piper/state/states.html

THOMAS: Legislative Information on the Net
http://thomas.loc.gov/

U.S. Army Corps of Engineers
       Civil Engineering Research Lab
       http://www.cecer.army.mil/
       Construction Engineering Research Laboratories
       http://www.cecer.army.mil:80/welcome.html
       Waterways Experiment Station (WES)
       http://www.wes.army.mil/
       WES – Structural Analysis Group
       http://sliris.wes.army.mil/

U.S. Government Collection
http://www.epix.net/~alf/usgov

6.1.4 Japan

Ministry of Foreign Affairs
http://infomofa.nttls.co.jp/infomofa
Provides a link to a number of information sources relating to Japan.

Ministry for International Trade and Industry (MITI)
http://www.glocom.ac.jp/NEWS/MITI-doc.html
Includes details of MITI's programme for the development of an advanced information infrastructure at:
http://www.glocom.ac.jp/WhatsNew/MPT.html

6.1.5 United Nations

UN Web Server
http://www.un.org
Details of UN agencies, documents, publications and photographs. As the header includes an 80k image the index may be accessed directly at:
http://www.un.org/textindex.html

United Nations Gopher
Gopher to: nywork1.undp.org
also via WWW at:
http://www.undp.org
World Trade, the U.N. Charter, World Currencies, The U.N. mission of Peace and much more.

6.1.6 Canada

The Canadian Parliament
http://www.parl.gc.ca
with a gopher server at:gopher.parl.gc.ca

Canadian Home Pages
http://info.ic.gc.ca
A complete listing of Canadian Government pages. This home page will be continually updated and new sites and URLs will be listed when available.

6.1.7 Hong Kong

Hong Kong Government Information Centre
http://www.info.gov.hk
A single access point to information published on the Internet by official and quasi-official organizations in Hong Kong. Includes: *Hong Kong in Figures* and *Hong Kong in Pictures* amongst other official publications.

Hong Kong Online Guide
http://www.hk.super.net/~webzone/hk.html
The Hong Kong Online Guide is an electronic guidebook for Hong Kong. Information on airlines, hotels, and tourist sites with many illustrations.

6.1.7 Australia

Parliament of Australia Home Page
http://www.aph.gov.au/
The Parliament of the Commonwealth of Australia is now offering a home page from which a variety of Australian Parliamentary information may be accessed. The WWW pages are still under development, with a trial of weekly Hansard and related information accessible from this home page as well as separate access to Senate, House of Representatives and Parliamentary Library information.

Australian Senate
http://senate.aph.gov.au/

Australian House of Representatives
http://www.aph.gov.au/house/

Australian Parliamentary Library
http:/library/aph.gov.au/library/
gopher://lib18.aph.gov.au

6.2 GOVERNMENT ORGANIZATIONS

BRANZ
http://www.branz.org.nz/
Building Research Association of New Zealand

BRE
http://www.bre.co.uk/

U.K. Building Research Establishment.
Information from the Energy Efficiency Office's Best Practice Programme is at:
http://www.bre.co.uk/bre/otherprg/eeobp/. A draft of BS1192 Part 5 on the structure
of CAD building project data is at: http://www.bre.co.uk/~itra.index.html. The BRE,
together with the University of Newcastle, is also developing 'The Construction
Information Gateway' as an interface to web resources. It is at: http://cig.bre.co.uk/

Centre Scientifique et Technique du Bâtiment
http://omega.sop.cstb.fr/

Canadian Centre for Architecture
http://cca.qc.ca/homepage.html

CIB W78
http://delphi.kstr.lth.se/w78
Conseil International du Bâtiment Working Group on IT in Construction.
A description of the CIB, its task groups, goals, seminars, members, mailing lists, and
links to other sites.

CIE
http://www.hike.te.chiba-u.ac.jp/ikeda/CIE/home.html
Commission Internationale de l'Eclairage. Publications, press releases, extracts from
CIE Journal.

Construction Industry Research and Information Association
http://www.gold.net/users/bm37/index.html
Construction research reports and information on CIRIA's activities.

CSIRO Division of Building, Construction and Engineering
http://www.ahuri.edu.au/
Australian building research organization.

Environmental Protection Agency
gopher://gopher.epa.gov:70/11
The EPA gopher includes EPA information locators such as ACCESS EPA (a directory
full of information that gives references to other sources, to the EPA online library
catalogue and to EPA gophers), EPA standards, rules, etc.

IRCAM
http://www.ircam.fr/
Institut de Recherche et Coordination Acoustique / Musique

Institute for Research in Construction. National Research Council Canada
http://www.irc.nrc.ca
Information on staff, research projects and publications. Some full-text items are included. French and English versions available.

Institute for Solar Energy Systems
http://www.ise.fhg.de/
At the Fraunhofer Institute at Freiburg, Germany.

International Standards Organisation (ISO)
http://www.iso.ch/welcome.html
Catalogue of ISO standards, details of committees and background to ISO.
Queries may be e–mailed to webmaster@isocs.iso.ch

Lawrence Berkeley Laboratory
http://www.lbl.gov
Access is provided to the library catalogue and publications list. The Lawrence Berkeley Laboratory has a Center for Building Science which has programmes in Building Technologies (including windows and daylighting), Energy Analysis and Indoor Air Quality.

National Institute of Standards and Technology
gopher://zserve.nist.gov:79/1
http://www.nist.gov/welcome.html
Includes information on their laboratory programs, such as the Materials Science and Engineering Laboratory and the Building and Fire Research Laboratory.

National Renewable Energy Laboratory
gopher://gopher.nrel.gov:70
Research in progress, NREL publications database, new energy information locator, solar radiation data and maps, wind energy resources maps and more.

National Science Foundation
gopher://stis.nsf.gov:70
NSF publications, awards, agencies, as well as links to other government gophers.

National Key Centre for Design
http://daedalus.edc.rmit.edu.au
'The National Key Centre for Design at the Royal Melbourne Institute of Technology exists to focus the work of Australian designers, researchers, industry and government on the changing relationship between design, production and consumption.' This site provides centre research papers and projects such as EcoReDesign ('a program to improve the environmental performance of manufactured products') and Eco Built

Environment ('an inquiry into the philosophy of environmental sustainability both for the design and the designers of the built environment') as well as links to other environmental design research centers, and to Internet sites relating to the built environment.

Solar Energy and Building Physics Laboratory
Laboratoire d'Energie Solaire et de Physique du Bâtiment
http://lesowww.epfl.ch/index.html
Includes information on research projects in daylighting and photovoltaics. It is also an excellent entry into some of the technical Internet sources related to building.

SOLSTICE
http://solstice.crest.org/
The online information service of the Centre for Renewable Energy and Sustainable Technology

Swedish Council for Building Research
http://www.bfr.se/
English homepage is at: http://www.bfr.se/building.htm
English language publications are at: http://www.bfr.se/library/tidn/sbr.htm

Swedish Institute of Steel Construction (SBI)
http://www.algonet.se/~sbi

TNO
http://www.tno.nl/instit/bouw/home.html
gopher://gopher.tno.nl/11/tno/bouw
Dutch construction research organization.

U.S. Department of Energy
http://appollo.osti.gov

VTT
http://www.vtt.fi/rte/bldtech.html
Finnish construction research organization.

6.3 SCHOOLS OF ARCHITECTURE

6.3.1 United Kingdom

Bath: University of Bath, School of Architecture and Building Engineering
http://www.bath.ac.uk/Departments/arch.html
Centre for Advanced Studies in Architecture (CASA)
http://bath.ac.uk/Centres/CASA/
Digital maps, urban models and design visualization.

Cambridge: University of Cambridge, School of Architecture
http://www.arct.cam.ac.uk/index.html
University of Cambridge, Martin Centre
http://www.arct.cam.ac.uk/mc/index.html

Cardiff: The Welsh School of Architecture
http://www.cf.ac.uk/uwcc/archi/
Computers in Teaching Initiative: Centre for the Built Environment
http://www.cf.ac.uk/cticbe/

Dundee: Duncan of Jordanstone College of Art, School of Architecture
http://bagpuss.architecture.dundee.ac.uk/

Edinburgh: Heriot Watt University, Edinburgh College of Art, School of Architecture
http://www.hw.ac.uk/ecaWWW/arch/arch.htm

Edinburgh: University of Edinburgh, Department of Architecture
http://www.caad.ed.ac.uk/arch/

Glasgow: Mackintosh School of Architecture
http://www.gla.ac.uk/Acad/Architecture/

Glasgow: University of Strathclyde, Department of Architecture and Building Science
http://www.strath.ac.uk/Departments/Architecture/index.html

Huddersfield: The University of Huddersfield, Department of Architecture
http://www.hud.ac.uk/schools/design_technology/architecture/arch_www/homep age/homepage.html
This site is being developed as an on-line resource for staff and students of the school. Apart from information about the school it contains WWW starting points, document and image archives and examples of student work.

Leicester and Milton Keynes: De Montfort University, School of the Built Environment
City Campus: http://www.benvle.dmu.ac.uk/
Milton Keynes: http://www.mk.dmu.ac.uk/depts/benv/

Liverpool: University of Liverpool, School of Architecture and Building Engineering
http://www.liv.ac.uk/Buildings/Building46.html

Liverpool: John Moore's University, School of the Built Environment
Undergraduate
http://www.livjm.ac.uk/university/courses/archst.htm
Postgraduate
http://www.livjm.ac.uk/university/courses/architpg.htm

London: the Architectural Association School of Architecture
http://www.gold.net/ellipsis/evolutionary/aa.html#top

London: University College London, the Bartlett School of Architecture
http://doric.bart.ucl.ac.uk/index.html

London: University of East London, School of Architecture
http://www.uel.ac.uk/faculties/arch/info.html
Centre for Environment and Computing in Architecture, Computing and Design Programme: http://www.uel.ac.uk/faculties/arch/#CAAD
The MSc(Generative Modelling) coursebook, the *Generative Modelling Cookbook* is at:
http://www.uel.ac.uk/faculties/arch/workbook.html

London: University of Greenwich (Dartford Campus), School of Architecture and Landscape
http://www.gre.ac.uk/academic/index.html

London: Kingston University, School of Architecture
http://www.king.ac.uk/university

Schools of architecture

London: University of North London, School of Architecture and Interior Design
http://lion.unl.ac.uk/courses/arch.html

London: South Bank University, School of Architecture and Civil Engineering
http://www.sbu.ac.uk/Architecture/home.html
Information about the school including their prospectus and newsletter, and student work. A tutorial on how to model the Barcelona Pavilion using UpFront.

Manchester: University of Manchester, School of Architecture
http://info.mcc.ac.uk/Arts/architecture/architecture.html

Newcastle: University of Newcastle, Department of Architecture
http://www.archit.ncl.ac.uk/

Oxford: Oxford Brookes University, School of Architecture
http://www.brookes.ac.uk/arch/archome.html
http://cs3.brookes.ac.uk/arch/archome.html

Sheffield: University of Sheffield, School of Architectural Studies
http://www2.shef.ac.uk/uni/academic/A-C/archst/

Ulster: University of Ulster, School of the Built Environment
http://www.ulst.ac.uk/SCOBE/index.html

York: York Institute of Advanced Architectural Studies
http://www.york.ac.uk/aux/init/res/iaas-w.htm

Computer-Assisted Learning in Construction and Property
http://www.salford.ac.uk/docs/depts/survey/staff/BSloan/cib/cib.html
This task group of the Conseil International du Batiment (CIB) is 'responsible for considering the application and development of computer-assisted learning (CAL) and computer-based training (CBT) within the education and training of the construction and property professions'. This site has information on the task group, and links to CAL/CBT related information on the web.

Computers in Teaching Initiative
http://info.ox.ac.uk/cti/
The U.K. Government has established a number of centres to co-ordinate computer applications in the teaching of various subjects at University level. The above URL provides links to all the current CTI centres but specific subject areas may be accessed directly:
Built Environment (Cardiff): http://ctiweb.cf.ac.uk/
Engineering (QM & W): http://www.ctieng.qmw.ac.uk/CTIEng.html

Art and Design (Brighton): http://www.bton.ac.uk/ctiad
Art and Architectural History (Glasgow): http://www.arts.gla.ac.uk/www/ctich/
Environmental Science (Aberdeen): http://www.clues.abdn.ac.uk:8080/

Anglia Polytechnic University. Department of the Built Environment
http://www.be.anglia.ac.uk/

ASCA
http://www.hw.ac.uk/ecaWWW/arch/asca
The Architecture Schools Computing Association

6.3.2 Europe (non UK)

Chalmers University of Technology, Gothenberg, School of Architecture (Sweden)
http://www.arch.chalmers.se/home-e.html

Chelyabinsk Technical University, Russia
Faculty of Architecture and Construction
http://www.tu-chel.ac.ru/base/f3/main.en.html

Czech Technical University, Architecture
gopher://isdec.vc.cvut.cz/11/.gopherdir/ctu/Architecture

Eindhoven, Netherlands: LAVA, The 'Lab voor Architectuur', Technische Universiteit Eindhoven, Faculty of Architecture and Planning
http://www.tue.nl/lava
Computer models in various formats, archives of ListServs and newsgroups, faculty home page information on the school, software for the virtual studio formerly operated at this site, student projects, essays and more.

Graz, Austria: University of Technology, Faculty of Architecture
http://www.tu-graz.ac.at/Carch
Studio projects, courses, events.

Kaiserslautern, Germany: University, Faculty of Architecture, Town and Environmental Planning,
http://www.uni-kl.de:80/FB-ARUBI/

Lausanne, Switzerland: Swiss Federal Technical Institute, Department of Architecture
http://dawww.epfl.ch/

Schools of architecture

Maribor, Slovenia
http://www.uni-mb.si/mb_arhitektura.html

Marseilles, France: GAMSAU, Groupe d'Etudes pour l'Application des Methodes Scientifiques a l'Architecture et l'Urbanisme. CAD research group:
http://gropius.cnrs-mrs.fr/
School of Architecture: http://www-gams.cnrs-mrs.fr/

Stockholm, Sweden: Royal Institute of Technology, Dept of Architecture and Planning
http://www,arch.kth.se/
Student projects organized into separate home pages, which document their designs through photographs, drawings and CAD images.

Stuttgart, Germany: Universität , Fakultät der Architektur und Stadtplanung
http://www.architektur.uni-stuttgart.de:1200/
A range of projects illustrated with computer rendered images.

Venice, Italy: Istituto Universitario di Architettura di Venezia
http://venice.iuav.unive.it/
Alternatively, http://www.iuav.unive.it or http://iuavbc.iuav.unive.it

Vienna, Austria: Technical University, EDV-Lab.
http://info.archlab.tuwien.ac.at/

Weimar, Germany: University, Department of Architecture, City and Regional Planning
http://www.hab-weimar.de/dummy/architektur.html
CAD Laboratory
http://www.hab-weimar.de/vradmin

Zurich, Switzerland: ETH, Architecture and CAAD
http://www.arch.ethz.ch/
http://caad.arch.ethz.ch/
The Chair of CAAD contains work on 3-D modelling research and projects from the 'Virtual Design Studio'.

eCAADe
http://www.liv.ac.uk/~arch/ecaade
The association for Education in CAAD in Europe

6.3.3 USA

Schools of Architecture and Academic Programmes
http://www.vnr.com/vnr/a_school.html

Association of Collegiate Schools of Architecture Western Region
http://uhunix.uhcc.hawaii.edu:3333/acsa_home.html
This server contains programme descriptions and admission requirements of the 23 ACSA colleges in the western region. The ACSA has as its principal membership the professional schools of architecture in both the United States and Canada. It exists for the purpose of improving the quality of architecture education.

Association of Collegiate Schools of Architecture Southwest Region
http://www.tulane.edu/~swacsa

Arizona State University, School of Architecture
http://128.171.44.6:3333/catalog/UA/ua_home.html

Arizona, College of Architecture and Environmental Design
http://aspin/asu.edu/provider/caed/caedhome.html
Academic info, plus student galleries and community projects.

Brown University, History of Art and Architecture Department
gopher://gopher.brown.edu/11/brown/departs/historyo

California College of Arts and Crafts, Department of Architecture / ACSA
http://128.171.44.6:3333/catalog/CCAC/ccac_home.html

California Polytechnic State University, San Luis Obispo, Architecture Dept:
http://www.calpoly.edu/~arch
College of Architecture and Environmental Design:
http://www.calpoly.edu/~caed

UCSB, Art and Architecture
gopher://ucsbuxa.ucsb.edu:3001/11/.Arts/.Art

California, University of, at Berkeley, Department of Architecture
http://128.171.44.6:3333/catalog/UCB/ucb_home.html
College of Environmental Design
http://www.ced.berkeley.edu/

Schools of architecture

California, University of, at Los Angeles, Department of Architecture and Urban Design
http://www.gsaup.ucla.edu/
Urban simulation team projects, class projects, faculty and student home pages, and more promised.

Carnegie Mellon, Department of Architecture
http://www.arc.cmu.edu/

Colorado University, College of Architecture and Planning
http://wallstreet.colorado.edu/ENVD_Mosaic_Files/A-P_Pages/A-P_HP

Columbia University, Graduate School of Architecture
http://www.cc.columbia.edu/~archpub
Of the four menu items the Digital Design Lab is the most interesting. It can be accessed directly at http://www.arch.columbia.edu and includes information on current DDL research projects; DDL Architectural Projects; and Computer-Aided Design Courses. 'The Digital Design Lab deals with issues surrounding the question of access to the Information Superhighway and focuses on the development of intuitive three-dimensional interfaces for multimedia and on-line learning environments.'

Cornell College of Architecture, Art and Planning
http://convex.cit.cornell.edu/
http://www.architecture.cornell.edu/
Various visualizations including pinhole camera images.
gopher://gopher.cornell.edu/11/.dirs/COURSES95/CSAP
Path: University courses/college of architecture, art and planning
Course descriptions by discipline. On the first Cornell institution menu the Cornell gopher may be searched by keyword, and 'architecture' turns up a variety of information such as the alumni list of the department (the firm at which they work is given, although the individual's name is coded).

Frank Lloyd Wright School of Architecture
http://128.171.44.6:3333/catalog/FLWSA/flwsa_home.html

Georgia Tech, College of Architecture
http://www.gatech.edu/coa/coa_home.html

Harvard Graduate School of Design
http://gsd.harvard.edu/GSD.html
School information, selected faculty and graduate student projects/research, and other information such as the library section.
gopher://gopher.harvard.edu/11/.courses/DES/main

Path: gopher courses.harvard.edu/Harvard University On-Line Course Catalogs/design, graduate school of
Information on the degree programs, facilities, courses, etc. The following can be searched by keyword: course descriptions, faculty information, and general information. Some of this information is also available at the web site.

Hawaii, University of, School of Architecture
gopher://gopher.hawaii.edu:70/11/Student/Cat/Schools/ARCH
Path: gopher gopher.Hawaii.edu/student information/1993-95UHM general and graduate information catalog/school-college information/ School of Architecture
Program descriptions, honours and awards, list of faculty.

Idaho, University of, Department of Architecture
http://128.171.44.6:3333/catalog/UI/ui_home.html

Illinois, University of, at Urbana-Champaign, School of Architecture
http://www.billboard.com/UnivIllArch/UIA.html

Kansas State University, Department of Architecture
http://www.ksu.edu/archdes/
A 4th year Computer Aided Design Studio is at:
http://www.ksu.edu/archdes/arch/index.html
The studio project is entitled 'Reality Center'. The students of the studio are challenged to come up with an architectural proposition which directly addresses the issues of reality, memory, orientation, dwelling and form in the context of the emerging world of virtual reality. Questions, comments, suggestions are welcome. Mahesh Senagala, Assistant Professor, Department of Architecture, Kansas State University, Manhattan, KS: http://www.ksu.edu/~yaksha

Kent State University School of Architecture and Environmental Design
http://arcrs4.saed.kent.edu/
Provides a gallery of faculty and student work, including rendered 3-D images and Photoshop images. Also links to class homepages and information archive of local architects.

Kentucky University, College of Architecture
http://www.uky.edu/Architecture/archhome.html
An interesting collection of 3-D images containing much innovative design work.

Massachusetts Institute of Technology School of Architecture
http://alberti.mit.edu/ap/ap.html
Descriptions of online classes including a virtual design workshop and a course called digital communities, a walkthrough/mpeg video of new school space, special projects

such as the current construction of studio space (The Design Studio of the Future) and more.

Massachusetts Institute of Technology, Media Lab
http://www.media.mit.edu/

Miami, University of, School of Architecture
http://rossi.arc.miami.edu/
Information on the school, local architecture ('Arquitectura Tropicana'), a virtual gallery of students' work containing models of various well-known buildings, courseware (of particular interest may be the online course 'Digital Design Studio'), faculty books in print, research (e.g. New South Dade Planning Charette) and other information.

Michigan, University of, College of Architecture and Urban Planning
http://www.caup.umich.edu

Minnesota, University of, College of Architecture & Landscape Architecture
gopher://gumby.arch.umn.edu/

Mississippi State University, School of Architecture
http://www.sarc.msstate.edu/online/online.cgi
Heavily graphics based site and so takes a while to load. Information about the school and its research units; contains various student homepages. To go direct to the student work use:
http://www.sarc.msstate.edu/work/work.cgi
To directly access the Digital Research and Imaging Lab's pages:
http://www.sarc.msstate.edu/dril/
A list of web architecture references are at:
http://www.sarc.msstate.edu/online/sources.html
The school also holds an ftp archive:
ftp://ftp.sarc.msstate.edu/

Montana State University, School of Architecture
http://128.171.44.6:3333/catalog/MSU/msu_home.html

NCSU School of Design (North Carolina State University)
http://www2.ncsu.edu:80/ncsu/design/

New Mexico, University of, School of Architecture and Planning
http://128.171.44.6:3333/catalog/UNM/unm_home.html

New York at Buffalo, University of, Architecture and Planning
http://arch.buffalo.edu:8001/

North Carolina State University (NCSU), Architecture
gopher://dewey.lib.ncsu.edu/11/library/disciplines/architecture

Oklahoma University, College of Architecture
http://www.uoknor.edu/architecture/
Scanned photographs of several student projects.

Oregon, University Department of Architecture
http://www-architecture.uoregon.edu/foyer.
Architectonics Studio
http://darkwing.uoregon.edu/~struct/
'An exploration of the current research, documentation and electronic courseware being developed by Chris Luebkeman.' Fascinating site featuring online courseware for structures in architecture, research and documentation, an online multiframe manual, and 'Connector' (correspondence and essays on teaching technology in architecture schools).

Oregon, University of, School of Architecture and Allied Arts
http://laz.uoregon.edu/

Portland State University, School of Fine and Performing Arts
http://www.ee.pdx.edu:80/depts/fpa/

Princeton School of Architecture
http://www.princeton.edu/~soa/
Standard information, but includes a text-only version and a form to send electronically to the school for additional information or to comment.

Rensselaer Polytechnic Institute, School of Architecture
http://www.rpi.edu/dept/science/Catalog/Architecture/
Lighting Research Center, School of Architecture
http://www.rpi.edu/dept/lrc/LRC.html

Rice University, Architecture
gopher://riceinfo.rice.edu/11/Subject/Architecture
Rice Design Alliance
http://riceinfo.rice.edu:80/ES/Architecture/RDA/RDA
This site holds full-text of many of the papers given in the spring lecture series on the virtual city, as well as information on the Design Alliance.

Schools of architecture

Southern California Institute of Architecture
http://128.171.44.6:3333/catalog/SCIARC/sciarc_home.html

Southern California, University of, School of Architecture
gopher://cwis.usc.edu/11/University_Information/Catalogue/School_of_Architecture
http://www.usc.edu/dept/architecture/
Computer visualizations used to explain more complex research topics.

Syracuse University, School of Architecture
http://soa.syr.edu/
A large site with many categories. CAD renderings are under the 'Images' heading.

Texas, University School of Architecture
gopher://gopher.utexas.edu:3003/11/pub/output/architecture
World Lecture Hall: Architecture
http://wwwhost.cc.utexas.edu/world/instruction/index.html#Architecture
Links to syllabi, essays, lecture notes and images of architecture courses from Columbia, MIT, University of Oregon, Syracuse, and the University of Virginia.

Tulane School of Architecture
http://www.tulane.edu/~tsahome/
Student projects, including excellent CAD graphics.

UCSB, Art and Architecture
gopher://ucsbuxa.ucsb.edu:3001/11/.Arts/.Art

UNLV, College of Architecture, Construction Management and Planning
http://www.unlv.edu/engineering/architecture_studies/index.html

Utah, University of, Graduate School of Architecture
http://128.171.44.6:3333/catalog/UU/uu_home.html

Virginia Polytechnic Institute, College of Architecture and Urban Studies
http://www.vt.edu/colleges/archi.html

Virginia, University of , School of Architecture
gopher://minerva.acc.virginia.edu/11/schools/architecture
http://minerva.acc.Virginia.EDU/~arch/
High quality computer renderings.

Washington State University, School of Architecture
http://www.arch.wsu.edu/

Individual student home pages of varying quality. Several designs include good computer graphics work.

Washington University in St. Louis, School of Architecture
http://www.cec.wustl.edu/arch/
Includes the graduate student handbook and other standard material, as well as course descriptions of selected courses.
Contains web links at
http://www.cec.wustl.edu/arch/links/Links.html

Washington University Centre for Architecture and Urban Planning
http://www.caup.washington.edu/
The graduate student homepages are of most interest for their architectural content, the undergraduate students pages provide links to a number of non-architectural sites.

Washington, University of, Department of Architecture
http://128.171.44.6:3333/catalog/UW/uw_home.html

Wisconsin-Milwaukee, University of, School of Architecture and Urban Planning
http://www.sarup.uwm.edu/
http://www.sarup.edu/

Woodbury University, Architecture Department
http://128.171.44.6:3333/catalog/WU/wu_home.html

6.3.4 Canada

British Columbia, University School of Architecture
http://www.architecture.ubc.ca/
Several student homepages displaying their project work.

Calgary, University, Faculty of Environmental Design, Architecture Program
http://128.171.44.6:3333/catalog/UC/uc_home.html

Carleton University School of Architecture
http://thrain.arch.carleton.ca/
http://www.arch.carleton
Contains several 3-D visualizations amongst the work carried out for the 'Harlem Project'.

McGill University School of Architecture
http://prometheus.architecture.mcgill.ca/

Schools of architecture

The prometheus option leads to 'student work, homepages and other design resources'. SiteX is material from 'a course which explores the notion of 'place' in cyberspace'.

Manitoba, University Faculty of Architecture
Environmental Design, Interior Design, Architecture, City Planning and Landscape Architecture
http://cad9.cadlab.umanitoba.ca/UofM.html
Several CADLAB projects are available at:
http://cad9.cadlab.umanitoba.ca
'Prairie Archnet' includes the Acanthus Virtual Gallery of work by 'prairie professionals, students of architecture and other notable contributors'; the Digital Warehouse (a student journal); and topical links which include interdisciplinary resources (the most extensive section at the moment), computers in design and planning, research programs and other Internet sources (21 for architecture).

Québec a Montréal, l'Université Département de Design
http://meenakshi.design.uqam.ca/

6.3.5 Australia

Adelaide, University Department of Architecture
http://www.arch.adelaide.edu.au/home.html

Canberra, Australian National University, Art and Architectural History
http://www.ncsa.uiuc.edu/SDG/Experimental/anu-art-history/home.html

Curtin University of Technology, Perth
School of Architecture, Construction and Planning
http://puffin.curtin.edu.au
This web site currently contains course and staff information, a large architectural computer visualization gallery (containing some 150 images) and links to student work through their WWW home pages.

Melbourne University
Faculty of Architecture, Building and Planning (Ictinus Network)
http://www.arbld.unimelb.edu.au/
Courses, faculty information, student work samples (in course notes section). Most interesting is their progressive plan to provide a networked environment (in the 'about the network' section).

New South Wales, University Faculty of the Built Environment
http://www.arch.unsw.edu.au/

Rayshade Objects Library, information on the faculty, tutorials (including some on autocad and Rayshade) and undergraduate research papers.

Sydney University, Department of Architecture
http://www.arch.su.edu.au/

Tasmania, University of, Department of Architecture
http://www.arch.utas.edu.au/Architecture_page.html

6.3.6 New Zealand

Auckland, School of Architecture, Property and Planning:
http://archpropplan.auckland.ac.nz/ArchPropPlan.html
Information about the University of Auckland school, ftp offerings, individuals' home pages, a virtual study tour (which includes computer constructions or reconstructions of various buildings such as the Barcelona Pavilion and the Hadrianic Baths at Leptis Magna), and a student gallery with student modelling and rendering projects.
WWW sources at
http://archpropplan.auckland.ac.nz/misc/sources1.html (schools)
http://archpropplan.auckland.ac.nz/misc/sources2.html (journals, papers, etc)
http://archpropplan.auckland.ac.nz/misc/sources4.html (planning related)
http://archpropplan.auckland.ac.nz/misc/sources5.html (libraries, catalogues)
http://archpropplan.auckland.ac.nz/misc/sources6.html (galleries)
http://archpropplan.auckland.ac.nz/Archivis/archivis.html (Architectural Visualization page)

Wellington, Victoria University, School of Architecture and Design
http://www.arch.vuw.ac.nz/index.html
Several categories to explore, including a range of student work.

Wellington, Victoria University: Society of Building Science Educators
http://brick.arch.vuw.ac.nz:85/index.html
About the society. Also includes an extensive listing of links at:
http://brick.arch.vuw.ac.nz:85/interesting_addresses.html

6.3.7 Far East

Singapore National University School of Architecture
http://www.arch.nus.sg/

The Global Design Studio contains products of studios: Y2 Parametrics Studio, International Virtual Design Studios, and PROG28 with ETH Zurich ('Exhibition Pavilions').
http://www.arch.nus.sg/globalstudio.html

Kyoto
Institute of Technology Design Research Group
http://woodpecker.dad.kit.ac.jp/serverFiles/welcome.html
Includes students projects.

Waseda University, Tokyo, Japan, Watanabe Lab. Dept. of Architecture
http://www.watanabe.arch.waseda.ac.jp
Students' works are the main contents now.
Media Design Lab., Waseda University, Tokyo, Japan
http://www.mdl.arch.waseda.ac.jp
'Where the wild things are.'

Hong Kong University School of Architecture
http://arch.hku.hk/
A large site, including many student home pages.

Hong Kong Chinese University, Department of Architecture
http://www.arch.cuhk.hk/
Many interesting projects, including the construction of a Song building. An extensive gallery of rendered images is available and the second year students have constructed their own home pages. An impressive site well worth looking at.

Tunghai University of Taiwan, Architecture Department
http://140.128.120.59/default.htm
Contains an amazing variety of high quality CAD work organized under the individual students' home pages.

See also WWW link collections which include school listings as a separate category, such as the schools section of the WWW virtual library for architecture
http://www.clr.toronto.edu:1080/VIRTUALLIB/ARCH/prog.html

Architecture: history and art

7.1 VIRTUAL GALLERIES

Acanthus Gallery
http://cad9.cadlab.umanitoba.ca
A project of the CADLAB of the Faculty of Architecture of the University of Manitoba and the Alberta, Saskatchewan and Manitoba Associations of Architecture. The Acanthus Virtual Gallery displays work by 'prairie professionals, students of architecture and other notable contributors'.

ACM Siggraph Internet Art Guide
http://siggraph.org/artresource/artguide/artguide.html
The Association for Computing Machinery's Special Interest Group on Graphics' Guide.

The Acropolis, Athens
http://atlas.central.ntua.gr.8080/webacropol/

Aedes Architecture Gallery, Berlin
http://www.netsign.de

Alvar Aalto Museum
http://www.cs.jyu.fi/~jatahu/aalto/homepage.html
Site for general Aalto information, as well as information about the museum.

American West Gallery
http://www.unl.edu/UP/gof/home.htm
A searchable database of photographs drawn primarily from the collections of the National Archives and Records Administration (U.S.) detailing the period of Western expansion. Most, if not all, are in the public domain.

Architecture Gallery
http://web.mit.edu/afs/athena/org/m/museum/www/archgallery.html
or

Virtual galleries

http://web.mit.edu/afs/athena/org/m/museum/www/architecture_online.html
The Architecture Gallery contains online versions of recent architectural exhibitions at the MIT Museum. The two exhibitions on the site in 1995 were 'William Robert Ware and the Origins of American Architectural Education' and 'From Louis Sullivan to SOM'.

Art Bin WWW page
http://www.algonet.se/artbin
Art Bin is a Swedish/international forum for art, literature, music, cultural politics, etc. Here you will find articles, essays, poetry, fiction, paintings and music as well as some rare classical and other source texts. The editorial language is English, but several texts are in their original languages, i.e. French, German, or Swedish. The Art Bin's editor is Karl-Erik Tallmo of Stockholm, Sweden. He is a writer and contributor of cultural articles to various Nordic dailies and magazines. The editor may be reached at e-mail: tallmo@nisus.se

Arthole
http://www.mcs.net/~wallach/paris/panic1.html
An eclectic mix of art from around the world featuring original works.

Art museums
http://www.yahoo.com/Art/Museums/

Art web sites
http://www.art.net/
http://www.art.net/links.html
Links to all sorts of arts and fine-arts related sites.

Avery Architectural Periodicals Index
http://www.ahip.getty.edu/ahip/Text_multdb-form.html
J. Paul Getty Trust's Art History Information Program has put the Avery Index of Architectural Periodicals on the web. Details on the Trust's other activities are at:
http://www.ahip.getty.edu/ahip/Text_home.html
Alternatively, for the Art History index
http://www.ahip.getty.edu/ahip/home.html

Big CityArt
http://www.tezcat.com/~honore
Architectural urban watercolor paintings of Chicago landscapes.

Birkbeck College, London
http://www.hart.bbk.ac.uk/
Site for art history, with links to several museums.

Museum of Science, Boston
http://www.mos.org
Basically an information server about the museum hours and programmes but more information and 'virtual exhibits' are promised in the near future.

Buckminster Fuller Exhibition
http://www.core77.com/Exhibition/index.html
Contemporary developments in design science, marking the birth centennial of Buckminster Fuller 1895–1995. An exhibition of innovations in design science and morphology and applications to architecture. Presented by Pratt Institute in cooperation with the Cathedral of St. John the Divine and the Buckminster Fuller Institute.

Center for Research in Computing and the Arts
http://crca-www.ucsd.edu/
Maintains a large number of links to art resources on the net.

Computer Museum, Boston
http://www.tcm.org/

Conservatoire National des Arts et Metiers
http://web.cnam.fr/

Cyber Gallery
http://gertrude.art.uiuc.edu/@art/gallery.html
An eclectic mix of art works.

Gallery Cyberia
http://www.easynet.co.uk/pages/cafe/galleria.htm
The U.K. Cyberia cafés also maintain a link to other art galleries:
http://www.easynet.co.uk/pages/cafe/gall.htm

DADArt Gallery
http://www.dada.it/dadart/
A virtual gallery opened on 14 July 1995, with four sections: architecture, poetry, painting and photography. DADA (Design-Architettura-Digitale-Analogica) are six architects that investigate new media.

Franklin Institute Science Museum
http://sln.fi.edu

Virtual galleries

Galleria Virtuale, Roma 2001
http://www.mclink.it/galleria-roma.html

Holography Museum
http://www.islandnet.com/~royal/index.htm
One of largest holographic galleries now on-line.

Hosokawa's Computer Graphics Gallery
http://www.mt.cs.keio.ac.jp/person/hosokawa/arts/cg.html

International Directory of Art Libraries
http://aaln.org/ifla-idal
The electronic version of the International Federation of Library Associations Section of Art Libraries International Directory of Art Libraries. A guide to over 3 000 institutions with specialized holdings in art and architecture.

The Israel Museum
http://www.macom.co.il/museum
Important archive and photographic exhibit. Some historical photos have been digitally enhanced for better legibility.

Joconde
http://www.culture.fr
The museums of France online. The database Joconde provides general public access to the collection records – and a small but growing number of their accompanying images – of more than 60 museums in France. Joconde already can reach records of designs, prints, paintings, sculptures, photographs, and art objects, representing 130 000 works of art and 10 000 artists, and an increasing number of inline GIF images.

Yves Klein Artworks
http://homepage.interaccess.com/~rotwang/
Art gallery site with many links to other art sites.

London, British Library
gopher://portico.bl.uk/
http://www.bl.uk/

London, British Museum
http://www.cs.ucl.ac.uk/local/museums/BritishMuseum.html

London, Science Museum
http://www.nmsi.ac.uk/

Information Superhighway exhibition.
http://www.tecc.co.uk/science_museum/

Louvre
http://www.louvre.fr/
or http://www.paris.org/Musees/Louvre/
U.K. mirror site
http://sunsite.doc.ic.ac.uk/louvre/

Louvre Web page
http://mistral.enst.fr/~pioch/louvre/
http://mistral.enst.fr/louvre/
The Web Louvre was set up before the real Louvre had a web page. Includes exhibits at the Louvre as well as a tour of Paris, the Eiffel Tower and the Champs-Elysees. Over 1 300 pages and over 800 graphics.

Metropolitan Museum of Art
http://www.metmuseum.org/
One of the largest art collections in the world. Images are under 'Collections':
http://www.metmuseum.org/htmlfile/gallery/gallery.html

University of Minnesota, Geometry Center
http://www.geom.umn.edu/
The Center maintains an interactive on-line geometry gallery:
http://www.geom.umn.edu/apps/gallery.html

Mobius Center
http://www.tmn.com/0h/Artswire/www/mobius/mobius.html
(Note that the /0h/ is the number not the letter.)
Boston's Artists Run Center For Experimental Work in all Media

Moholy-Nagy Symposium
http://128.175.47.160/Events/Moholy-Nagy/Symposium.html
The University Gallery at the University of Delaware invites you to explore our new WWW home page, with information and images related to our upcoming centenary celebration of the birth of Hungarian modernist Laszlo Moholy-Nagy, a premier artist, designer, filmmaker, teacher and theorist of the twentieth century. This page also contains a link to the Arts page at the University of Delaware.

Montreal Museum of Fine Arts
http://www.interax.net/tcenter/tour/mba.html
The Montreal Museum of Fine Arts, Canada's oldest art museum, was founded in 1860 by a group of devoted art lovers belonging to the Art Association of Montreal. The

Virtual galleries

Museum is justly proud of the some 26 000 works in its Permanent Collection, which has established its reputation worldwide.

Musée National des Techniques
http://web.cnam.fr/museum/

National Arts Guide
http://www.national-arts-guide.co.uk/uk/home.html
Britain's art galleries and information on exhibitions.

OTIS Home Page
http://sunsite.unc.edu/otis/otis.html
This eclectic gallery contains everthing from traditional works of art to post-modern and beyond. People are encouraged to submit their own works and thus this is a showcase for much new and imaginative talent. There are numerous links to the home pages of other artists.

Pittsburgh, Andy Warhol Museum
http://www.warhol.org/warhol/

Pompidou Centre
http://www.cnac-gp.fr/index-e.html
English language index
http://www.cnac-gp.fr/horaires.html
Exhibition of work by computer artist Lillian Schwartz.

RIBA Architecture Centre
http://www.slumberinggiant.co.uk
The 'Products of Desire' exhibition available on-line.

Norman Rockwell Gallery
http://www.gus.com/artgallery/rockwell_list.html

Ruskin School of Drawing and Fine Art
http://www.ruskin-sch.ox.ac.uk/
Designed by the artist Jake Tilson, this site includes work from 'The Laboratory', a scheme intended to promote new work in the visual arts.

Smithsonian Institute
http://www.si.edu/
A virtual tour of the world famous institute.

The Temple University Gallery of the Arts
http://betty.music.temple.edu
Provides many links to other fine-arts sites and fine-arts information related sites.

Vatican City museums
http://www.christusrex.org/
Sistine Chapel
http://www.christusrex.org/www1/sistine/O-Tour.html
Over 160 images from the Sistine Chapel ceiling.
Many other images of items from the Vatican Museums are held in IBM's digital library:
http://www.ibm.com/features/library/vatican
Rome Reborn – Vatican Exhibition
http://sunsite.unc.edu/expo/vatican.exhibit/Vatican.exhibit.html

Video On Line Exhibition
http://www.vol.it/HTML_UK/MOSTRE_INGLESE/
Guggenheim exhibition on post-war Italian style, and the Venetian exhibition on the Renaissance. Also includes links to net sites relating to the exhibits.

Virtual Library Museums Page
http://www.comlab.ox.ac.uk/archive/other/museums.html

WebArt
http://www.webart.com/

World Art Resources
http://www.cgrg.ohio-state.edu/Newark/artsres.html
Maintained by the Ohio State University at Newark, Art Gallery
http://www.cgrg.ohio-state.edu/~mkruse/osu.html
A list of links to art galleries and exhibitions is at:
http://www.cgrg.ohio-state.edu/Newark/galleries.html

World Wide Arts Resources
http://www.concourse.com/wwar/default.html
Maintains a list of galleries and on-line exhibitions organized by subject matter:
http://www.concourse.com/wwar/galleries.html

Frank Lloyd Wright Gallery
http://flw.badgernet.com:2080/gallery.htm

7.2 IMAGE RESOURCES

AcIS Imaging and Hypertext Projects
http://gutentag.cc.columbia.edu/imaging/html/imaging.html
A joint project of AcIS (Academic Information Systems) and Columbia University Libraries. It includes 2000 digitized images (e.g. of Paris maps, Calatrava bridges and miscellaneous other topics). Home of the Digital Image Access Project.

ADAM – Art, Design, Architecture and Media Resources
http://www.adam.ac.uk/
This project, run by Tony Gill at Surrey Institute of Art and Design, has its own mailbase discussion list, ADAM–NEWS. To join send 'join adam-news firstname lastname' to mailbase@mailbase.ac.uk.

Images from Ann Arbor (University of Michigan Library)
gopher://libra.arch.umich.edu/11/AnnArbor

Ansel Adams: Fiat Lux
http://bookweb.cwis.uci.edu:8042/AdamsHome.html
Ansel Adams, the renowned photographer, exhibits his portfolio for the whole world to see. Hundreds of images, but the liberal use of thumbnails makes for quick and effiecient viewing.

Architectural Gopher Database
gopher://library.berkeley.edu
Select 'Research Databases' and then 'Architecture'.
A variety of architectural data, including links to other gopher sites. The downloadable documents include drawings as well as text files.

The Architecture of Islam
http://www.co.caltech.edu/~mahmoudi/Art.html

Architecture and Visualisation
http://bau2.uibk.ac.at/erwin/Arch/archinc.html
A selection of pointers put together by Erwin Zierler at the University of Innsbruck.

Architecture Images
gopher://servo.hs.jhu.edu
Select 'Images' and then 'Architecture'
A collection of architectural design images.

Architecture Image Repository
ftp://ftp.sunet.se/pub/pictures/architecture

Architecture of Atlanta
http://www.gatech.edu/3020/architecture/intro/homepage.html

Art and Architectural History
http://www.arts.gla.ac.uk/www/ctich/artlinks.html
Part of the U.K. Government's Computing in Teaching Initiative. Many links to related sources.

Art Liaison Virtual Gallery
gopher://artspeak.dorsal.org
A visually rich site but unfortunately the gopher site requires the downloading of images before viewing. A web site is planned.

ArtServe
Australian National University, Institute of the Arts
http://rubens.anu.edu.au/
Islamic architecture
http://rubens.anu.edu.au/islam2/index_1.html
2500 images of classical architecture of the Mediterranean Basin, survey of Islamic architecture, and some 10 000 images of European sculpture and architecture from classical to 19th century. To go directly to the searchable architecture database, use the URL: http://rubens.anu.edu.au/architecture_form.html.
There is also a searchable book on Greek and Roman Cities of Western Turkey.

ArtSource
http://www.uky.edu/Artsource/artsourcehome.html
ArtSource provides text bibliographies and guides to information on art and architecture (with more art than architecture). The archive of the ARLIS-L discussion group is stored here. Items may also be downloaded by ftp from:
ftp://convex.cc.uky.edu/pub/artsource

Athens
http://www.arch.columbia.edu/DDL/paperless/keller/Angelidakis2.html
Andreas Angelidakis documents the unauthorized postwar construction in Athens.

Dan Cornish's Architecture Web Site
http://www.cornishproductions.com.
This site presents recent work of leading architects in still photographs, video, audio, VRML and other media.

DESIGN Architecture
http://www.cornishproductions.com/
Recent works of various architects illustrated by photographs, audio and animation.

Digital Image Center
University of Virginia Fiske Kimball Fine Arts Library
http://www.lib.virginia.edu/dic/colls/arh102/index.html
Images from an architecture history class, on Renaissance and Baroque architecture in France and Italy.

Diocletian Palace
http://www.ncsa.uiuc.edu/SDG/Experimental/split/split1.html
Lots of images, plus text, contributed by Michael Greenhalgh, Department of Art History, Australian National University.

DIVA (Digital Images – Visual Arts)
http://www.monash.edu.au/diva
Mostly Australian Art and Architecture images.

Doors of Perception
http://mmwww.xs4all.nl/home.html
An avant-garde site maintained by Mediamatic in Amsterdam.

Ellipsis
http://www.gold.net/ellipsis/ellipsis.html#top
Avant-garde contemporary architecture.

Encyclopaedia of Virtual Environments
http://www.cs.umd.edu/projects/eve/eve-articles/TOC.html

Fractal Images
http://www.rain.org/~ayb
Freaky fractals.

French architectural projects (Photographs)
gopher://gopher.hs.jhu.edu/11/–%3eImages/Architecture

Gallery
gopher://unix5.nysed.gov:70/11/K-12%20Resources/Arts%20%26%20Humanities/Gallery
JPEG images of paintings by over 100 famous artists from all periods, e.g. Botticelli, Chagall, Dali, Escher, Goya, Klimt, Michelangelo, Munch, Picasso, Raphael, Tenniel.

Graffiti Page (Art Crimes)
http://www.gatech.edu/desoto/graf/Index.Art_Crimes.html
Contains photographs of graffiti from around the world.

Graphics Archive
ftp://nic.funet.fi
Log in as 'pictures' and follow the path /pub/pics/

Greek and Roman Cities of Western Turkey
http://rubens.anu.edu.au/turkeybook/toc1.html

Greek Architecture
gopher://libra.arch.umich.edu/11/GreekArchitecture

Hadrian's Baths at Leptis Magna
http://archpropplan.auckland.ac.nz/People/Bill/hadrians_bath/hadrians_
bath.html
Computer reconstruction by University ofAuckland

Hawaii
http://www.hcc.hawaii.edu/hawaii/
Images of Hawaii by the University of Hawaii.

Hawaiian Architecture 1995 J.L. Morton.
http://www.lava.net/~ada/
Aloha. Hawaii plantation housing is one of the unique architectural styles of the
Hawaiian Islands. The homes were built by the sugar plantation owners to house the
workers who were imported from Japan, China and the Philippines.

Hong Kong Contemporary Architecture
http://www.ncsa.uiuc.edu/SDG/Experimental/anu-art-history/hongkong.html

**Imaging Systems Laboratory, Department of Landscape Architecture, University
of Illinois, Urbana-Champaign**
http://imlab9.landarch.uiuc.edu
The lab's 'activities have concentrated on environmental perception research related to
the visualization of environmental impact, with emphasis on methodological studies and
on preference and choice modelling'. The site includes full-text of publications for most
projects, lists of publications and grants received, and bibliographies in the lab's areas
of research.

Islamic Architecture
http://rubens.anu.edu.au/islam2/index_1.html

Islamic Architecture in Isfahan (Thomas C. Rochford)
http://www.anglia.ac.uk/~trochford/isfahan.html

Italian Art and Architecture
http://www.eat.com/architecture/index.html
Sponsored by Van den Bergh Foods, Inc.

Images from Japan
http://www.cs.uidaho.edu/~marc9442/japan.html

Jerusalem in the 19th Century
http://www.macom.co.il/museum/photo-2/index.html

Melbourne (20th Century Architecture)
http://www.monash.edu.au/diva/ozarch.html

MIT Museum Architectural Collection
http://web.mit.edu/afs/athena/org/m/museum/www/architecture.html
More than 15 000 thesis and project drawings by students of MIT's Department of Architecture from 1873 and 1968.

Image Archive of the University of Minnesota, College of Architecture and Landscape Architecture
gopher://gumby.arch.umn.edu/1D-2%3a13330%3aImages

Images of Napoli
http://www.na.infn.it/Images/images.html

Netlink: Architecture
http://honor.uc.wlu.edu/net/classes/Architecture.html
List of FTP sites for architecture images (and some texts).

Ottawa, Canada
http://www.cisti.nrc.ca/pio/intro.html
Parliament Buildings and Parliament Hill.

Palladio Slide Collection, University of Michigan
gopher://libra.arch.umich.edu/11/Palladio

Philadelphia Region
http://www.honors.drexel.edu/
A guide to old covered bridges.

Photographic Images
ftp://ftp.netcom.com/pub/bbrace
Contains 5000 JPEGs and GIFs of Brad Brace's own interpretation of post-modern photography.

PHOTONet
http://www.scotborders.co.uk/photon/netindex.html
Photon magazine of Scotland produces this index of fantastic photos from sites all over the world.

The Place
http://gertrude.art.uiuc.edu/ludgate/the/place.html
A collection of digital art.

Pompeii Forum Project at the Univeristy of Virginia
http://jefferson.village.virginia.edu/pompeii/page-1.html

Portfolio IV
http://www.arc.cmu.edu/portfolio
A student publication that exhibits studio work of the Carnegie Mellon University Department of Architecture.

QuickTime site
ftp://ftp.netcom.com/pub/fl/flypba/QuickTime

Ray-traced 3D web pict site
http://www-cse.ucsd.edu/users/bsteuer/

Renaissance and Baroque Architecture
http://www.lib.virginia.edu/dic/colls/arh102/index.html
There is a gopher server on:
gopher://gopher.virginia.edu
Architectural History course at the University of Virginia.
There is a detailed archive of works by Brunelleschi:
http://www.lib.virginia.edu/dic/colls/arh102/two/two.html
Filippo Brunelleschi, Lesser Works / Florence / and Beyond
http://www.lib.virginia.edu/dic/colls/arh102/three/three.html
http://www.lib.virginia.edu/dic/colls/arh102/four/four.html
http://www.lib.virginia.edu/dic/colls/arh102/five/five.html

Smithsonian Institute Photographic Archive
ftp://photo1.si.edu

mirrored at ftp://sunsite.unc.edu
Huge database of articles and pictures.

Sydney Opera House
http://www.monash.edu.au/diva/utzon.html

Syracuse University
http://mirror.syr.edu/image/strip.html
The architecture of the American Strip.

Tokyo
http://www.gold.net/ellipsis/guides/tokyo/introduction/index.html
Architecture guide. The index of buildings is at:
http://www.gold.net/ellipsis/guides/tokyo/buildings/index.html

UCLA Architecture Slide and Photograph Library
University of California, Berkeley
http://www.mip.berkeley.edu/mip/collections/arcslide.html
Access to the SPIRO image collection. Some 5 000 digital images.

Vatican City
http://www.christusrex.org/www1/citta/0-Citta.html

Venice Portfolio
gopher://gopher.iuav.unive.it/11/%20Venice%20Portfolio

Vision and Art
http://psych.hanover.edu/Krantz/art/
A tutorial on the technical aspects of colour and vision.

WSA/CTICBE Architectural Image Database
http://ctiweb.cf.ac.uk/image/
A prototype searchable database being compiled by the Welsh School of Architecture in collaboration with the CTI Centre for the Built Environment.

7.3 VIRTUAL CITIES

Africa
http://www.sas.upenn.edu/African_Studies/Home_Page/Country.html
Links to home pages of all African countries.

Alice Springs
http://www.world.net/Travel/Australia/NT_info/NTTC/as.html

Amsterdam
http://dds.nl/home.shtml/hoofdmenu
The City Council's page

Architects Abroad Inc
http://www.rahul.net/arctour/
A commercial travel company specialising in architectural tours.

Atlanta
http://www.city.net/countries/united_states/georgia/atlanta/

Australia
http://www.csu.edu.au/education/australia.html
http://www.csu.edu.au/australia.html
These two sites attempt to collect all Australian resources at the one place.

Beijing
http://www.ihep.ac.cn/tour/bj.html

Bermuda
http://www.microstate.com/pub/micros/forbes/forbes2.html
Extensive information about the island. More visual images are at:
http://www.bercol.bm/Bermuda/Bermuda.HTML

Boston
http://www.std.com/homepages/std/boston.html
The Boston Information Server has a wide range of information on the Metro-Boston Area.

Brazil
http://www.city.net/countries/brazil/
A site devoted to pictures of Brazil is at:
http://guarani.cos.ufrj.br:8000/Rio/Todas.html

Brighton
http://www.pavilion.co.uk/brighton
Amongst other things, fly through a VRML model of the town.

Brugge
http://www.brugge.be/brugge/

Virtual cities

Information about the 'Venice of the north'.

Cambridge, On-Line City
http://www.worldserver.pipex.com/cambridge

Cambridge (Pub-guide)
http://www.cityscape.co.uk:81/bar/pubguide.html

Cambridge, MA
http://www.ai.mit.edu/projects/iiip/Cambridge/homepage.html
City Hall: http://www.ai.mit.edu/projects/iiip/Cambridge/city.hall.html

Camino del Soul (Ecuador)
http://gopher.usfq.edu.ec/0c:/ecuador/guia.html
Virtual visit to Ecuador. The entire page is in Portuguese.

Canada
http://www.fleethouse.com/fhcanada/fhc_epl.htm
A comprehensive source of links on Canadian travel.

Cape Town, South Africa
http://www.aztec.co.za/users/hammond/virtualc.htm
Jump on a virtual Double Decker bus for a tour of Cape Town, South Africa, stopping at the city's best web sites.

Central Park, NYC
http://www.centralpark.org/~park/

Champs Elysees
http://www.iway.fr/htbin/champs_elysees.cgi?page=index.html

Chicago
http://www.math.uic.edu/touring_chi.html
An alternative site for Chicago is the Chicago Information System: the home page has a collection of downloadable photographs and the tourism link leads to pages on Fine Arts and Museums. CIS is at:
http://reagan.eecs.uic.edu/tourism.html

City.Net
http://www.city.net
Information on cities around the globe. Includes many links to cities which have their own informative web pages.

Cracow, Poland
http://www.uci.agh.edu.pl
gopher://gopher.uci.agh.edu.pl
Links to Polish Network Resources, a JPEG photo collection and travelogue/tourist guide by Michael Rozek of Stanislaw Staszic University of Mining and Metallurgy that presents historical facts and cultural traditions about Poland.

Cybertown
http://www.cybertown.net
Cybertown is a rapidly growing virtual community in Southwestern Wisconsin. Platteville, WI is the pilot city with many more to come.

De Digitale Stad (The Digital City)
http://www.dds.nl/
A true virtual 'digital city' on the web. This place teems with people and links resembling streets and sidewalks throughout the town are littered all over the place, making navigation questionable until you begin to realize that any large metropolis is tough to navigate (with or without a map) when you first arrive. There are reportedly over 10 000 regular 'inhabitants' of this digital city and more come to visit every day. People have set up permanent shops and dwellings and there are many 'nooks and crannies' to discover just like old back alley ways in a real large city. Getting lost is half the fun here but please do visit the Town Hall as this has links to the 'outside' world of Amsterdam and provides info on services and other assorted sundries within the digital city and actual Amsterdam. This is the best 'virtual city' on the web.

Detroit
http://detroit.freenet.org/index.html

Digital Communities
http://alberti.mit.edu/arch/4.207/homepage.html
Notes for a course given at MIT School of Architecture.

Disneyland
http://www.best.com/~dijon/disney/parks/disneyland/

Edinburgh
http://www.efr.hw.ac.uk/EDC/Edinburgh.html

Egypt
http://pages.prodigy.com/guardian/egypt.htm
Presents reliable links to Egypt and Egyptology resources throughout the web. Categories include: General Egypt Resources, Pyramids, Art and Music, Sites and Monuments, Hieroglyphs, Egypt Today.

More links to Egyptian Archeology sites are at:
http://ce.ecn.purdue.edu/~ashmawy/egypt.html
There is a section on the reconstruction of the pyramid of Djoser and links to several
map and photograph archives.

EXPO
http://sunsite.unc.edu/expo/ticket_office.html
Plentiful links to various virtual 'web tours' found across the globe. This site includes
links to the Vatican tour (Rome), a Russian tour and many others.

Flanders Coast
http://www.flandercoast.be
Offers information about accommodation, tourism, travel and business at the coastal
region of Belgium.

Florence
http://marco.ing.unifi.it/florence/florence.ht

Florida Keys
http://Florida-Keys.info-access.com/
Information about the Florida Keys including the marine sanctuary, diving, fishing and
the Everglades National Park. Includes links to other resources for information about
the Florida Keys and Key West.

Le serveur France
The URL for the Minsitere des affaires Etrangères
http://www.france.diplomatie.fr
French history, geography, institutions, political parties, economy, education, science,
culture.

France in the world : foreign policy, development aid, defense policy, the European
Union, France's humanitarian action, French language and Francophony, Cultural and
scientific cooperation.

French news : Official foreign policy statements, Cultural events, Exchange rates.

Practical information : Going to France (visiting, taking up residence, studying,
learning French), French people abroad, Useful addresses (embassies and consulates),
French firms.

Other sources of French information include:
The WebFoot's Guide to France
http://pond.cso.uiuc.edu/ducky/docs/france/
Ecila Index Internet Resources in France
http://www.ceic.com/ecila/
Page de France
http://gplc.u-bourgogne.fr:8080/pdf/Welcome.html

Internet en francais
http://www.uqat.uquebec.ca/~wwweduc/franc.html
The French Connection
http://www.anu.edu.au/french/french.html
French Travel Gallery
http://www.webcom.com/~wta/
French Resources on the Web
http://hapax.be.sbc.edu/home.html
Conseil Regional d'Aquitaine
http://dufy.aquarel.fr/
FranceScape (tm)
http://www.france.com/francescape/top.html
FranceLINK
http://www.iia.org/~siembor/francelink/index.html

Genoa
http://afrodite.lira.dist.unige.it:81/~pan/GENOVA/genova.html

Germany
http://www.chemie.fu-berlin.de/outerspace/www-german.html
A comprehensive listing of German web servers.

Greece
http://www.algonet.se:80/~nikos/greek.html
A good set of links with a particularly detailed description of the city of Patros.

Greenwich CT.
http://townline.com/local/grnhome.htm

Helsinki
http://www.spellbound.com/helsinki/index.html
A virtual tour.

Hollywood
ftp://ftp.netcom.com/pub/jc/jclark/web/wehowebl.html

Hollywood
http://www.hollywood.com
The Internet's premiere source of multimedia entertainment, information and previews.
Hundreds of photos, video, sound and multimedia clips, movie trailers and more.

Hong Kong
http://www.hkta.org

Architecture: history and art   **153**

Virtual cities

Sponsored and maintained by Hong Kong Tourist Association, this site is a comprehensive guide and planning tool for vacation and business travel, featuring information on tours, hotels, transportation, food and restaurants, shopping, nightlife, culture, festivals, events.

Hyde Park Corner
http://www.cs.ucl.ac.uk/cgi-bin/tube/hyde_park_corner

India
http://spiderman.bu.edu/misc/india/
Many links to Indian States and Cities. More Indian cities are at:
http://www.indiaworld.com/open/rec/travel/index.html

The (In-) Visible City
http://indycad.archlab.tuwien.ac.at/model.html
On-line information is available on the information server of TU Vienna (info.tuwien.ac.at) under 'International Activities'.

Isfahan
http://www.anglia.ac.uk/~trochford/isfahan.html
A guide to the historic city, concentrating on architecture and historic monuments.

Italy
http://www.mi.cnr.it:80/WOI/
The index includes a pointer to 'List of Towns' with connections to most of the major cities.

Japan
http://www.ntt.jp/japan/explore/index.html
Access to city information through a 'clickable' map.
City-Net provides an alternative set of links to 9 major cities at:
http://www.city.net/countries/japan/
The Japan National Tourist Agency is at:
http://www.jnto.go.jp

The Jerusalem Mosaic (Information on Jerusalem)
http://shum.cc.huji.ac.il/jeru/jerusalem.html

Johannesburg's Active Access network
http://www.active.co.za
Johann Visagie's home page. Many travel links.

Kansas
http://www.city.net/countries/united_states/kansas/

Las Vegas
http://www.city.net/countries/united_states/nevada/las_vegas/

Linz, Austria
http://www.gup.uni-linz.ac.at:8001/CityOfLinz/index_engl.html

London
http://www.city.net/countries/united_kingdom/england/london/
There is also a 'London Guide' with many photographs at:
http://www.cs.ucl.ac.uk/misc/uk/london.html

Los Angeles
http://www.city.net/countries/united_states/california/los_angeles/
A specifically architectural tour is at:
http://www.cf.ac.uk/uwcc/archi/jonesmd/la/

Manchester
http://www.u-net.com/manchester/tourist/home.html

Maps of World Cities
http://www.lib.utexas.edu/Libs/PCL/Map_collection/world_cities/
Part of the Perry-Castañeda Library Map Collection. Down loadable maps for virtually everywhere. The general index is at:
http://www.lib.utexas.edu/Libs/PCL/Map_collection.html

Megacities 2000
http://valley.interact.nl/MEGACITIES
In addition to providing a mailing list, conferences, and links to net sites, this project, undertaken for Unesco by the International Academy of Architecture, is developing a 'Codex Megacities', 'to cover all aspects of urban management and development, [which] has to take into account the enormous variety of problems and solutions that go together with the geographic, cultural and economic diversity of urban life over the world'. The substantial beginning to this codex is posted here.

Melbourne
http://www.cs.monash.edu.au/melbourne/melbourne.html

Montana
http://www.mt.gov/

Virtual cities

The State of Montana home page provides the link to Yellowstone National Park. Detailed descriptions of the Park's terrain and geography are available together with a park tour and several images.

Naples
http://www.weblink.com/naples
Welcome to Naples, Florida!

Netherlands Tourist Information
http://www.xxlink.nl/cities
http://www.xxlink.nl/nbt
These are two linked pages and each has particular information on the Netherlands. Includes pictures, maps, guidebooks, images, sight-seeing information, restaurants, accommodation and more.

New Orleans
http://www.neosoft.com/~bigeasy/
Mardi Gras live on the net.

New York City WWW sites
http://www.pubadvocate.nyc.gov/~advocate/index.html
http://www.escape.com/eMall/exploreny/ny1.html
http://www.city.net/countries/united_states/new_york/new_york/
The first web site is put up by the Public Advocate's office and is designed to make the Big Apple more user-friendly. Lots of New York information and links.

New Zealand
http://www.city.net/countries/new_zealand/
The Victoria University, Wellington maintains an information site at:
http://www.vuw.ac.nz/govt/nzinfo.html

Orlando
http://www.globalnet.net/golda02.html
http://www.iu.net:80/orlando/

Pacific Rim
http://gnn.com/gnn/bus/wview/cityhogh/pacific.html
Access to 19 Pacific Rim cities.

Pakistan
http://www.rpi.edu/~ansars/paksa_locker/pak_mosaic/paksa_www.html
The Pakistan Students' Association at Rensslaer Polytechnic Institute maintain this site with links to several city pages, including many pictures.

Paris home page
http://web.urec.fr/france/france.html
Other Paris web sites include:
http://www.city.net/countries/france/paris/
http://www.paris.org
http://meteora.ucsd.edu:80/~norman/paris

Phoenix
http://arizonaweb.org/City/Phoenix/

Pittsburgh
http://www.city.net/countries/united_states/pennsylvania/pittsburgh/

Poland
http://www.urm.gov.pl:80/
The Government's list of places to see.

Portland, Oregon
http://www.ee.pdx.edu/depts/fpa/html/portlandtour.html
Visual tour of downtown.

Quebec
http://www.quebecweb.com/tourisme/
A virtual tour of the Quebec tourist regions.

Redwood Country
http://www.northcoast.com/unlimited/unlimited.html
A virtual guide to Northern California's coast.

Rome
http://www.virtualrome.com/virtualrome

Russia
http://www.kiae.su/www/wtr/
A Moscow–based service providing much information about Russia. Some links are in Russian so the pages may be garbled if you do not have a Cyrillic font. Information on Cyrillic fonts may be found at http://www.elvis.ru (really) or see RFC-1489.

Virtual Riviera
http://www.riviera.fr

Virtual cities

St. Louis
http://www.st-louis.mo.us/

Santiago, Chile
http://www.dcc.uchile.cl/chile/turismo/santiago.html
Detailed information about the city.

Scotland
http://www.fastnet.co.uk/scotland.
Spotlight on Scotland is an informative and regularly updated general interest magazine for anyone with an interest in Scotland.

Seattle
http://www.city.net/countries/united_states/washington/seattle/

Singapore
http://www.dataperipherals.com/html/singweb.html
A complete listing of related web sites and web pages from government links, to educational, to commercial and technical. The Singapore Tourist Promotion Board maintain a site at:
http://www.ncb.gov.sg/sog/sog.html
The Singapore On-line Guide is also at:
http://www.travel.com.sg/sog

Spain
http://www.uji.es/spain_www.html
An interactive map offers links to many regions and cities in Spain.

Sri Lanka
http://www.city.net/countries/sri_lanka/

Sydney
http://www.bio.uts.edu.au/sydney/sydney.html
A virtual tour of Sydney, Australia, with many images.

Telepolis
http://www.lrz-muenchen.de/MLM/telepolis.html
Exhibition and Symposium on the Interactive and Networked City
Organized by the Goethe-Institute, Luxemburg, the German contribution to 'Luxemburg, Cultural City of Europe 1995'. The on-line city Telepolis represents the vision and literal utopia of a global society based on digital media and computer networks, cable and satellite links and the vision of a new environment which opens up in data space and eventually will become inhabited and fully furnished, so to speak.

Telepolis is a mega-city, which is developing from old cities – barely comprehensible, polymorphic, mesmerizing, and constantly renewing itself, while growing at breakneck speed. It exists wherever interfaces make entering it possible; but only those possessing the necessary technical means will be able to gain entrance. So far, Telepolis has been only partially colonized. There are still many empty spaces ready to be populated and shaped at will – a virtual space waiting paradoxically to be discovered and invented at the same time. Telepolis promises more individual freedom, liberation from the restrictions of space, the opportunity of novel forms of experience, action, and communication. What, however, will communication and urban life look like in the networked city? How could a better coordination of ecological and economic aspects be achieved in the future? What challenges does the city of the 21st century pose to city planners and architects? Will the city become superfluous, with more and more civic functions being taken over by the networks? The Telepolis exhibition and conferences will not limit themselves, as is the case with many similar events, to presenting the new environment in virtual space, but will focus on the interfaces between human beings and machines, between mind and information, between real and virtual space. Although Telepolis is situated in a siteless space, it will be anchored in physical space. Coordination between these two spaces will be the central task of the information society. The different traditional aspects of the city – gate, streets, downtown, entertainment, education and science, social institutions, art, production, and housing – serve as starting points for the demonstration and explanation of the manner in which the real and the virtual world overlap. Thus Telepolis, being more than a metaphor for the interactive and networked city, demonstrates the current and future role played by telecommunication in social life.

Text of the City
http://mirror.syr.edu/analcity.html
Course description and eventually course products of ARC 500-18, The Text of the City: An Analysis of Space, Form, and Information in the City, a course taught at the School of Architecture Syracuse University. 'Through the application of computer based multimedia programs this studio will develop methods for the reading and documentation of information that is critical to the fundamental significance of certain urban environments.'

Tokyo
http://www.city.net/countries/japan/tokyo/
Part of City-Net Japan.

Travel and Tourist information Web site
http://www.digimark.net/rec-travel
Everything you want to know about all parts of the world that you may want to travel to. Even virtual web travellers will find this a useful tool. Includes the CIA World Fact Book online and the U.S. State Dept travel advisories.

Architecture: history and art

Turkey
http://ultb.rt.edu:80/~oak3489/Turkish_page.html
Links to museums, palaces, mosques and other sites of architectural interest.

USA CityLink
http://www.neosoft.com/citylink
http://www.NeoSoft.com:80/citylink/
Travel and city data and a whole lot more. Contains information on States and many cities within the USA. Numerous links to city-based pages across the US. Alternatively, take the Cybertour at:
http://www.std.com/NE/usatour.html

Vancouver
http://view.ubc.ca/

Venice
http://www.iuav.unive.it/wetvenice/wetvenice.html

Venice Urbanism forum
http://cidoc.iuav.unive.it
Some students from the University of Architecture in Venice are working in a forum about an innovative project for a new vision and organization of Venice. The themes of the projects are: the connection of the city with the world nets; the reorganization of the museums system; the destiny of the old industrial areas.

The Virtual Tourist
http://wings.buffalo.edu/world/
Graphic overview of web sites across the globe. A great place to find out about many places around the world. Excellent resource with lots of links.

The White House WWW site
http://www.whitehouse.gov/
Contains information, links and virtual tours of the White House.

Wien – 80 tage Urban exercises
http://www.lot.or.at/LOT/80TAGE/
A virtual 'parcours' for artistic explorations of the city, architecture and urbanity as part of the architecture festival 80 tage Wien. 'Urbanism and cultural life belong together like the gel to hair...', writes Paolo Bianchi at the beginning of his essay Stadt Koerper Denken (City Body Thought), thus initiating a pleasurable exploration of the city and urban subjectivities. Urbanism stands for the contradictory, infathomable as well as artificial and civilisatory aspects of urban culture. It refers to the fascinating dimension

of cities. The various communication and image levels of the digital networks gives the trajectory of such exercises, and in general the urban discourse, a new dimension with new images and new ideas about the city and urban planning. Urban characteristics are increasingly being moved to the virtual space. At the beginning still based on the notion of the global village, ideas of digital urbanism and cybercity now assume a concrete form. A cultural leap or the threat of derealization? Architecture, what is constructed, continues to act against this. Interplay between real city and virtual city, possible nodes and questions as to the state and circumstances of urban and virtual structures are the subject of artistic works. Special invitations, essays and statements make up the range of discourse. Enjoy the exercises!

Sabine Bitter: Connecting framing locations

Andrea Neuwirth: Ort un Ort Eine Unordnung und Umordnung staedtischer Strukturen

Helmut Weber: Looping walkin' on structure, NYC, Mexico City, Wien

Juerg Meister: WWW

Essays von

Paolo Bianchi: Stadt Koerper Denken

Bart Lootsma: Bodysnatchers

Mariette van Stralen / Bart Lootsma: Occupation: Leisure

Bazon Brock: Metropole gegen metropolis? Urbanitaet als postulat

Organized by LOT project: http://www.lot.or.at/LOT/

Sabine Bitter: bitter@interport.net

Helmut Weber: weber@thing.or.at

Juerg Meister: meister@mecad.co.at

The LOT Site itself (http://www.lot.or.at/LOT/) is organized in three sections:

- Urban Exercises

  The newest addition: Possible Urbanities, an essay by William Menking, architecture theorist, New York. Updated versions of some of the LOT group artworks, take a look at: on condition, on formation. Essays from: Paolo Bianchi, Bazon Brock, Bart Lootsma, Mariette van Stralen

- Station

  Ideas and background information about the intention of the LOTsite

- Extensions

  Contributing to mobility is updated ITEA, a project by Michael Smith, New York, is coming soon. Next rooms, a site from Juerg Meister on architecture will be announced soon.

There is a more conventional (official) Vienna Tourist Information guide at:
http://www.atnet.co.at/Tourism/Vienna/

If all of this virtual touring whets the appetite for the real thing, a listing of all internet sources on airports and airlines is maintained at:
http://www.bekkoame.or.jp/~dynasty/

All industry web sites are hot-linked and a free e-mail alert on new sites will be sent to anyone who registers with the host site.

Architecture: history and art

Worldwide rail timetables can be found at:
http://www.cse.ucsd.edu/users/bowdidge/railroad/rail-gopher.html
European rail information is at:
http://www.eurorail.com/
and Eurostar is available through:
http://www.itl.net/barclaysquare/

7.4 INDIVIDUAL ARCHITECTS AND DESIGNERS

The Alvar Aalto Museum
http://www.cs.jyu.fi/~jatahu/aalto/homepage.html

William Adams, Kippen Condominiums, 1991
http://www.cf.ac.uk/uwcc/archi/jonesmd/la/surf/kippen.html
Computer Reconstruction, University of Cardiff.

Leon Battista Alberti: an Architect's Architect.
http://www.olivetti.it/oliart/alberti/albertig.htm
Leon Battista Alberti (1404–1472).

Joao Batista Villanova Artigas
http://www.lsi.usp.br/%7Eartigas/home/thearchitect/
Artigas, The Architect. 'When we talk about Artigas, we are talking about a master: his work contributed decisively to characterize Brazilian architecture.'

Arcosanti, an Urban Laboratory
http://www.getnet.com/~nkoren/arcosanti/arcosant.html

Richard Buckminster Fuller, Geodesic Dome
http://www.futuro.usp.br/rod/text/buckminster_fuller.html
Dome Project, Synagetics Institute
http://cs1.sfc.keio.ac.jp/~t93827ya/dome/dome.html

Eisenman Architects, and Richard Trott & Partners
The Greater Columbus Convention Center, 1993
http://arcrs4.saed.kent.edu/Architronic/v3n1/v3n1.05.html

Graced Places: The Architecture of Wilson Eyre
http://www.upenn.edu/GSFA/Eyre/Eyreintro.html

Frank O. Gehry & Associates, Edgemar Shopping Mall, 1989
http://www.cf.ac.uk/uwcc/archi/jonesmd/la/surf/edgemar.html

Frank O. Gehry & Associates, Chiat Day Offices, 1991.
http://www.cf.ac.uk/uwcc/archi/jonesmd/la/surf/chiat.html
Computer Reconstructions, University of Cardiff.

Charles Rennie Mackintosh
http://www.glasgow.gov.uk/cityva/crm/index.htm
On-line guide to a major exhibition of his work organized as part of Glasgow's Visual Arts 1996 project. The centrepiece of the exhibition is a reconstruction and refurbishment of the Ladies Luncheon Room from Miss Cranston's Ingram Street Tea Room.

Richard Meier
Douglas House:
http://www.arch.unsw.edu.au/exhibits/rayshade/ca1-93s2/jojnlim.htm
Computer reconstruction, University of New South Wales.
Smith House:
http://www.cc.columbia.edu/~archpub/BT/SMITH/smith.html
Computer reconstruction, University of Columbia.
Getty Center for the Arts, Westwood Hills, 1984–1997:
http://www.cf.ac.uk/uwcc/archi/jonesmd/la/auto/getty.html
Computer reconstruction, University of Cardiff.

Moriyama & Teshima
Ontario Science Centre, 1969: http://www.magic.ca/mtarch/osc.html
Scarborough Civic Centre, 1973: http://www.magic.ca/mtarch/scc.html
Metropolitan Toronto Reference Library, 1977: http://www.magic.ca/mtarch/mtl.html
Science North (Science Museum), 1984: http://www.magic.ca/mtarch/scin.html
Niagara Parks: A 100-Year Vision, 1988: http://www.magic.ca/mtarch/nia.html
Ottawa-Carleton Centre, 1990: http://www.magic.ca/mtarch/oc.html
Canadian Embassy, Tokyo, 1991: http://www.magic.ca/mtarch/emb.html
York University Vari Hall, 1991: http://www.magic.ca/mtarch/vari.html
Bank of Montreal Inst. for Learning, 1993: http://www.magic.ca/mtarch/bofm.html
Owen Public School, 1993: http://www.magic.ca/mtarch/gallery.html
Bata Shoe Museum, 1995: http://www.magic.ca/mtarch/bsm.html

Andrea Palladio, Il Redentore Church
http://www.arch.unsw.edu.au/exhibits/rayshade/church/thumbs.htm
Computer reconstruction, University of New South Wales.
MIT's Palladio project is reported at:
http://alberti.mit.edu/projects/palladio.html

Individual architects and designers

Cesar Pelli, Pacific Design Centre, Beverly Hills, 1975
http://www.cf.ac.uk/uwcc/archi/jonesmd/la/dtown/pdc.html
Computer reconstruction, University of Cardiff.

Jozef Plecnik
http://www.ijs.si/slo/ljubljana/plecnik.html

Richard Rogers, the PatCentre
http://www.cc.columbia.edu/~archpub/BT/PATCENT/patmenu.html
Computer reconstruction, University of Columbia.

Mies van der Rohe, the Barcelona Pavilion
http://archpropplan.auckland.ac.nz/People/Mat/barcelona/barcelona.html
Computer reconstruction, University of Auckland.

Aldo Rossi
Art Gallery, Fukuoka (Japan)
http://archpropplan.auckland.ac.nz/People/Tania/rossi/rossi_artgal.html
Computer reconstruction, University of Auckland.

Adele Narde Santos, La Brea/Franklin Social Housing, Hollywood, 1993
http://www.cf.ac.uk/uwcc/archi/jonesmd/la/dtown/labrea.html
Computer reconstruction, University of Cardiff.

Rudolph Schindler, Pueblo Ribera
http://www.cc.columbia.edu/~archpub/BT/P_RIB/p-rib.html
Computer reconstruction, University of Columbia.

SOM, Lever House
http://www.cc.columbia.edu/~archpub/BT/LEVER/lever.html
Computer reconstruction, University of Columbia.

Louis Sullivan
http://www.geocities.com/CapitolHill/2317/sullivan.html

Henry Vaughan, Amasa Stone Memorial Chapel, 1911
http://arcrs4.saed.kent.edu/Architronic/v3n3/v3n3.04.html

Frank Lloyd Wright
in Winconsin: http://flw.badgernet.com:2080/
Seth Peterson Cottage: http://flw.badgernet.com:2080/sethpet1.htm
Taliesin: http://flw.badgernet.com:2080/gallery.htm

8

Practice and management

8.1 BUSINESS RELATED SITES

8.1.1 General business sites

Best Business Sites
http://techweb.cmp.com:2090/techweb/ia/13issue/13topsites.html
Annotated guide to the best 25 business web sites as determined by 'Interactive Age'.

Business Information Sources
http://www.dis.strath.ac.uk/business/index.html
Annotated guide, maintained by Sheila Webber, editor of the Institute of Information Scientists' newsletter, *Inform*.

Commercial Usage of the Net
http://pass.wayne.edu/business.html

Cyberpreneur's Guide to the Internet
http://asa.ugl.lib.umich.edu/chdocs/cyberpreneur/Cyber.html
or gopher://una.hh.lib.umich.edu
select 'inetdirstacks' then select 'cyberpreneurship'
This is an excellent gopher resource for the individual or company either investigating or already doing business on the Internet. This gopher resource provides a huge compendium of Internet business related information: e-mail lists, other gophers, web pages, newsgroups and a host of other pointers for the online entrepreneur. The site is well organized and broken down into areas or topics. The WWW address version of CGI is a graphical version of the gopher with many links to other resources.

Digicash
http://digicash.support.nl/
Latest news on Cybercash.

Business related sites

EINet Galaxy Business index
http://www.einet.net/galaxy/Business-and-Commerce.html

Europages
http://www.europages.com
This mulitiligual service brings European suppliers to the world's fingertips by providing company data on 150 000 suppliers from 25 European countries. There is also over 100 pages of economic analyses as well as important business information on the main European markets.

Interesting Business Sites
http://www.rpi.edu/~okeefe/business.html

Internet Business Directory
http://ibd.ar.com

Internet Business Guide
gopher://gopher.hkkk.fi/:70/11/HKKK/InternetBusinessGuide
The full text of the 500 page *Internet Business Guide* is available in 15 chapter length files. Alternatively, as a 1.2 Mb file by anonymous ftp from:
ftp://gopher.epas.utoronto.ca
in the directory /pub/datalib/misc/sternberg.txt
Further details may be found at Phoenix Systems Synectics web site:
http://www.phoenix.ca/Phoenix/whatsnew.html/Internet_Business_Guide

Open Market Commercial Sites Index
http://www.directory.net

Small Business Administration Home Page
http://www.sbaonline.sba.gov/
Offers information on the SBA's mission and overview of the SBA. Whilst this is an exclusively U.S. based organization this well written home page not only provides some useful information but is a good example of how to organize business pages on the web.

Small Business Help Center
http://www.kclink.com/sbhc/
An often overlooked WWW site that has pointers and information for operators of small businesses or those who plan to start a small business.

Web Success
http://www.kdcol.com/~ray/index.html
An on-line magazine showcasing examples of successful web marketing. Shows how good ideas are generated and transformed into effective web sites.

Yahoo's Business Resources
http://www.yahoo.com/Business/
http://www.yahoo.com/Business/Miscellaneous

8.1.2 Computer related

ArchiCAD Gallery
http://www.aloha.net/~rexmax/archicad_gallery.html

AutoCAD links
http://www.autodes.com/autodes/coolinks.html

Autodesk
http://www.autodesk.com/
ftp://ftp.autodesk.com/
The home of AutoCAD.

Bentley Systems
http://www.bentley.com/
Microstation.

CADALYST Magazine
Home Page:
http://www.advanstar.com/cadalyst
Gopher service:
gopher://gopher.enews.com/11/magazines/alphabetic/all/cadalyst

CADENCE Magazine
http://whiz.mfi.com/cadence

Cadkey Corp
http://www.cadkey.com/

CAD Resources on the Net
http://www.renature.com/instarc/cad_net.html

Computer Hardware, Software, Magazines and Information
http://boss.cpcnet.com/personal/wgogle/computer.html
242 computer related links and growing.

Business related sites

David Marsden's AutoCAD links
http://nyx10.cs.du.edu:8001/~dmarsden/autocad.html

Intergraph
http://www.intergraph.com/
AEC Products
http://www.intergraph.com/doc-train/paec.html
AEC Products Pricelist
http://www.intergraph.com/doc-train/aec.html
AEC Documents
http://www.intergraph.com/doc-train/daec.html
AEC Training Courses
http://www.intergraph.com/doc-train/taec.html

Robert Brown's CAD Software WWW resource
http://www.iucf.indiana.edu/~brown/hyplan/wood.html#CAD

Softdesk Auto-Architect LT Specifications
http://www.softdesk.com/oem/specs/aaltspec.htm
Auto-Architect LT is a complete architectural CAD application that addresses the needs
of the home builder. Auto-Architect LT combines 3D CAD capabilities including an
easy-to-use graphic interface.

Ventana's AutoCAD Resource Archive
http://www.vmedia.com/vvc/onlcomp/autocad/resource.html

Ventana AutoCAD Online Companion
http://www.vmedia.com/vvc/onlcomp/autocad/index.html

8.1.2.1 Multimedia/video information and video archives on the Internet

Cornell Theory Center
http://www.tc.cornell.edu/Visualization

Internet Multicasting Service (Carl Malamud)
http://www.town.hall.org

Internet Talk Radio (Carl Malamud)
http://juggler.lanl.gov/itr.html

Los Alamos National Lab video encoding and video server
http://bang.lanl.gov/video

MICE (Multimedia Conferencing for Europe)
http://www.cs.ucl.ac.uk/mice/mice.html

MICE Seminars and Media on Demand servers
http://www.it.kth.se/~klements/vatplay.html

MIT Laboratory for Computer Science online video
http://www.lcs.mit.edu
http://tns-www.lcs.mit.edu/cgi-bin/vs/vsbrowser
http://tns-www.lcs.mit.edu/cgi-bin/vs/vsdemo
MIT is experimenting with the VUSystem Application for video files. The lab is also running trials with live video via the Internet.

MPEG Video Archive (Europe)
http://www.eeb.ele.tue.nl/mpeg/index.html

MPEG Video Archive (U.S.A.)
http://www.acm.uiuc.edu/rml/Mpeg

Multimedia File Formats on the Internet – a Beginner's Guide
http://ac.dal.ca/~dong/contents.html
An extensive multimedia guide for novice Internet users. It explains the file formats for texts, compressed files, games, software, pictures, sound and music, movies, foreign languages, etc. It also explains the ways to identify the different files and how to download and use the files. There are many pointers within the guide that may be used to download files. This data is mostly PC oriented but some of the information is essential even for Mac users and is general enough to be of importance for all.

NCSA Exhibits
http://www.ncsa.uiuc.edu/General/NCSAExhibits.html

Rob's New Multimedia Lab
http://www.acm.uiuc.edu/rml
This site is co-sponsored by the Association for Computing Machinery

Scientific Video archives at CRS4
http://www.crs4.it/Animate/Animations.html
Centre for Advanced Studies, Research and Development, Sardinia, Italy.

Video Webalog
http://figment.fastman.com/vweb/html/vidprod.html
An e-zine full of video data.

Virtual Reality Testbed (Sandy Ressler)

http://nemo.ncsl.nist.gov/~sressler/OVRThome.html

National Institute of Standards and Technology site.

Sandy Ressler is exploring the possibilites of offering virtual reality to users of the net. A glimpse of this is shown in 'Inline Graphics Surrogate Travel'. An inline picture of an area is shown and users 'click' on where they want to go inside this virtual world.

WAXWeb (The Discovery of Television among the Bees)

http://bug.village.virginia.edu:7777

One of the classic Internet sites. The site consists of the script of the film, 600 pages of supplementary text material related to the film, 2 000 stills (that went to make up the film), 600 MPEG video clips, and the entire audio track of the film in English, French, German and Japanese. Any part of the film may be viewed, in any order, and whilst viewing, it is possible at any time to 'jump out' of the film to read hyper-text comments related to the making of the film or related to the script. In addition it is possible to add or create additions to the script.

WWW Graphics Page

http://www.best.com/~bryanw

Maintained by Bryan Woodworth, the site is structured in two sections:

1. The FAQ desk

Graphics information; Internet Service FAQ pages; Miscellaneous FAQs.

2. Computer Support Areas

Macintosh MPEG players, contact sheet makers, dl/gl/fli viewers, etc. IBM PC MPEG players, JPEG viewers, a link to the Xing Technology FTP site, and official QPEG support site for North America (including the latest version of QPEG, along with a link to Oliver Fromme's homepage in Germany). Unix/X-Window MPEG source, movies. QuickTime Support Links; Archie link; Winsock support area.

8.1.3 Design related

Alberta Business Index, Architecture and Construction Services

http://www.infostream.ab.ca/busdir/secidx11.html

Archinet

http://www.archinet.co.uk

Web showcase for U.K. architects, including Fosters and Farrell.

Architect's DataBase

http://www.fmdata.com.

Over 1 200 project profiles in a web–searchable database with links to the archtects, engineers and consultants who worked on them.

Architectural Firms on the Web
http://www.intellinet.com/~afmccauley/index.htm
Andrew F. McCauley (afmccauley@intellinet.com) is establishing a list of architects and Architectural firms who have home pages on the World Wide Web. He is an architect based in Little Rock, Arkansas, and intends the list to become a resource for anyone interested in finding an Architect or an Architectural Office. The list is U.S. based and categorized by state, and sometimes cities within states.

Architects On-Line
http://news/arch_ol/jul95pag/index.htm.
'For RIBA Memebers or anyone else interested. A survey, conducted by the RIBA (Royal Institute of British Architects) IT (Information Technology) Group, to find out how many of you there were, in the UK, produced about 24 responses. Not many! Most of those were on Compuserve. If you weren't contacted or didn't respond please do so to Ashley Clough (sac@ash-c.demon.co.uk) who is a Member of the RIBA IT Group. Whilst there is much hype surrounding the 'Information-Highway', information and services may only appear if the providers know that there is an audience. Your presence may influence the Architectural Institutes in Europe like the EUA (European Union of Architects) and individual Member Institutes.'– Tim Aikin Architects On-Line.

Architectural visualization
http://ournet.clever.net/edifika/hp.html
Modelling, ray tracing, simulations, computer animation and more.
email: edifika@clever.net

Thomas Bollay, Architect
http://www.architect.com/ThomasBollayAssoc/Bollay/

British Architects On-line
http://www.dircon.co.uk/pringco/baol/baol.html
Regularly updated library of architects' brochures (includes Michael Hopkins).

Builder's Graphics and Custom Home designs WWW page
http://www.primenet.com/~mrclark/builders.html
Head on over here to see how construction-based and architectural companies can effectively use the WWW.

Careers: Architect, Builder or Engineer
http://www.etc.bc.ca/apase/scitech/arch_car.html
This category links activities for students with career interests in architecture, construction or all types of engineering.

Business related sites

CHA Architects
http://www.houstonet.com/cha
Specialists in commercial structures.

City Wide Alert E-zine
http://www.isisnet.com/Alive
An article about choosing an architect appeared in this Nova Scotia e-zine.

Creative Tech
http://www.creativetech.com
Describes services of 'a small firm that specialized in providing computer services to architects, including advanced rendering and walk-through animations.'

The Designer's Guide to the Internet
http://www.zender.com/designers-guide-net/
Offers a look at the Internet from a designer's perspective. Mike Zender and his coauthors offer practical suggestions, directions and insights for creating design-related services on the Internet. The book, published by Hayden books, can be found online in its entirety.

Directory of Professional Services
http://www.profnet.co.uk/profnet
Listings of architectural practices.

Eric C. Evangelista, Architect
http://www.iit.edu/~evaneri/
On-line business.

Susan Grant. Architect on the Move
http://www.cba.uh.edu/~phaedra/1stsista.html
Sista Showcase. In 1992, Susan Grant became the first african american woman to be licensed as an architect in the state of Illinois (along with Irma Ward) since 1949.

Pat Harrison, Architect
http://ucdenvdes.ucdavis.edu/data/design/faculty/bios/harrison.html
Professor Patricia Harrison has developed her research on housing for underrepresented population in coordination with the Rural California Housing Corporation of Sacramento (non-profit) and Community Development.

NETCAD Corporation
http://www.netcad.com/cad/

Practice and management

Provides the opportunity to display CAD portfolios on the net. Examples may be viewed at: http://www.netcad.com/aec/archs/Archco.html

O'Donnell, Wicklund, Pigozzi and Peterson
http://www.automatrix.com/owp/
An architectural firm that has set up a site with good links to other services, including architectural schools and research centres.

Paris-Anglophone Architecture and Construction
http://www.paris-anglo.com/data/rubriques/arch.html

Stephen Perrella: information architect
For those interested, further explanations of my work may be found at:
http://mmol.mediamatic.nl
or
http://www.mediamatic.nl/WhoisWho/Perrella/StephenPerrella.html

Shawn's Internet Resume Centre: Architecture/Construction
http://www.inpursuit.com/sirc/architec.html

John Stonum, Architect
http://deepthought.armory.com/~jstonum/
Environmentally-sensitive visionary architecture. Design Approach: our small office enables us to provide responsive, quality professional service on schedule and within budget. We understand the necessity of working closely with the owner, consultants and government agencies.

Survey of Architects' Use of Computing Technology
http://www.co.calstate.edu/AEC/
Survey of the use of computers by Californian architects.

Threshold
http://cybercom.net/~cyberian/threshold
Web site dedicated to architecture, landscape design and planning. Maintained by architect Dennis Pang in Boston, MA.

8.2 ASSOCIATIONS AND SOCIETIES

Acoustical Society of America
http://sunspot.nosc.mil/asa

Associations and societies

ACSA, Association of Collegiate Schools of Architecture Western Region
http://uhunix.uhcc.hawaii.edu:3333/acsa_home.html

American Cultural Resources Association
http://www.mindspring.com/~wheaton/ACRA.html
The American Cultural Resources Association (ACRA) is a professional business association for the promotion of the professionalisation of the cultural resources consulting industry and its many disciplines. Member firms consult in history, archaeology, historic preservation, architectural history, historical architecture, planning, landscape architecture, etc.

American Institute of Architects (AIA)
http://www.aia.org/
The AIA Home Page includes Selecting an Architect, Careers, Art and Science of Architecture (includes Award-winning architecture and the anticipated research abstracts), American Architecture Foundation, and Classroom Resources K-12.

American Institute of Architects, Baltimore Chapter
http://www.goucher.edu/aia
Describes architectural firm members of the chapter, giving information on number of employees, years of practice, number of recent design awards, and areas of speciality.
Other AIA Chapters with Web sites are:
San Mateo County California Chapter
http://www.webcom.com/~smccaia/
Philadelphia Chapter
http://www.libertynet.org/~aia

American Society of Architectural Perspectivists
http://www.asap.org/

American Society for Civil Engineers (ASCE)
http://www.asce.org/asce/index.html
ASCE maintains a site for progress information on U.S. construction industry metrication:
http://www.infi.net/~cstone/comindex.htm
ASCE Engineering Mechanics Division
http://venus.ce.jhu.edu/emd/

Arts and Crafts Society
http://www.arts-crafts.com/
An interactive electronic community dedicated to the philosophy and spirit of the original Arts and Crafts Society. Contains an 'Archive' area with links to Arts and Crafts related sources.

Association for Computer-Aided Design in Architecture (ACADIA)
http://www.clr.toronto.edu/ORG/ACADIA/home.html
The Association is for tutors of CAD in Schools of Architecture. The site contains information on membership, officers, steering committee and a conference paper database.

Belgian Architects' Association
http://www.brenda.be/nav
The Nationaal Architekten Verbond provides information on practice law, competitions, exhibitions, etc.

Bolivia – Instituto de Ensayo de Materiales
http://www.undp.org/tcdc/spec510.htm
Geotechnical Services.

British Board of Agrément
http://cig.bre.co.uk/bba/bbahome.htm

Building Centre Trust
http://www.cityscape.co.uk/usres/ez97/

Building Environmental Performance Analysis Club (BEPAC)
gopher://nisp.ncl.ac.uk/11/lists-a-e/bepac
Mailing list.

Canadian Centre for Architecture
http://cca.qc.ca/homepage.html

Canadian Institute for Research in Construction
http://www.irc.nrc.ca/

Canadian Society of Landscape Architects
http://www.clr.toronto.edu:1080/ORG/CSLA/brochure.html
Includes the origins of the profession in Canada, and the objectives of the society.

Chartered Institution of Building Services Engineers
http://www.bre.co.uk/org/cibse
The institution's publications list and details of conferences, as well as links to suggested HVAC info sources, building engineering sources and British engineering institutions.

Associations and societies

CIE (Commission Internationale de l'Eclairage)
http://www.hike.te.chiba-u.ac.jp/ikeda/CIE/home.html
Technical, scientific and cultural non-profit organization devoted to international cooperation and exchange of information among its member countries on all matters relating to the science and art of lighting.

Construction Industry Computing Association (CICA)
http://www.cica.org.uk/users/fj23/CICA/

Construction Industry Research Association (CIRIA)
http://www.ciria.org.uk/ciria

Construction Specifications Institute
http://www.aec-info.com/~aec/csi/index.html
History, membership categories and code of ethics.

Cooperative Network for Building Researchers (CNBR)
gopher://daedalus.edc.rmit.edu.au/

Design Online
http://www.dol.com/Root/designonline.html

Design Research Society
http://www.mailbase.ac.uk/lists-a-e/design-research
A multi-disciplinary association. The site contains links to a variety of design related sources.

eCAADe
http://www.liv.ac.uk/~arch/ecaade
The association for Education in CAAD in Europe.

Electronic Resource Network of Architecture, Engineering and Construction (AECNET)
http://www.aecnet.com
For information contact Drew Linsalata on info@aecnet.com

Energy and Climate Information Exchange (ECIX)
ftp://igc.org/pub/ECIXfiles

Energy Efficiency and Renewable Energy Network (EREN)
http://www.eren.doe.gov

ICARIS
http://www.fagg.uni-lj.si/ICARIS
'ICARIS is an experimental research network related to integrated CAD in civil engineering and architecture.' It includes bibliographies, full-text papers, a searchable civil engineers' calendar of events and EDITEC and WG78 membership databases.

Illuminating Engineering Society of North America (IES)
http://www.ksu.edu/~kenbeyer/ies.html
The IES mission is 'to advance knowledge and to disseminate information for the improvement of the lighted environment to the benefit of society'.

Institute of Civil Engineers
http://www.ice.org.uk/

Institute of Electrical Engineers (IEE)
http://www.iee.org.uk/

International Association of Lighting Designers
http://www.aecnet.com/IALD/IALD.html

International Association for Solar Energy Education (IASEE)
http://www.hrz.uni-oldenburg.de/~kblum/iasee.html

International Building Performance Simulation Association (IBPSA)
gopher://nisp.ncl.ac.uk/11/lists-f-j/ibpsa
Mailing list.

International Council on Monuments and Sites
http://hpb1.hwc.ca:10002/Welcome.html
Documents, information on its committees and links to net sources on protection of cultural property.

International Standards Organisation
http://www.iso.ch

Israel Arts and Science Academy
http://multinet.co.il/www/misc/iasa/iasa1.html.

Netherlands Architecture Institute
http://www.nai.nl

Professional Engineers Association of New Zealand
http://www.ipenz.org.nz/

Royal Architectural Institute of Canada
http://www.inforamp.net/~aec/arch/raic/index.html#Library

Royal Institute of British Architects
http://www.riba.org
Information on exhibitions, lectures and services.
See also the Architecture Centre at:
http://www.slumberinggiant.co.uk/archcent.html

Royal Institute of Chartered Surveyors (RICS)
http://www.cityscape.co.uk/users/fa08/ricshome.htm

Society of Architectural Historians, Southern California
http://www.ccsf.caltech.edu/~mac/sah/index.htm
The group's objectives, activities and calendar, as well as items of general interest to architecture and urban design in southern California.

Society of Building Science Educators
http://brick.arch.vuw.ac.nz:85/index.html
About the society. Also includes an extensive listing of links
http://brick.arch.vuw.ac.nz:85/interesting_addresses.html

Society of CAD Engineers
http://www.cadsociety.org
A non-profit professional organization dedicated to the continued growth of its members by keeping them informed, educated, and effective in their respective disciplines.

See also WWW Link Collection Sites with an Associations category, such as Yahoo:
http://www.yahoo.com/science/engineering/civil/construction/institutes
and CIBSE's British Engineering Institutions:
http://www.bre.co.uk/org/cibse/briteng.htm

8.3 INDUSTRIAL DESIGN, INTERIOR DESIGN, ETC.

Cohousing
http://everest.cs.ucdavis.edu/~stanifor/cohousing.html
General information, information about specific communities, and an extensive cohousing resource guide to additional sources
http://seclab.cs.ucdavis.edu/~stanifor/CRG/welcome.html

Construction and Real Estate (CARE) Information System
http://www.bre.polyu.edu.hk/CAREinfo
Site of the Hong Kong Polytechnic University Department of Building and Real Estate, the Construction and Real Estate Information System has menu choices for Hong Kong, China, Elsewhere (on the net) and Product Data Index. The department also offers movie clips on the construction industry and the department .
http://www.bre.polyu.edu/hk/DoBRE/Movies/

CORE – Industrial Design Resources
http://www.interport.net/CORE/
The net spot for industrial design, set up by two Pratt graduate students. Go directly to the Resource Lab for information on events, jobs, associations, links, schools, manufacturers and parts suppliers, and more.
http://www.interport.net/CORE/resource/index.html

DesignOnline
http://www.dol.com/designonline.html
Information on design associations, conferences, people (including resumes) and various design disciplines including industrial design, graphic design, architecture, furniture design, fine arts, photography, advertising, new media, fashion and interior design.

Domespace
http://www.iway.fr/domespace/
Illustrated exhibit of 'the house that turns with the sun'.

Ewa Planation Village Slide Show
http://www.lava.net/~ada/ewaslide.html
Two bedroom Bond type home for Ewa Plantation workers.
©1995 Architect Design Associates.

Home Styles
http://homestyle.com/hs/
Information on how to choose a home design, and on the home plans and home plan publications that they sell. Links to related sites in home repair, interior design, real estate and others.

Housing Related Links
http://www.primenet.com/~mrclark/links.html
Builders, landscaping, home automation, virtual tours, home products, realtors.

OBD Company Profiles
http://www.inca.net/obd/links/0014.html

50 new model homes for inspection.

Steve's Alternative Housing Archive
http://www.uel.ac.uk:80/pers/16405
Homelessness, legislation, policy, design and repair are some of the categories, but this very individual site is worth looking at. Access is sometimes difficult and it may be necessary to enter at a higher level (http://www.uel.ac.uk/) and select the Alternative Housing Archive link.

Summers House Plans
http://www.cyberstore.ca/FosTech/Real_Estate/Summers/profile.html
Current projects by designer William Summers, with information on sites available for purchase along with the house plans.

This New House
http://www.thisnewhouse.com/tnh/
Resource guide associated with U.S. TV show.

Virtual Design Center
http://www.vdc.com
The VDC is a 'communication and marketing system serving the needs of contract manufacturers, service providers and interior designers worldwide'. Typical areas include furniture, floor covering, lighting, office furniture dealers and facility consultants. Information on trade shows, publications, dealers and products.

WaterFront/ Sunshine Dreams Real Estate
http://www.islands.com
'This page, and the information it will direct you to, specializes in presenting some of the most beautiful, unique, and picturesque real estate available in Florida and the Caribbean.'

Robin White Interiors
http://www.discoverdesign.com/rwhite.html
As a Professional Member of ASID since 1983, Ms. White serves on many committees and is currently a board member. She has served as a board member for the Hospitality Industry Association and has been involved in the Architectural Heritage Foundation.

WWW Virtual Library: Design
http://www.dh.umu.se/vlib.html
Annotated, not extremely comprehensive, but covering a wide range of design professions, including fashion design, graphic design, environmental design, industrial design and interactive design.

WWW Virtual Library: Furniture and Interior Design
http://www.i3.se/furniture.html
Although architecture makes up the bulk of the list of academic sites, the miscellaneous and commercial sites are of interest.

9

Building construction

9.1 CONSTRUCTION INDEX SITES

AEC Net
http://www.aecnet.com
The Electronic Resource Network of Architecture, Engineering and Construction. AECNet provides World Wide Web services, Internet access and an Internet based bulletin board service for professionals in the architecture, engineering and commercial construction industry. The BBS software is free and can be had via anonymous FTP to ftp.aecnet.com in the /pub/aecnet/ directory (both Windows and Mac available).

The AEC InfoCenter provides a keyword search engine to retrieve a variety of data. It holds a database of over six thousand building product manufacturers organized using the Masterformat system from the Construction Specifications Institute. The code directory includes contact information for every code and regulatory agency in every state in the US.

The Construction Information Gateway
http://cig.bre.co.uk/
A U.K. host to a variety of construction services.

Building Industry Exchange (BIX)
http://www.building.org/
'The global exchange center for building industry businesses, resources and communications.'

The Building and Home Improvement Products Network
http://www.build.com/
Pointers to materials manufacturers, trade associations, builders merchants and general internet sites to do with building and construction.

Civlist
http://rampages.onramp.net/~shilston/shilston.html
An increasingly comprehensive list of, mainly, civil engineering sites maintained by Jay Shilstone.

Proconet
http://www.cityscape.co.uk/users/fa08/menu.htm
A U.K. based site maintained by chartered surveyor Mark Wilderspin set up with the intention of providing a gateway to property and construction web sites.

Reading University MSc(Project Management)
http://www.reading.ac.uk/~kcrsmstr/prac_www.html
A list of pointers, maintained by Steve Simister, to illustrate the range of construction industry web sites available.

9.2 SCHOOLS OF CIVIL AND ENVIRONMENTAL ENGINEERING

9.2.1 USA and Canada

Auburn University, College of Engineering
http://www.eng.auburn.edu/

Brigham Young University, Civil and Environmental Engineering
http://www.et.byu.edu/~cewww

Bucknell University
http://www.bucknell.edu/~svensson/ce/cehome.html

California Institute of Technology, Southern California Earthquake Center
http://scec.gps.Caltech.edu

California State University, Civil Engineering
http://www.ecst.csuchico.edu/ce.html

Carleton University, Civil and Environmental Engineering
http://www.civeng.carleton.ca/
Carleton University Civil Engineering software list
http://www.civeng.carleton.ca/csce/software/
Movie of Tacoma Narrows Bridge failure
http://www.civeng.carleton.ca/Exhibits/

Carnegie Mellon University, Civil and Environmental Engineering
http://www.ce.cmu.edu:8000/

Case Western Reserve University, Ohio
http://www.cwru.edu/CWRU/Dept/Engr/eciv/eciv.html

Clemson University, South Carolina
http://www.eng.clemson.edu

Cornell University, College of Engineering
http://www.engr.cornell.edu/CE.html
Engineering Library
http://www.englib.cornell.edu/

Dartmouth College, Thayer School of Engineering
http://caligari.dartmouth.edu/thayer/thayer.html

Environmental Research Institute of Michigan (ERIM)
http://www.erim.org/

Georgia Institute of Technology, Civil and Environmental Engineering
http://www.ce.gatech.edu/ce.html
EPITOME Project:
http://www.ce.gatech.edu/Projects/Epitome/epitome.html
College of Architecture, Building and Construction
http://www.gatech.edu/coa/coabc.html

Indiana University
http://www.indiana.edu

Kansas State University, College of Engineering
http://www.engg.ksu.edu/
has good links to references at:
http://www.engg.ksu.edu/information/references.html

Lehigh University
http://www.lehigh.edu
Center for Advanced Technology for Large Structural Systems (ATLASS)
http://www.lehigh.edu/~inatl/inatl.html

Michigan Technological University, Civil and Environmental Engineering
http://www.geo.mtu.edu/civil/

New Jersey Institute of Technology, Civil Engineering
http://www.njit.edu:8010/njIT/Schools/NCE/civil.html

North Carolina State University at Raleigh, College of Engineering
http://www.eos.ncsu.edu/coe/coe.html
VIMS project
http://vims.ncsu.edu

Northwestern University
http://www.civil.nwu.edu
Infrastructure Technology Institute Library Services Program
http://iti.acns.nwu.edu/library/index.html
Advanced Cement Based Materials
http://www.civil.nwu.edu/ACBM/

Notre Dame, Civil Engineering and Geological Sciences
http://www.nd.edu/Departments/EN/CEGEOS/lists.html

Ohio Northern University, Engineering Department
http://www.onu.edu/Engineering/

Princeton University
http://soil.princeton.edu
Directory of Transportation Resources
http://dragon.princeton.edu/~dhb/

Purdue University School of Engineering
http://ce.ecn.purdue.edu

Southwest Texas State University
Edwards Aquifer Research and Data Center
http://eardc.swt.edu:80/

Stanford University, School of Engineering
http://www-ee.stanford.edu/soe.html
Center for Integrated Facility Engineering
http://gummo.stanford.edu/html/ICM/CIFE.html
CICEE Project Abstracts
Bridging the A/E/C gap – an interdisciplinary computer supported course at Stanford
University:
http://synthesis.stanford.edu/Docs/ProjAbs/cicee/bridge_gap.html

State University of New York at Buffalo
http://www.eng.buffalo.edu/dept/cie/index.html

Schools of civil and environmental engineering

Texas Agricultural and Military University (College Station)
http://info-civil.tamu.edu/

University of Alberta, Canada, Water Resources Engineering
http://maligne.civil.ualberta.ca

University of California at Berkeley
http://www.ce.berkeley.edu
Partners for Advanced Transit and Highways (PATH)
http://www-path.eecs.berkeley.edu
Northern California Earthquake Center
http://quake.geo.berkeley.edu
UC Berkeley ASCE Student Chapter Home Page
http://ce.berkeley.edu/~asce/

University of Cincinnati, College of Engineering
http://decon.coe.uc.edu/

University of Colorado at Boulder
http://bechtel.colorado.edu
Civil Engineering Department
http://civil.colorado.edu

University of Florida at Gainesville, Civil Engineering
http://www.ce.ufl.edu/

University of Hawaii, College of Engineering
http://www.eng.hawaii.edu/

University of Illinois, Civil Engineering
http://mahogany.cen.uiuc.edu/COE/newcoe.html
Center for Cement Composites and Advanced Construction Technology
http://www.cen.uiuc.edu/COE-Info/research/labs.html

University of Manitoba, Department of Civil and Geological Engineering
http://www.ce.umanitoba.ca/

University of Miami, Engineering Department
http://coeds.eng.miami.edu/CoEinfo/overview.html

University of Michigan, Materials Engineering
http://www.engin.umich.edu:80/dept/mse

M.I.T. Civil and Environmental Engineering
http://web.mit.edu:80/org/c/civenv/www/

University of New Brunswick, Canada, Fire Science Centre
http://www.fsc.unb.ca:80/

University of New York
National Center for Earthquake Engineering Research (NCEER)
http://nceer.eng.buffalo.edu

University of North Carolina
Institute for Transportation Research and Education
http://itre.uncecs.edu/

University North Carolina, Charlotte, College of Engineering
http://www.coe.uncc.edu/catalog/HTML/coe.col.html

University of Oregon, Structural Engineering
http://darkwing.uoregon.edu:80/~struct/

University of Portland, Multnomah School of Engineering
http://www.up.edu/

University of Southern California, Structural Control
http://cwis.usc.edu/dept/civil_eng/structural/concrete/ConHome.html

University of Texas, Civil Engineering
http://www.ce.utexas.edu

University of Victoria, Faculty of Engineering
http://www-engr.uvic.ca/

University of Washington, Seattle, College of Engineering
http://www.engr.washington.edu/

University of Washington Department of Civil Engineering
http://ce.washington.edu/

University Wisconsin-Madison, College of Engineering
http://trans4.neep.wisc.edu/COE.proto

Virginia Technical University
http://www.eng.vt.edu

Schools of civil and environmental engineering

Virginia Tech. geotechnical division
http://geotech.ce.vt.edu
Virginia Tech., Multimedia Statics programme
http://128.173.52.118/Succeed/statics
SUCCEED Project:
http://succeed.ee.vt.edu/index.html
Graphical presentation of standard concrete and aggregate test techniques.
http://succeed.edtech.vt.edu/Indexes/Materials%20Engineerin.html

Washington University at St. Louis, Department of Civil Engineering
http://www.cive.wustl.edu/cive/

9.2.2 Australasia

Curtin University of Technology, School of Civil Engineering
http://www.cage.curtin.edu.au/civil/

Deakin University, Engineering and Technology
http://altair.et.deakin.edu.au

Monash University, Civil Engineering
http://civil-ftp.eng.monash.edu.au/default.htm

University of Melbourne
High Performance Concrete in Australia
http://aqua.civag.unimelb.edu.au/~pendyala/hsc

University of Tasmania, Department of Civil and Mechanical Engineering
http://info.utas.edu.au/docs/beasley/civenghp.htm

9.2.3 Europe

9.2.3.1 Belgium
Catholic University of Leuven, Civil Engineering Department
http://www.bwk.kuleuven.ac.be/

9.2.3.2 France
Centre for Advanced Engineering Education (ESIEE)
http://www.esiee.fr:80/

9.2.3.3 Italy
University of Parma, Civil Engineering
http://magoo.cedi.unipr.it/civile/dipartimento.civile/index-eng.html

9.2.3.4 Netherlands
Delft Technical University, Department of Civil Engineering
http://www.ct.tudelft.nl/
Concrete Structures.
http://dutcb35.tudelft.nl/welcome.html

9.2.3.5 Norway
University of Trondheim, Civil Engineering
http://www.pvv.unit.no/~oes

NorwegianTechnical University, Civil Engineering
http://www.unit.no/NTH/nth-eng.html
Institutt for Geoteknikk
http://www.geotek.unit.no

9.2.3.6 Poland
Warsaw Agricultural University, Department of Structural Mechanics
http://alpha.sggw.waw.pl/~kaminski/dept0.html

9.2.3.7 Slovenia
University of Ljubljana
http://www.fagg.uni-lj.si/

9.2.3.8 Sweden
Chalmers University of Technology, School of Civil Engineering
http://www.vsect.chalmers.se/
Concrete Department
http://www.vsect.chalmers.se/~cse/Betong/Betong.html

9.2.3.9 Switzerland
ETH Zurich, Laboratory of Building Materials
http://ibwk28.ethz.ch/TOPIC/topic.html

9.2.3.10 United Kingdom
Cambridge University, Department of Engineering
http://medusa.eng.cam.ac.uk/

Schools of civil and environmental engineering

Imperial College Department of Civil Engineering
http://rankine.cv.ic.ac.uk

Leeds University, Civil Engineering
http://itts02.leeds.ac.uk/civil/civil.htm

Napier University, Building & Surveying
http://bs-www.napier.ac.uk/Construction.html
Contains a number of pointers to related sites.

Queen Mary and Westfield College, Software for Engineering Education
http://www.ctieng.qmw.ac.uk/CTIEng.html

University of Bradford
http://www.brad.ac.uk/acad/civeng/civhome.html

University of Bristol
http://www.fen.bris.ac.uk/civil/

University of Durham, Geotechnical and Geological Engineering
http://www.dur.ac.uk/~des0dt/

University of Edinburgh , Science and Engineering
http://www.ed.ac.uk/edinfo/scieng/civilengbs_menu.html

University of Portsmouth, Civil Engineering
http://www.civl.port.ac.uk:80/

University of Reading, Construction Management.
http://www.rdg.ac.uk/kqFINCH/Home_CM.html
Navigator Project – Time lapse photography of construction.
http://www.rdg.ac.uk/kqFINCH/wkc1/mac/DBA/Navigator.html

University of Salford
http://www.salford.ac.uk/docs/depts/survey/CIB/cib.html
CIB W-89 CAL in Construction

University of Strathclyde, Department of Civil Engineering
http://www.strath.ac.uk/Departments/Civeng/index.html
Virtual Reality Construction Site Project.
http://www.strath.ac.uk/Departments/Civeng/conman/vcproject.html

University of Wales at Swansea, Masonry research
http://www.swan.ac.uk/civeng/research/masonry/masonry.htm

9.2.3.11 Ukraine
Kyiv State Technical University
Department of Construction and Architecture.
http://www.undp.org/tcdc/ukr99.htm

Odessa State Academy of Construction and Architecture
http://www.undp.org/tcdc/ukr49.htm

9.2.4 Other countries

Pontificia Universidad Catolica de Chile, Faculty of Engineering
http://www.ing.puc.cl:80/

The University of Tokyo, Concrete Laboratory, Tokyo, Japan.
http://concrete.t.u-tokyo.ac.jp/

Korea Advanced Institute of Science and Technology
http://cair-archive.kaist.ac.kr/kaist/dept.html

University of Natal, South Africa, Computing Centre for Water Research
http://aqua.ccwr.ac.za/

9.3 GENERAL BUILDING CONSTRUCTION

ABAM Engineers
http://www.abam.com/~abam/

Acer Consultants
http://www.ibmpcug.co.uk/~acer

AECNet
http://www.aecinfo.com

Alpha-DIDO
http://www.compulink.co.uk/~hr/
A general information source providing full-text access to technical papers, standards, etc. Maintained by Geoffrey Hutton.

Alternative Building Books
http://www.indra.com/jade-mtn/bldgbooks.html
How To Be Your Own Contractor. Save over 20% on building projects without hammering a nail. The author shares his 32 years' experience as a general contractor and covers everything from choosing a site to landscaping.

Arch-Online NY
http://www.arch-online.com
Arch-Online NY is an architectural and construction resource index focused on the New York Area.

C.E. Ball and Partners
http://www.compulink.co.uk/~ceball/welcome.html
U.K. quantity surveying and construction cost management group. The site is maintained by Andrew Hudson and provides links to U.K. construction IT initiatives such as the CITE (Construction Industry Trading Electronically) home page: http://www.compulink.co.uk/~ceball/cite.html/

Beargrass Engineers
http://beargrass.com/
Environmental engineers

Becoming a Building Contractor
http://www.wa.gov/lni/build.htm
Becoming a Building Contractor. The Consultation and Compliance Services Division of the Department of Labor and Industries administers the states building contractor laws. The site explains the requirements for operating as a specialty contractor.

Before Hiring A Contractor
http://www.wa.gov/lni/before.htm
If you are a consumer interested in having work done by a contractor, this brochure can help you by explaining how the Washington state contractor registration program works.

BIW (Building Information Warehouse)
http://www.biw.co.uk
U.K. based information exchange for construction industry professionals.

Black and Veatch
http://www.bv.com/
Contractors.

BM International Domespace
http://www.branch.com/dome/

Botolph Construction
http://www.worldserver.pipex.com/nc/Botolph_Const

BouwWeb
http://www.bouwweb.nl

BRAC/Presidio Remedial Action.
Reports of several projects, e.g.:
Building 637 – Crissy Field.
http://www.envcleanup.gov/b637.html
Cleanup Site. Description. Former gas station for the Presidio motor pool. The Army closed the station in 1989. Contractor. Montgomery Watson – engineering, design, analysis and workplans...
Building 950. Cleanup Site.
http://www.envcleanup.gov/b950.html
Description. Originally constructed as a storage facility for materials, vehicles and equipment. Contractor. International Technology Corporation. Type of Contamination. Lead. Type of Cleanup Activity. Excavation.and disposal.
Building 976 – Target Range.
http://www.envcleanup.gov/b976.html
Cleanup Site. Description. Former outdoor firing range. Contractor. International Technology Corporation. Type of Contamination. Suspected lead. Type of Cleanup Activity. Excavation and disposal.

British Board of Agrément
http://cig.bre.co.uk/bba/bbahome.htm

Bryant Group Plc. Building Services, Contruction & Contracting.
http://www.milfac.co.uk/milfac/u2166.html
Cranmore House, Cranmore Boulevard, Solihull, West Midlands B90 4SD.

Building Centre
http://www.buildingcentre.co.uk
Online product information.

Building Online
http://www.buildingonline.com
Product information.

Building Survey: Markle Hall through McKelvy House
http://www.lafayette.edu/library/special/survey/m.html
Markle Hall. Location: North of High Street, opposite the Quad. Date Built: 1929.
Architect: Charles Z. Klauder, Philadelphia. Contractor: Breig Brothers, Scranton, PA.
Originally the John Markle Hall of Mining.

Lorna Burrell
http://dolphin.csudh.edu/~david/burrell/lorna.html
Lorna Burrell. 43 years of Real Estate experience in all phases of Real Estate. Licensed
Real Estate Salesperson. Licensed Building Contractor. Land Developer. Former Bank
Escrow Officer and Manager of R.E. Loan Dept. Grandmother.

Canadian Engineering Network
http://www.transenco.com/
Site for information exchange between engineers, architects, suppliers and contractors.

CARE infosys: World
http://www.bre.polyu.edu.hk/CAREinfo/World/
Department of Building and Real Estate Construction and Real Estate related pages.
World Contractor Guide. Australia. University of New South Wales, Faculty of the
Built Environment (with links to other sites) Canada. ICI World Real Estate Network.

CIB
http://bcn.arch.ufl.edu/cib/html
Conseil International du Bâtiment.

CIRIA
http://www.gold.net/users/bm37/index.html
Construction Industry Research and Information Association.

Civlist
http://rampages.onramp.net/~shilston/civlist.html
Large listing of Civil Engineering resources.

Commercial Property Journal
http://www.insightinfo.co.uk/builserv.html
Building Services and Development Consultants. The UK Commercial Property Journal
Lists companies by district and by county:
North East London: http://www.insightinfo.co.uk/a2londne.html
East London: http://www.insightinfo.co.uk/a2londe.html
North London: http://www.insightinfo.co.uk/a2londn.html
North West London: http://www.insightinfo.co.uk/a2londnw.html
South West London: http://www.insightinfo.co.uk/a2londsw.html

West London: http://www.insightinfo.co.uk/a2londw.html
London West Central: http://www.insightinfo.co.uk/a2londwc.html
London East Central: http://www.insightinfo.co.uk/a2londec.html

Conduit
http://www.conduit1.com
Specialist construction site.

Construction and Architecture
http://www.k-net.com/kbdir/oregon/or_port/architec.html

Construction Industry Research Centre (CIRC)
http://www.irc.nrs.ca/
The Canadian CIRC is bilingual. The English homepage is at:
http://www.nrc.ca/irc/irc.html
To go straight to the table of contents:
http://www.nrc.ca/irc/irccontents.html

Construction Online
http://www.io.org/~conston/
An intensive effort to develop online resources for construction. Includes software and shareware downloads, home pages for members, and many links to other construction sites.

Construction Site
http://www.morpheus.com/construc/home.html
Links to several construction related sites

The Construction Site
http://www.constr.com/
A directory of contractors, architects, engineers, construction equipment and materials suppliers.

Contractor Information Database
http://www.asia1.com.sg/cidb/coninfo.html
Contractor information. Firms doing general building works. Firms doing civil engineering works. Firms doing piling work. CIDB-SISIR ISO 9000 Certified contractors. Construction statistics. Training programmes etc.

Craftsman Book Company
http://ns1.win.net/~contractor/cbc/items/cgttbc.htm
1992-93 Contractor's Guide to the Building Code. By Jack Hageman, 544 pages, 5-1/2 x 8-1/2. This completely revised edition explains in plain English exactly what the

Uniform Building Code requires. Based on the most recent code, it covers many changes.

Craftsman Product Index
http://www.swcp.com/~coach/craftsman/prdidxa.htm
Craftsman Alphabetical Product Listing.
1992-93 Contractor's Guide to the Building 0-934041-67-9 $28.00.
A Treatise on Stairbuilding and Handrailing 0-941936-02-3 $22.95.
Basic Engineering For Builders 0-934041-83-0 $34.00
Bookkeeping for Builders 0-934041-42-3 $19.75
Builder's Comprehensive Dictionary 0-934041-50-4 $24.95
Builder's Guide to Accounting Revised 0-934041-18-0 $2.50
etc.

CSIRO
http://philpc.mel.dbce.csiro.au/index.htm
Structural Engineering, in Melbourne, contains a link to some shareware engineering software.
Division of Building Construction and Engineering
http://www.dbce.csiro.au/

Custom Building
http://www.finel.com/cb33480.html
Owner/Builder Alliance Inc. Be your own contractor – save thousands. As the Owner/Builder you will, with our help, obtain the permit, negotiate sub-contractor bids, obtain materials, etc.

Design or Construction Opportunities – Definitions
http://fcn.state.fl.us/dms/dbc/oppor1z.html
Florida Department of Management Services. Division of Building Construction. Design or Construction Opportunities Detail Report.

Dictionary of Architecture and Construction
http://www.technical.powells.portland.or.us/stacks/archcon.html

Document Center
gopher://doccenter.com
A commercial U.S. service where it is possible to order on-line a large number of codes and standards. A similar service is available in the U.K. through AlphaDIDO:
http://www.compulink.co.uk/~hr/

Dot & Line Construction Co. Oregon
http://www.k-net.com/kbdir/oregon/or_corva/architec.html

EE/CSE Building Project Status Reports.
e.g. Building Project Status Report 4/28/95.
http://bauhaus.cs.washington.edu/building/reports/4.28.95.html
This Week. Contractor continues to concrete the perimeter walls that form the outside walls of the two basement levels. The walls are 18 ins thick, 38 feet high and 48 feet wide and contain approx. 65 cubic yards of concrete.
Building Project Status Report 6/26/95
http://bauhaus.cs.washington.edu/building/reports/6.26.95.html
This Week. The final lower basement to first floor perimeter wall pour was completed last Friday. Contractor will form and pour the first brick corbel ledge which will eventually support the brick facing.
Project Status Report 9/21/95.
http://www.cs.washington.edu/building/reports/current.html
This Week. The Contractor continues to form and pour walls and floor slabs. All of the first floor slab and the westernmost portion of the 2nd floor slab have been concreted. The contractor is now preparing for the next 2nd floor slab pour.

EINet Galaxy Civil Engineering Page
http://galaxy.einet.net/galaxy/Engineering-and-Technology/Civil-and-Construction-Engineering.html

Engineers' Virtual Library
http://epims1.gsfc.nasa.gov/engineering/engineering.html

EU Official Journal
http://epin1.epin.ie
Home page with information on contracts and companies.

Fairfax County Licenses, Permits, and Regulations
http://www.eda.co.fairfax.va.us/fceda/do_bus/b_regs.html__24029-6
Air Pollution Control and Hazardous Materials Permits. Alcoholic Beverage Licenses. Building, Electrical, Mechanical and Plumbing Permits/Construction. Business, Professional and Occupational Licenses (BPOL).

Farm Structures
http://quiknet.com/farm/farmstru.html
Selecting and Working with a Farm Building Contractor. Ventilation for Warm Confinement Livestock Buildings. Lightning Protection for Missouri Farms and Homes.

Federal Building Company
http://www.federalbuilding.com/

A Design/Build Remodeling Contractor. Office and Showroom 3630 Park Boulevard Oakland, CA 94610. Fax 510/482-0306 Phone 510/482-0300. Since 1925. License No. 285785. Visit our web showroom.

FM Data
http://www.fmdata.com
FMdatacom members have instant access to a continually updated database of facilities projects including cost, square footage and project-team information. Membership also includes access to facilities news, an on-line glossary, member discussion groups and judiciously selected links to important facilities and building-related web sites.

Georgia Tech, Construction Research Centre
http://www.gatech.edu/coa/news/no3/13crc.html
Symposium on 'Global Future of the Construction Industry'.

Glavproject Ltd, Bulgaria: Contractor
http://www.undp.org/tcdc/bul10.htm

Global Construction Network
http://www.gcn.net:80/index.html
Pointers to Construction sites.

Harvest Building Services, Inc.
http://www.columbus.org/chamber/membership/member/H/1712.html
General Information: 647 Park Meadow Rd. Westerville, OH 43081.

Home Owners' Page – Contractor Categories
http://www.weblink.com/homeowners/categories.html
Contractors Listed by Category. Architects. Building Inspectors (see also Structural Engineers), Carpenters and Cabinet Makers (see also Handymen/women, Remodelers).

Huntsville City Licenses and Permits
http://www.ci.huntsville.al.us/ci_services/faq/223.htm
City Licenses and Permits. Animal Licenses. Building Permits. Business License. Contractor or Sub-Contractor Licenses. Doing Business With Contractors. Parade Permits.

International Christian Building Ministries
http://www.supptec.com/business/icbm.htm
Psalms 127:1. Churches. Homes. Renovations Consulting Services. General Contractor Construction Management. C. Thomas Vaughan 813-867-0452. E-Mail Address: icbm@supptec.com. Support Technologies Corp.

InterPRO Construction Industry Links
http://www.ipr.com
Interpro Resources Inc is a site specifically for the construction industry and maintains many links to directories and contracting firms, e.g.
InterPRO-AEC Services
http://www.ipr.com/interpro/location/united_states/cd01001.html
Lists of General Building Contractor firms are referenced at this location. The lists are sorted according to the home location of company.
InterPRO-AEC Construction Publications
http://www.ipr.com/interpro/publicat/pb361.html

KBS-Media Lab
http://delphi.kstr.ith.se/kbs

Kleenway Building Maintenance Services Inc.
http://www.valuenetwork.com/sab/busdir/genbs/to.on.ca.kleen.html
Kleenway Building Maintenance Services Inc. 3991 Chesswood Drive Toronto, ON, Canada M3J 2R8. Kleenway Building Maintenance Inc. has been providing complete janitorial and related services for more than 15 years.

Kuwait Mosque Construction Project
http://www.moc.kw/Users/mosque/arci.html

National Building Specification
http://arch20.newcastle.ac.uk/nbs/nbshome.htm

NFSD: Disaster Handbook
http://www.agen.ufl.edu/~foodsaf/dh5.html
Buildings. Checking Damaged Buildings. Choosing a Contractor. Electrical Systems & Appliances. Home Clean-up and Renovation: Building Damage. Floors. Walls. Siding, Doors and Windows. Finding and Repairing Leaks in Roofs. Restoring Flooded Water Systems.

PIRS On-Line
http://biz.rtd.com/insa/index.html
On-Line Information Service for Construction and Design Professionals. Information Systems and Automation, Corp. (INSA, Corp.) of Tucson, Arizona is providing access to PIRS On-Line, the On-Line Product Information Retrieval System for Architecture, Engineering, and Construction. PIRS On-Line provides information and communications to meet the needs of the A/E/C community. Offering a one point solution that brings together information from Professionals in the field, Software developers, Building product manufacturers, Codes and regulations and other sources.

On-line Resources for Construction
http://www.copywriter.com/ab/constr.html

Planning and Code Enforcement
http://www.ilstu.edu/~mjtomlia/forccom/bloom/plancode.htm
Building Safety Division. This Division is responsible for the following: Construction Permits. Plan Review and Approval. Contractor License and Registration. Inspections. Investigations.

Pride Industries Building Maintenance
http://www.worldtouch.com/pride/build.maint.div.html
Property maintenance and management services. Pride Industries is fully insured and maintains a California State Contractor's License and a Pesticide Applicator's License.

Raytheon
http://www.raytheon.com/rec
Engineers and contractors.

RBC Construction Contractor Services
http://www.aecnet.com/rbc/constrct.htm
Services for the construction contractor. Civil engineering. Site and Building Layout. Boundary and Topographic Surveys. Soil and Vegetative Mapping. Land Use and Wetlands Permits – Local, State and Federal. Drainage Studies. Structural engineering.

Real Estate Companies
http://www.sunvalleyid.com/realest/construc.htm

Sabo and Zahn, Construction Law Attorneys
http://www.webcom.com/~sabozahn/
Services, information on the attorneys including Sabo's book *Legal Guide to AIA Documents*, and links to law and construction related WWW sites.

Sampson Construction.
http://slv.net/slvbnet/felton/sampsonc.htm
Paul Sampson. General Building Contractor - Lic #583016. Serving all of Santa Cruz County. Remodels. Decks. Concrete. Home Repairs. Sampson Construction - 265 Madrona Road, Felton, Ca 95018 - (408) 335-3808.

Vitruvius Corporation
http://com.primenet.com/ssp/TVC/

Specializing in Insurance Claims. Earthquake, Fire, Wind, and Water damage. Commercial or Residential properties. Insurance Claims. Retrofitting. General Building Contractor. Main office located in Los Angeles, CA. 91105.

Keith Ward and Associates
http://www.paston.co.uk/lionet/kwa.html
Norwich-based firm of quantity surveyors.

Waste Disposal Home Page
http://www.cybergate.com/~silver/HOME.HTML
Guidelines for all types of waste removal.

Wimpey
http://www.wimpey.com.uk/wimpey
U.K. contractor.

Winter Park Construction
http://www.wpc.com
A contracting firm whose site includes a 'Glossary of Construction Terms for the Buyer and Builder' and 'Humorous Construction Definitions' for such terms as 'bid opening,' 'project manager,' 'OSHA' and 'completion date'.

Worldwide Contractor Guide
http://dino.worldpub.com/contractors.htm
Worldwide Contractor Guide. AEC InfoCenter's Building Product Library. AEC InfoNet: Architecture, Engineering, Building Construction.

Yahoo Civil Engineering Page
http://www.yahoo.com/Science/Engineering/Civil_Engineering/

9.4 CONSERVATION AND RENOVATION

Alberquerque, New Mexico, Kimo Theatre
http://www.cabq.gov/kimo/restore.html
Description of the on-going restoration of this listed building.

Bexhill-on-Sea, De La Warr Pavilion
http://www.heritage.co.uk/heritage/delawarr.html
Explanation of the restoration of the classic international style pavilion.

Boulder Restoration Projects
http://www.boulder.org/dreams.html

Discussion and walkthrough of historic commercial and residential districts, highlighting specific architects and restoration projects (with illustrations).

California State Historical Building Code
http://134.186.213.51/shbc/shbcintr.htm
The intent of the State Historical Building Code (SHBC) is to protect California's architectural heritage by recognizing the unique construction problems inherent in historic buildings and offering an alternative code to deal with these problems.

Cluny Abbey
http://www.research.ibm.com/xw-P4205-snapshots.html
Images of the extraordinary reconstruction of the Abbey.

Detroit, Michigan
http://www.oit.itd.umich.edu/~tfadoir/pw/tours.html
The historic districts of Detroit described by the architectural preservation society.

Dresden, Frauenkirche
http://www.ibm.com/sfasp/teamwork.htm
How computers played a major role in the restoration of the church.

London, The Globe Theatre
http://www.globe.jhc.net
Not so much conservation as reconstruction.
http://www.delphi.co.uk/delphi/stories/9508/16.Globe/archi.html
The Architect's Vision. Apart from Sam Wanamaker, the other key figure in realizing the reconstruction was the architect Theo Crosby and his practice, Pentagram.

Louisiana State Museum
http://www.yatcom.com/meworld/museum/lastate.html
The Museum was established to preserve the State Historic properties in 'Vieux Carre'. Details of specific buildings are included.

Montreal
http://www.cam.org/~fishon1/archit.html
Historic Montreal.

New Bedford's Architectural History
http://www.umassd.edu/SpecialPrograms/DFinnerty/homepage.html
Interactive tour of four Federal Style buildings in New Bedford's Waterfront Historic District. Discussions of the architecture, people and businesses associated with each building and an explanation of the efforts involved in restoring and preserving the buildings.

New Orleans, Gallier House
http://www.yatcom.com/meworl/museum/gallierhouse.html
Historical restoration of the former residence of James Gallier Jr., a leading New Orleans architect.

Ohio's Statehouse
http://www.ohio.gov/ohio/statehouse/welcome.html
Interactive explanation of the restoration project in process at the Ohio Capital Square Complex.

Paris, Notre Dame
http://www.paris.org/Monuments/NDame/
The history and restoration of the cathedral.

Preserve/Net
http://www.crp.cornell.edu/

Royal Commission on the Historical Monuments of England
http://www.rchme.gov.uk

Salem Architecture in the 17th and 18th Centuries
http://www.star.net/salem/houses.htm
The commercial and residential structures of early Salem, including furnishings and fittings.

San Jose, California, St. James' Square
http://www.preservation.org/st.james.html
Description of the overall plan and important historic buildings.

University of Virginia, Rotunda
http://jefferson.village.virginia.edu/decalcomania/home.html
'Thomas Jefferson's Rotunda Restored: a pictorial review with commentary'.

Washington State University, Lewis Alumni Center
http://www.wsu.edu:8080/WSU_Alumni/alumctr.html
The architectural and historical aspects involved in the conversion of this historic building into the alumni centre.

9.5 BUILDING STRUCTURES

Engineering Software Exchange
http://www.best.com/~lidial

Bridge Engineering home page
http://www.best.com/~solvers/scsolutions.html

Computational Mechanics Corporation
http://cmc2.akcess.com
Finite element analysis software.

Computational Mechanics Co.
http://www.comco.com
Engineering software company.

CivilServe Software
http://forum.gaertner.de/ggu/civil.htm
German software company.

Fabric Structures Database
http://www.arch.buffalo.edu/~samsudee
Hidhayathullah Samsudeen has established a database for tensile and pneumatic fabric structures.

Finite element analysis homepage
http://www.vtt.fi/rte7/femspost.html
At the Technical Research Centre, Finland.

FElt homepage
http://www-cse.ucsd.edu/users/atkinson/FElt
More Finite Elements.

Pavenet - Pavement Engineering Site
http://www.mincad.com/au/engineering/pavenet/
Software for road design and analysis.

9.6 BUILDING MATERIALS

AEDILE
http://www.smart.it/Aedile/welcome.html
AEDILE, located in Italy, contains the web sites of 3 Building Industry International Trade Shows (featuring more than 1000 exhibitors each) plus several home pages of companies that are among the leading manufacturing firms in this field (mostly ceramic tile producers at the moment), and is constantly growing.

Brick Sculpture
http://www.brickstone.com/
Specialist site for brick murals. The company is based in Lincoln, Nebraska.

Builder and Decorators' Sourcebook
http://www.ljp.com/sourcebook
On-line reference to 4 800 manufacturers, distributors and retailers of building and decorating products.

Builder Net
http://www.deltanet.com/users/builder
An interactive catalogue of building products.

French Architectural Technology
http://www.generation.net/~slaberge/index.htm

Instant Data – Online product information
http://www.demon.co.uk/instant/
Instant Data is a new online building product information service on the WWW. Specifiers: use it to find suppliers and products using alphabetical and CI/SfB indexes. Suppliers: get your name, telephone number and products in front of specifiers.

Masonry fireplace home page:
http://www.olympus.net/biz/buckley/rumford.html
Rumford fireplaces and much other information about the masonry industry as it relates to fireplaces and chimneys.

New Zealand Products Database
http://www.bitz.co.nz/ralenti

Prime Materials (Asphalt)
http://rampages.onramp.net/~prime

Reggiani Ltd, Lighting Catalogue
http://info.co.uk/reggiani/

SAIEDUE - Building Components and Internal Finishing Trade Show
http://www.smart.it/SAIEDUE/welcome.html

Thomas Register
http://www.thomasregister.com:8000/
Supplier Finder. Register of U.S. manufacturers; able to locate product or service and retrieve information on the companies who offer that product or service.

Wavin (plastic pipes)
http://www.wavin.dk

Wood and Stone Carving
http://www.catch22.com/agrell
Classical hand-carving in wood and stone.

Woodworking
http://access.digex.com/~mds/woodwork.html
Articles and reports on woodworking, with links to other woodworking sites.

9.7 BUILDING SERVICES

9.7.1 General references

European Union Building Technology Newsletters
http://erg.ucd.ie/thermiewww/newsletters.html

Chartered Institution of Building Services Engineers
http://www.bre.co.uk/org/cibse
The institution's publications list and details of conferences, as well as links to suggested HVAC info sources, building engineering sources and British engineering institutions.

Paul Milligan's HVAC Collection
http://www.elitesoft.com/sci.hvac/

Extensive links on HVAC (categories include schools and labs, government resources, solar, industry groups, efficiency and commercial sites), FAQ and information on the newsgroup sci.engr.heat-vent-ac.

Society of Building Science Educators
http://brick.arch.vuw.ac.nz:85:/index.html
Many links to building science related sites.

9.7.2 Acoustics

Acoustical Society of America
http://sunspot.nosc.mil/asa

Acoustics, Lighting and General Environment
http://wwwetb.nlm.nih.gov/monograp/ergo/acoustic.html

Acoustics newsgroup
news:alt.sci.physics.acoustics

Acoustics Research Laboratory
http://sti.larc.nasa.gov/RandT/RandT/SectionM/M14.html

Auburn University, Acoustics Page
http://www.eng.auburn.edu/department/me/research/acoustics/Acoustics.html

Helsinki Technical University, Acoustics Laboratory
http://www.hut.fi/English/HUT/Units/Faculties/S/Acoustics/index.html

Instituto de Aczstica's WWW Acoustics Server
http://www.ia.csic.es/Acoustics.html

IRCAM
http://www.ircam.fr/accueil/r-et-d-e.html
Research and Development at IRCAM.

ISEN Research, Acoustics Department
http://wwwserv.isen.fr/recherche/acoustique.html

Penn State University, Department of Acoustics
http://www.acs.psu.edu/Acoustics.html
Center for Acoustics and Vibration
http://kirkof.psu.edu/cav/

University of Salford, Department of Applied Acoustics
http://www.salford.ac.uk/docs/depts/acoustics/homepage.html

TOPS Group V: Acoustics
http://www.larc.nasa.gov/tops/Groups/V.html

Yahoo Acoustics Index
http://akebono.stanford.edu/yahoo/Science/Acoustics/

9.7.3 Lighting

CIE (Commission Internationale de l'Eclairage)
http://www.hike.te.chiba-u.ac.jp/ikeda/CIE/home.html
Publications, press releases, extracts from CIE Journal.

Illuminating Engineering Society of North America (IES)
http://www.ksu.edu/~kenbeyer/ies.html
The IES mission is 'to advance knowledge and to disseminate information for the improvement of the lighted environment to the benefit of society'.

Lawrence Berkeley Laboratory (LBL)
http://www.lbl.gov
Access is provided to the library catalogue, publications list and project descriptions. The Lawrence Berkeley Laboratory has a Center for Building Science which has programs in Building Technologies (including windows and daylighting), Energy Analysis and Indoor Air Quality.
Full-text of the 1994 and 1995 issues of the Lawrence Berkeley Lab Science newsletter on energy are available
http://eande.lbl.gov/CBS/NEWSLETTER/CBSNEWS.html

Lighting Images Technology
http://www.light-link.com/
The 'Design Gallery' displays various designers schemes.

Lighting Research Center, Rensselaer Polytechnic Institute (LRC)
http://www.rpi.edu/dept/lrc/LRC.html
Overview of the center and its projects, abstracts from the National Lighting Product Information Program and DELTA (Demonstration and Evaluation of Lighting Techniques and Applications) and links to lighting sources on the net (and to net sources on energy, optics, patents and standards as well).

LightNET
http://www.aecnet.com/lightnet/home.html
A central source of on-line lighting information created by the cooperative efforts of AECNet, Illuminating Engineering Society of North America, International Association of Lighting Designers and the Lighting Research Center at Rensselaer Polytechnic Institute.

Lighting Resource
http://www.webcom/com/~lightsrc/
This site offers an extensive set of links to net sources on lighting, the capacity for ordering lighting products, and even web site set up services. It also includes articles, an archive and new product pages.

Solar Energy and Building Physics Laboratory (Laboratoire d'Energie Solaire et de Physique du Batiment)
http://lesowww.epfl.ch/index.html
Includes information on research projects in daylighting and photovoltaics, and the software they are developing. It is also an excellent entry into some of the technical Internet sources related to building. Daylight Laboratory at EPFL-LESO Lausanne
http://lesowww.epfl.ch/daylighting/daylighting_laboratory.html

9.7.4 Safety

Canadian Centre for Occupational Health and Safety (CCOHS)
CCOHS has developed a guide, 'Using the Internet to Access Health and Safety Resources'. The guide gives details on how to join health and safety mailing lists and newsgroups, locations of library catalogues and web health and safety resources. Further details are available from CCOHS Customer Services on custserv@ccohs.ca

Center for Safety in the Arts
gopher://gopher.tmn.com:70/11/Artswire/csa
Chart of toxic woods is of interest. Also includes links to other health and safety gophers.

Health and Safety Executive
http://www.open.gov.uk/hse/hsehome.htm
Notes on the CDM Regulations are at:
http://www.open.gov.uk/hse/fod.htm

Institution of Occupational Health and Safety
http://www.iosh.co.uk/

Material Safety Data Sheets
gopher://atlas.chem.utah.edu:70/11/MSDS
MSDS Online. A database of Material Safety Data Sheets (MSDSs) from the University
of Utah.

Occupational Safety and Health Administration (OSHA)
http://www.osha.gov/
A division of the U.S. Department of Labor, with links to other government resources.
The entire OSHA Act of 1970 online.

10

Environment and energy

10.1 INDEX SITES

Environmental Sites on the Internet
http://www.lib.kth.se/~lg/envres.htm
Larsgöran Strandberg's extraordinary list of links.

Mike Donn's Building Science Educators' Useful Addresses
http://brick.arch.vuw.ac.nz:85/interesting_addresses.html
Extensive list of links including energy and environment sites.

World Wide Web Virtual Library: Energy
http://solstice.crest.org/online/virtual-library/VLib-energy.html
This list covers energy policy, sources, distribution, generation and transmission. It also includes alternative and renewable energy sources, including energy efficiency.

World Wide Web Virtual Library: Environment
http://ecosys.drdr.virginia.edu/Environment.html

WWW Environmental Servers
http://kaos.erin.gov.au/other_servers/other_servers.html

10.2 GENERAL ENVIRONMENTAL SOURCES

Air Infiltration and Ventilation Centre (AIVC)
http://www.demon.co.uk/aivc/
AIVC maintain the International Energy Agency (IEA) Buildings and Community Systems Implementing Agreement homepage, which includes links to the IEA's research annexes:
http://www.demon.co.uk/bcs/

Building Energy Standards Program, US Department of Energy
http://ased.pnl.gov:2080/bp/besp/

Building Environmental Services
http://spartan.mohawkc.on.ca/Building/courses/desea521.htm
EA521 Building Enviromental Services. Research and analysis of building mechanical and electrical service systems. Standards and codes and energy saving techniques related to heating, lighting and ventilation. Course Outline.

Building Services I
http://gil.ipswichcity.qld.gov.au/comm/tafe/subjects/8895.html
TBG332. Building Services I. Pre-requisite(s): TBG131, TBG231. Broad knowledge of building services related to plumbing and drainage, with emphasis on installation requirements and planning.
Building Services II
http://gil.ipswichcity.qld.gov.au/comm/tafe/subjects/8897.html
TBG334. Building Services II. Pre-requisite(s): TBG231. The installation requirements for mechanical and electrical equipment in buildings and co-ordinating the work of on-site sub-contractors.

Building Services 3
http://spartan.mohawkc.on.ca/Building/courses/desar635.htm
AR635 Building Services 3. Calculations and development of mechanical and electrical contract documents for a project. Course Outline.

Building Services, Basic Course
http://www.fht-esslingen.de/institute/aaa/evtgrund.html
Building Services, Energy, Environment (Diese Seite gibt es auch in Deutsch). The course of studies includes the planning, construction and operation of heating, ventilation, airconditioning systems, energy and water supply, sewage and waste.

Center for the Analysis and Dissemination of Demonstrated Energy Technologies (CADDET)
http://www.ornl.gov/CADDET/caddet.html

Charter 88
http://www.gn.apc.org/charter88/

COMBINE 2 (COmputer Models for the Building INdustry in Europe)
http://erg.ucd.ie/combine.html
COMBINE is a major research project. It seeks to develop an operational computer-based Integrated Building Design System (IBDS). This site provides background information on COMBINE 2, project updates, outlines of design tools software and a contacts list.

EAC – Environmental Internet Resources
http://www.cfn.cs.dal.ca/Environment/EAC/EAC-Home.html

Energy Management Association of New Zealand
http://pacwww.chch.cri.nz/ema/ema.html

Energy Research Group
Faculty of Engineering and Architecture, University College Dublin
http://erg.ucd.ie/

Energy Research Unit, Rutherford Appleton Laboratory
http://www.rl.ac.uk/departments/tec/eru.html

Energy Sector Information Server
Department of National Resources Canada
http://es1.es.emr.ca/

Energy Systems Research Unit
http://www.strath.ac.uk/Departments/ESRU/esru.html
Extensive publications list, description of projects, products and courses. ESRU 'focuses on the development of simulation based design tools for predicting the energy/environmental performance of demand side systems such as buildings; heating, cooling and power plant; and the technologies to harness renewable sources such as solar and wind energy'.

Engineering Technology: Building Services Bill of Quantities
http://www.biw.co.uk/et/product/bill_of_quants_hvac/hvac_bofq.htm
Example of multi–media on the Internet. Bill of Quantities for HVAC: CAWS:U10 General Supply Extract.

Envirolink Directory of Web Sites
http://envirolink.org/envirowebs.html

Environment Canada
http://www.ns.doe.ca

Environmental Courses
http://www.foe.co.uk/infosyst/other_services/env_courses.html

Environmental Information Catalog
gopher://infoserver.ciesin.org/11/catalog

General environmental sources

Environmental Organisation Directory
http://www.rain.org/~eis/

Environmental Organisations e-mail list
http://www.foe.co.uk/infosyst/env_email.html

US Environmental Protection Agency
http://www.npr.gov/NPR/Reports/EPA_Main.html
EPA PPIES Server
http://www.epa.gov/
http://wastenot.inel.gov/pies
Many environmental links.

Environmental Resources Information Network (ERIN) Australia
http://kaos.erin.gov.au/erin.html
List of WWW environmental servers
http://kaos.erin.gov.au/other_servers/other_servers.html

Global Energy Network International
http://www.cerf.net/geni/Text/GENI_Directory.html

Global Network for Environmental Technology
http://gnet.together.org

GRID-Arendal
http://www.grida.no
United Nations Environment Programme.

Guide to Internet Environmental Resources
http://www.cfn.cs.dal.ca/Environment/EAC/briggs-murphy-toc.html

Index of Environmental Acronyms (ERIN)
http://kaos.gov.au/general/acronyms.html

Information Center for the Environment (ICE)
http://ice.ucdavis.edu/

InfoTerra
gopher://pan.cedar.univie.ac.at/11/UNEP
Environmental database.

LBL Center for Building Science News
http://eande.lbl.gov/CBS/NEWSLETTER/CBSNEWS.html

Full-text of the 1994 and 1995 issues of the Lawrence Berkeley Lab newsletter on energy.

Linkages – Environment and Development
http://www.iisd.ca/linkages/index.html

National Centre for Alternative Technology
http://www.foe.co.uk:80/CAT/

National Environmental Information Resource Center (NEIRC)
http://www.gwu.edu/~greenu/

National Interactive Directory – Building Services
http://www.insightinfo.co.uk/relocate/exnbuild.html
Building Services and Development Consultants. A and Q Partnership.

Oak Ridge National Laboratory
Environmental Sciences Division
http://jupiter.esd.ornl.gov/

Pandora Systems Environmental List
gopher://path.net:8001/11/.subject/Environment

THERMIE Journal
http://www.demon.co.uk/tfc/thermie.html
The official publication of the European Commission's THERMIE project.

United Nations Environment Programme (UNEP)
gopher://nywork1.undp.org/
United Nations Conference on Environment and Development (UNCED).
gopher://infoserver.ciesin.org/11/human/domains/political-policy/intl/confs/UNCED

10.3 ENERGY CONSERVATION; RENEWABLE ENERGY

Alternative Fuels Data Center
http://afdc2.nrel.gov/
Maintained by the U.S. Department of Environment.

Centre for Renewable Energy and Sustainable Technology
http://ie.uwindsor.ca/other_green.html

Energy Efficiency and Renewable Energy Network
http://www.eren.doe.gov
Information on EREN and links to energy and other information resources.

Energy Efficient and Environmentally Responsible Housing in Canada
http://web.cs.ualberta.ca/~art/house/
'Intended to be a small archive, containing information about, and pointers to information about Energy Efficient and Environmentally Responsible housing in Canada.' Includes information about R-2000 homes, and the Advanced Houses program. List of resources on and off the Internet.

Frisse Wind
http://www.design.nl:80/friswind/
The Amsterdam wind turbine cooperative.

Home Energy Magazine
http://www.eren.doe.gov/ee-cgi-bin/hem.pl
Issues from 1993 and 1994 online, with plans to add them back to volume 1, 1984.

National Renewable Energy Laboratory
gopher://gopher.nrel.gov:70
Under 'Research in progress' you find the NREL publications database and information about the various divisions including the Photovoltaic Division and the Buildings and Energy Systems Division. Under Information Sources/ NREL Information Systems find the solar radiation data and maps, wind energy resources maps and more.

Renewable Energy Network
http://www.eren.doe.gov/

Solstice
http://solstice.crest.org
'Site for energy efficiency, renewable energy, and sustainable technology information and connections.' A good starting point, with menu options including databases, company profiles, case studies, and organizations, as well as topical categories like renewable and alternative energy sources.

US Department of Energy
Environmental Technology Development Plan
http://www.etd.ameslab.gov/etd/overview.html

US National Renewable Energy Laboratory
http://www.nrel.gov

World Conservation Monitoring Centre
http://www.wcmc.org.uk/

10.4 SUSTAINABLE DESIGN

Alternative Energy Resource List
http://www.foe.co.uk/pubsinfo/infosyst/

Ames Lab Green Pages
http://www.etd.ameslab.gov/etd/library/greenpg.html

Center for Clean Technology (UCLA)
http://cct.seas.ucla.edu

Consortium on Green Design and Manufacturing (CGDM) at UCBerkeley
http://euler.berkeley.edu/green/cgdm.html

Earth Council's Web – Sustainable Development
http://terra.ecouncil.ac.cr/ecweb.html

EcoNet
http://www.econet.apc.org/lcv/econet_info.html
Energy resources
http://www.igc.apc.org/igc/www.energy.html
Environmental Directory
http://www.igc.apc.org/igc/www.eco.html

The Eco-Village Network
http://www.gaia.org
Founded in June 1994, its goals are to support the development of sustainable human settlements, to assist in the exchange of information amongst the settlements and to make information available about Eco-Village concepts and sites.

Electronic Green Journal
http://gopher.uidaho.edu/1/UI_gopher/library/egj/
Published by the University of Idaho Library.

Environmentally Conscious Design and Manufacturing Infobase
http://ie.uwindsor.ca/ecdm_lab.html
This site of the Department of Industrial and Manufacturing Systems Engineering at the University of Windsor in Ontario lists publications in the field, and links to 'green engineering' home pages and to recycling web pages.

Environmentally Conscious Design and Manufacturing Laboratory at the University of Windsor
http://ie.uwindsor.ca/ecdm_lab.html
Mailing list: http://ie.uwindsor.ca/ecdm_list.html
Database: http://ie.uwindsor.ca/ecdm_info.html

Electronic Green Journal
http://gopher.uidaho.edu/1/UI_gopher/library/egj/

Gary Shea's Resource Guide for Straw Bale Construction
http://www.xmission.com/~shea/straw
'This page is an attempt to draw together as much available information as possible on Straw Bale construction history, technique, literature and resources, both on and off the Internet.'

The Global Environment Facility (GEF)
http://www.worldbank.org/html/gef/geffiles/gef.html
GEF provides grants and concessional funding to recipient countries for projects and programs that protect the global environment and promote sustainable economic growth. The objective of this web site is to provide on–line information on all GEF activities.

GreenClips
http:solstice.crest.org/environment/greenclips
gopher://gopher.igc.apc.org:70/11/pubs/greenclips
You can subscribe from greenclips@aol.com. 'GreenClips is a summary of recent articles in the media on environmental news. It has a special focus on sustainable design for buildings, green architecture and related government and business issues. The one–page digital summary is published every two weeks.'

Green Design Initiative at CMU
http://www.ce.cmu.edu:8000/GDI/

International Environmental Agreements On-line
http://sedac.ciesin.org/pidb/pidb-home.html
The Consortium for International Earth Science Information Network (CIESIN) and its Socioeconomic Data and Applications Center (SEDAC) make available the Policy Instruments Database (PIDB), an on-line tool for browsing and searching of text, summaries and status of treaties and other international agreements related to global environmental change and sustainable development. The PIDB allows users to ask basic questions about environmental treaties such as 'Which treaties are in force for a given

country?'; 'Which treaties had entered into force by a given date?'; and 'What is the text of a given treaty?'. In many cases it is also possible to link directly to the international bodies responsible for overseeing the treaties and to other related information resources.

The New Environmentalist
The Journal of Sustainability
http://198.69.129.152/

Solstice
http://solstice.crest.org/
Sustainable energy and development.

O2W3
http://www.wmin.ac.uk/media/O2/O2_home.html
Focused on environmentally–conscious design, this site has information on the mission of O2 and its global network, articles and projects from the international design workshop it sponsored in November 1993, information on the October 1995 design event in Kyoto and the Global Network Newsletter (including an article on Ecotourism).

10.5 SOLAR ENERGY

Arizona State's Solar Energy Index
telnet://csi.carl.org
Path: telnet csi.carl.org/ Other Library Systems/ Carl Corporation Network Libraries – Western US (Menu 1)/ Arizona Libraries/ Other
ASU Libraries Specialized Collections and Databases. Journal articles, patents, technical reports and pamphlets on alternative energy sources.

International Energy Agency Solar Heating and Cooling Programme
http://www-iea.vuw.ac.nz:90/
Describes the programme.

International Solar Energy Society
http://www.ises.org/

National Climatic Data Center
http://www.ncdc.noaa.gov/ncdc.html

Solar Energy and Building Physics Laboratory
http://lesowww.epfl.ch

Information on passive solar architecture, daylighting and photovoltaics. Many links to other sites of interest at: http://lesowww.epfl.ch/other_links.html

Solar Energy Industries Association Members Database

http://solstice.crest.org/renewables/seia_database/seiadb.html

Solar energy products offered by members of the Solar Energy Industries Association (SEIA), including photovoltaics, solar thermal building products and solar components and materials. SEIA is a trade group for manufacturers and service suppliers; the SEIA homepage is: http://solstice.crest.org/renewables/seia/index.html.

Solar Energy Stops on Route 66

http://www.rt66.com/rbahm/solar.html

Ray Bahm's solar energy site with information on organizations, businesses, data and resources, index to journal Solar Energy and links to other sites.

SolarPACES

http://www.demon.co.uk/tfc/SolarPACES.html

The International Energy Agency's Solar Power and Chemical Energy Storage Systems. This page is maintained by The Franklin Company Consultants Ltd., publishers of *SunWorld*, the official magazine of the International Solar Energy Society. *SunWorld* is at: http://www.demon.co.uk/tfc/sunworld.html

Solar Radiation Data

http://solstice.crest.org/renewables/solrad/index.html

Allows you to specify a particular place, then download the solar radiation and climate summary data. There is also a lot of background information here.

Student Solar Information Network

http://lesowww.epfl.ch/ssin/ssin.html

In addition to their newsletter, this group maintains a comprehensive list of net solar energy sources.

Environment and energy

11

Planning and landscape

11.1 PLANNING AND LANDSCAPE SCHOOLS

School of Planning and Landscape Architecture Degree Programs
Degree Program Summaries
http://aspin.asu.edu/provider/caed/Planning/PLDegrees.html

University of Arkansas, Center for Advanced Spatial Technologies (CAST)
The Center was established at the University of Arkansas in September of 1991 in order to bring together the considerable expertise of a network of researchers with a long-standing history of GIS development at the University. As a multi-college organization, CAST unites personnel from the Fulbright College of Arts and Sciences, the College of Agriculture and Home Economics and the School of Architecture in the common goal of introducing and making GIS technologies available to a wide variety of researchers and professionals and to furthering the field through basic and applied research.
CAST focuses on research, data development, undergraduate and graduate education, user service and professional education in GIS and related technologies. Much of CAST's research efforts involve new approaches to spatial data and the development of new methodologies for analysis of these data, providing products to a variety of different audiences. Cooperative programs developed by CAST are designed to bring together the benefits of academic research and development, the resources of state and federal agencies and the private sector to provide the state and region with effective spatial technologies, trained practitioners and low-cost digital data.

University of California at Davis
http://ucdenvdes.ucdavis.edu/data/lda/faculty/facultypage.html
Landscape Architecture Faculty Pages. Generic Landscape Architecture Faculty Page. Environmental Design Program.

University of Canberra
gopher://services.canberra.edu.au/11/Faculty/Environmental_Design

CAP Department of Landscape Architecture
http://www.bsu.edu/cap/landscape/landscape.html

Landscape Architecture involves applying natural and aesthetic principles to the planning, design, preservation and management of the land in response to social and ecological problems and for public health and safety.

Colorado State Landscape Architecture Faculty
http://www.lance.colostate.edu/~cm082310/fac.html
Colorado State University. Landscape Architecture Faculty. Merlyn Paulson, BLA Utah State, MLA II Harvard University. Jeff Lakey, BSLA Oregon State, MLA II Harvard University. Brad Goetz, BSLA Colorado State, MLA II Harvard University.

University of Guelph
http://tdg.uoguelph.ca/nav/LA_startingpoints.html

University of Hannover
http://www.laum.uni-hannover.de/

University of Idaho
http://ian.aa.uidaho.edu/larch/program.html
The Department of Landscape Architecture is housed with the interrelated professions of art, architecture and interior design in the College of Art and Architecture. The department offers a professional four-year degree programme.

University of Illinois
http://imlab9.landarch.uiuc.edu

University of Minnesota, Center for Urban and Regional Affairs (CURA)
http://www.umn.edu/cura
One of the U.S.'s foremost applied research and service centres. CURA runs over 150 projects per year, successfully linking University faculty and students with community groups and government organizations, all addressing critical societal issues affecting people in Minnesota.

Technical University, Munich
http://www.edv.agrar.tu-muenchen.de/hello.html

Oklahoma State University
Department of Horticulture and Landscape Architecture
http://www.okstate.edu/OSU_Ag/asnr/hort/schmoll/wwwpage.html

University of Oregon. Department of Landscape Architecture
http://laz.uoregon.edu/departments/landscape/laindex.html
AAA Web Server Landscape Architecture Index Page

Rutgers Centre for Urban Policy Research
http://www.rutgers.edu/CUPR/

Texas Agricultural and Military University
Master of Landscape Architecture
http://archone.tamu.edu/laup/mlaup.html
Master of Landscape Architecture. Candidates are encouraged to conduct applied research in pursuit of their degree. Program Requirements.

Virginia Commonwealth University, Urban Studies and Planning
http://www.vcu.edu/hasweb/usp/usp.html
Links to related sites and abstracts of articles from JAPA.

11.2 GENERAL PLANNING AND LANDSCAPE SITES

American Society of Landscape Architects
http://www.asla.org/asla/
Apart from membership information, contains a landscape architecture gateway to links of interest on the web.

The Los Angeles Forum for Architecture and Urban Design
http://www.ccsf.caltech.edu/~mac/sah/ephem/webforum.htm
The Forum is a relatively new element in the arena of discussions about architecture in Los Angeles, and hosts two or three series of typically thought-provoking speaker presentation/discussions annually.

Bridging the Urban Landscape: Tours
http://hamlet.phyast.pitt.edu/exhibit/tours.html
The Neighborhoods: In Alphabetical Order. Super CyberTour of Pittsburgh. The Road You're On (K-6 Tour). Take a Walk down Fourth Avenue. Go Random. Search By. Off the Screen Tour. Pittsburgh Portraits by Joseph Stella...

Campus Landscape Simulation
http://gaudi.sk.tsukuba.ac.jp/projects/UD/index_ja.html

Canadian Society of Landscape Architecture
http://www.clr.utoronto.ca:1080/ORG/CSLA/CSLA.csla.html
The CSLA is administered by a ten-member Board of Governors comprised of one representative from each component association, a President and a President-Elect. The primary objectives of the Canadian Society of Landscape Architects, the CSLA, are to represent the profession of Landscape Architecture in Canada:
http://www.clr.toronto.edu/ORG/CSLA/CSLA.objs.html

Planning and landscape

223

Cultural Landscape Bibliography
http://www.cr.nps.gov/phad/clbib.html
Cultural Landscape Bibliography: An Annotated Bibliography on Resources in the National Park System. by Katherine Ahern. Edited by Leslie H. Blythe and Robert R. Page. Park Historic Architecture Divison. Cultural Landscape Program. Washington Office. 1992.
Cultural Landscape Bibliography
http://www.cr.nps.gov/phad/nwrobib.html
Cultural Landscape Bibliography. Pacific Northwest Region. Coulee Dam National Recreation Area (CODA). Gilbert, Cathy A. The Historic Landscape of Fort Spokane: A Preliminary Study, Coulee Dam National Recreation Area. 1984.

Equinox Design Group
http://www.magicnet.net/~toddmac/equinox.html
Equinox Design Group. Landscape Architecture Site Planning Digital Imaging Computer Consulting Web Page Graphics. Registered Trainer for MiniCad and Blueprint and the forthcoming Graphsoft CAD for Windows. PO Box 561135 Orlando, FL 32856-1135.

Everglades Landscape Modeling
http://kabir.umd.edu/Glades/ELM.html
Landscape modeling in the Florida Everglades.

Garden Net
http://www.olympus.net/gardens/point04.htm
A guide to gardens, arboreta and herbariums.

The Garden Shed Landscape
http://www.garden.co.nz/lscape.htm
Links to various landscape sites at this address. Many of them originate from landscape departments of universities around the world. Others are pages initiated by organizations.

GIS Beginners Tutorial
http://info.er.usgs.gov/research/gis/title.html

GIS data resources
http://www.laum.uni-hannover.de/gis/gisnet/data.html

GIS Resources on the Internet
http://www.lib.berkeley.edu/UCBGIS/
Index site for Geographic Information Systems.

GIS World
http://www.gisworld.com/mag/gw/index.html
GIS World Journal's index page.

GIS WWW Server
http://www.laum.uni-hannover.de/gis/gisnet/wwwgis.html

The Great Globe Gallery
http://hum.amu.edu.pl/~zbzw/glob/glob1.htm
A collection of over 200 different views of the Earth on maps and globes.

Guidance on Landscape Engineering
http://www.engei-hs.oyama.tochigi.jp/Japanese/guide/land/guidance.html

Kew, Royal Botanic Gardens
http://www.rbgkew.org.uk

Landscape and Urban Planning
http://www.elsevier.nl/catalogue/SA2/245/23150/23154/503347/503347.editors.
html
Landscape and Urban Planning. An International Journal of Landscape Ecology, Landscape Planning, and Landscape design. Editorial Board. Editor-in-Chief: J.E. Rodiek, College of Architecture, Texas A & M University, College Station, TX 77843-3137, USA.

Landscape Architect and Geometry
http://www.educ.state.ak.us/AKCIS/cacs\pla12812.txt
PLAN 12812 course. You are computing a bid to do the gardens around a client's new house. You need to calculate the cost of mulch and the cost of labor to spread the mulch. The mulch is spread at a depth of 2 inches....

Landscape Architecture Newsgroups
Newsgroup alt.architecture
Newsgroup alt.architecture.alternative
Newsgroup alt.planning.urban
Newsgroup alt.politics.greens
Newsgroup alt.save.the.earth
Newsgroup bionet.agroforestry
Newsgroup bionet.plants
For a listing of related newsgroups see:
http://tdg.uoguelph.ca/nav/LA_newsgroups.html

LOT, a project by Viennese artists Sabine Bitter and Helmut Weber, understands itself as an area of individual artistic investigations on phenomenas of global mobility, urbanism and the aesthetics of public communication and media structures.
http://www.ping.at/users/LOT/
Projects on view now:
URBAN EXERCISES:
urbanity, artistic investigations, state of affairs created as a forum for artistic statements and further contribution on architecture, art and theory, with Andrea Neuwirth (Vienna) beitrag zur beweglichkeit (contributing to mobility), in German, an international art project on mediastructures, mobilty and cultural shifts.
LOT Project: home@lot.or.at
http://www.ping.at/users/LOT/
sabine bitter: bitter@interport.net
helmut weber: weber@thing.or.at
juerg meister: meister@mecad.co.at

John McDermon's Collection of Planning Related Sites
http://www_cic2.lanl.gov/planning/planhome.html

Museum Graphics - Landscape California, Wyoming and the Southwest
Ansel Adams Note Cards. Landscape: California, Wyoming and the Southwest. Museum Graphics Note Card A-002: Moonrise, Hernandez, $1.50. Museum Graphics Note Card A-028: Sand Dunes, Sunrise, $1.50. Museum Graphics Note Card A-039: Arches, North Court,...
http://bookweb.cwis.uci.edu:8042/MuseumGraphics/LandsCal.html

Planning Commissioners' Journal
http://www.webcom.com/~pcj/
Many links to planning related sites.

Planning Information
http://huduser.aspensys.com:/84/habitat.html
The clearinghouse will serve as a focal point for selected United Nations, U.S. Department of Housing and Urban Development, and Habitat II information.

Planning Resources on the Internet
http://www.lib.berkeley.edu/ENVI/cityweb.html
The UC Berkeley Library website for planning. Apart from much specialized Californian data there are U.S. Census data and other statistics and links to related sources.

Solano Lighting – Landscape Lighting.
http://www.ispot.com/golights/landscape.html

Solano Lighting has several years of experience in designing both 120 and 12 volt landscape systems.

Survey-Net
http://www.survey.net
Online polls and demographics where results are instantly available; the results of these surveys are freely republishable; current polls cover everything from politics, sex, Internet demographics, shopping, shareware to religion.

Utah State University Botanical Gardens
http://ext.usu.edu/resource/bot/ygbot.html
Landscape Demonstration Gardens. Utah State University Extension and the Utah Agriculture Experiment Station created and maintains a beautiful botanical garden in Farmington, Utah.

VLTi – GPS
http://www.realtime.net/virtual/gps.htm
Virtual Landscape Technologies, inc. Global Positioning Systems. Trimble GPS Mapping Products.

White Horse Landscape
http://www.netaxs.com/~ladson/whl_high.htm
High Tech Words. Hey, we have to deliver our message via the medium that is appropriate to reach our target market. If someone spends their time surfing the net, then they are probably neglecting their turf.

WWW Virtual Library Landscape Architecture
http://www.clr.toronto.edu:1080/SALA/

11.3 ECOLOGY AND RESOURCE MANAGEMENT

Arcosanti, an Urban Laboratory
http://www.getnet.com/~nkoren/arcosanti/arcosant.html
The construction of Arcosanti, a prototype for an energy-efficient town combining architectural and ecological concepts, began in 1970. The site is located in the high desert of Arizona, 70 miles north of metropolitan Phoenix, in a 4000-acre preserve managed by the Cosanti Foundation. Paolo Soleri has designed Arcosanti as an 'urban laboratory' to demonstrate his view of architecture, ecology and urban planning. When complete, Arcosanti will house aproximately 5000 people, providing an urban infrastructure with work places, cultural centres and service facilities, while allowing access to and interaction with the surrounding natural environment. The community is planned to serve as a research and study centre for the social, economic and ecological

implications of its architectural framework. At the present stage of construction, Arcosanti consists of various mixed-use buildings and public spaces constructed by 4000 past Workshop participants, Each year more than 60 residents host 40 000 visitors, conduct educational seminars for over 400 people, and are involved in the construction of the project. Now Arcosanti has its own web site, allowing detailed access to many levels of the project.

Antenna
http://antenna.apc.org/

Biodiversity and Ecosystems Network
http://straylight.tamu.edu/bene/bene.html

BioTechWeb WWW Site
http://midigod.fhda.edu/BioWebHome.html
BioTechWeb is a cooperative project sponsored by the Community Colleges Biotechnology Consortium and participating biotechnology firms of the greater San Francisco Bay and Silicon Valley area. BioTechWeb is intended to enhance opportunities for education and employment in the field of biotechnology through the shared use of technical, human and corporate resources.

BioTechWeb is a work in progress. Current college and industry participants include Syntex Corporation and De Anza College. In the weeks and months ahead, we hope to add many more community college/corporate biotech partners to these pages. BioTechWeb is the first phase of a much larger school-to-work project which will include Software Engineering, Health Care and a variety of other professions.

BioTechWeb is hosted by De Anza Community College (Cupertino, CA, USA), the Biotech Consortium of San Francisco Bay Area community colleges and the NOVA Private Industry Council.

Carbon Dioxide Information Analysis Center
http://cdiac.esd.ornl.gov:80/cdiac/

Earth Watch – Environmental Research
http://gaia.earthwatch.org/

Ecological Society of America
http://www.sdsc.edu/SDSC/Research/Comp_Bio/ESA/

Eco–Net (Institute for Global Communications project)
http://www.econet.apc.org/icr/econet_info.html
environmental directory: http://www.igc.apc.org/igc/www.eco.html
gopher://gopher.igc.apc.org
select 'Econet Environment'

Both the web and gopher sites provide information on a wide variety of ecological issues and topics. Climate, development of lands, pesticide use and pollution are just a few of the covered topics. There are many links to other ecological and environmental resources including the National Wetlands Inventory, the Electric Green Journal at the University of Idaho and many more.

Eco–Village Network
http://www.gaia.org
The Eco–Village Network was founded in June 1994. This site provides information about the network, whose aims are: to support the development of sustainable human settlements, to assist in the exchange of information amongst the settlements and to make generally available information about Eco–Village concepts and sites.

EcoWeb
http://ecosys.drdr.virginia.edu/EcoWeb.html

EnviroLink Network
gopher://envirolink.org
Contains an environment watch report and information on endangered species, energy, environmental laws, environment groups, environmental newsletters and more.

Environmental Ethics
http://www.cep.unt.edu/

Environmentally Conscious Design and Manufacturing Infobase
http://ie.uwindsor.ca/ecdm_lab.html
This site of the Department of Industrial and Manufacturing Systems Engineering at the University of Windsor in Ontario lists publications in the field, and links to 'green engineering' home pages and to recycling web pages.

EnviroWeb
http://www.envirolink.org
This is an 'outgrowth' of the EnviroLink Network and has to be one of the best thought out and laid out web sites around. It contains beautifully done pages that don't take years to download the images. Collaborative ventures between public schools are here courtesy of the Environmental Education Network along with many other on-going projects. A wealth of information comes from many sources including the Enviro Products Directory and of course links back to the 'parent' network, the EnviroLink Network.

Friends of the Earth
http://www.foe.co.uk/

Ecology and resource management

Green Action Glasgow
http://www.envirolink.org/orgs/greenaction/

GreenDisk (paperless Environmental Journal)
ftp://ftp.igc.apc.org/pub/GREEN_DISK/

Green Engineering
http://ie.uwindsor.ca/other_green.html
WWW database.

GreenNet UK
http://www.gn.apc.org/

Greenpeace International (Amsterdam)
http://www.greenpeace.org/
GreenPeace World Wide Web Home Page
http://www.cyberstore.ca/greenpeace/index.html

IGC EcoNet
http://www.econet.apc.org/

InfoTerra – Environmental Database
gopher://pan.cedar.univie.ac.at/11/UNEP

RMIT (Royal Melbourne Institute of Technology) National Key Centre for Design
http://daedalus.edc.rmit.edu.au
gopher://daedalus.edc.rmit.edu.au:70
'The National Key Centre for Design at RMIT exists to focus the work of Australian designers, researchers, industry and government on the changing relationship between design, production and consumption.' This site provides centre research papers and projects such as EcoReDesign ('a program to improve the environmental performance of manufactured products') and Eco Built Environment ('an inquiry into the philosophy of environmental sustainability both for the design and the designers of the built environment'), as well as links to other environmental design research centres.

O2W3 Homepage
http://www.wmin.ac.uk/media/O2/O2_home.html
Many links to related sources.

Rocky Mt. Institute
http://solstice.crest.org/efficiency/rmi_homepage/rmi_Homepage.html
Description of the institute and its seven foci, including green development. Publications lists are included.

Water Resources Gopher
gopher://gopher.c-wr.siu.edu:70/11
Not run by the government, but it does include some government-produced information, such as the USGS WRSIC Research Abstracts.

Young's Life Cycle Assessment Site
http://www.ecf.toronto.edu/~young
Information on LCA, including bibliography of publications, software, university groups. Some links to green design sites as well.

11.4 PLANTING

AGINFO Gopher (Agricultural Info Gopher), University of Delaware
Gopher: //bluehen.ags.udel.edu
Created by the University of Delaware College of Agricultural Scientists, this site offers a wealth of information to the landscaper and gardener. The archive is filled with information to help both amateur and professional growers. The AGINFO plant database and Cooperative Extension directories are filled with information on thousands of plant species and provide graphics and pictures on every type of shrub and tree imaginable.

Agricultural Gopher (PENPAGES)
Gopher ://penpages.psu.edu
The Penn State College of Agricultural Sciences archives over 13 000 files including newsletters, reports, bibliographies and fact sheets. Also contains sources from many other Universities such as the Center for Sustainable Agriculture at Iowa State and Ohio State.

British Trees
http://www.u-net.com/trees/home.html

Forestry Library (University of Minnesota)
gopher://minerva.forestry.umn.edu/1

The Garden Gate
http://www.prairienet.org/ag/garden/homepage.htm
Contains a collection of gardening resources including many pointers to other related information. Has links to subjects such as 'The Teaching Garden', Internet Resources, virtual gardens to visit and lots more.

Planning and landscape

Gardening Gopher (The Virginia Cooperative Extension Gopher)
Gopher://gopher.ext.vt.edu:70/11/vce-data/hort/consumer
Horticulural information, gardening tips, pest management, ecological news, general environmental information and plant fact sheets.

Roses FAQ site
http://www.mc.edu/local/nettles/rofaq-top.html
Well written and concise information on growing roses. This FAQ contains detailed information on rose care and growing.

Texas A&M Horticultural Program
http://aggie-horticulture.tamu.edu/
A complete agricultural information site. Links to several sites, including Cornell University and the Virginia Tech Consumer Horticultural Information Site. Also includes information on weed and pest control and organic gardening issues.

Glossary

A

anonymous ftp
Anonymous file transfer protocol. Allows access to public files through the Internet by the use of the 'user ID' anonymous. *See also* ftp.

Archie
An indexing system developed at McGill University for cataloguing *anonymous ftp* sites. *See* 3.7.

archive
The storage of similar-subject files on an Internet host (usually an *anonymous ftp* server) thus creating an archive of subject specific data. These files may be condensed (archived) using special software techniques which require the file to be 'extracted' in order to be used.

ARPA
Advanced Research Projects Agency. Originally DARPA (Defence ARPA). The U.S. government agency which funded the establishment of *ARPAnet*, the precursor of today's *Internet*. *See* 2.1.

ARPAnet
Advanced Research Projects Agency Network. Established in 1968 this network established the protocols and methodologies still used by the *Internet*. *See* 2.1.

AUP
Acceptable Use Policy. The official policy statement regarding use of a network.

B

backbone
A central network connecting other networks together. *See* 2.4.

BITNET

Because It's Time Network. An academic network based around IBM (rather than *ARPAnet*) protocols. Now part of the Corporation for Research and Networking *(CREN). See* 2.1, 2.3.

bookmark

An address stored in *Archie* or a *WWW browser* for easy access.

browser

A *client* program for accessing the *WWW. See* 3.11.3.

C

CCITT

Comité Consultatif International de Télégraphique et Téléphonique. Part of the United Nations International Telecommunications Union (ITU) responsible for making technical recommendations regarding telephone and data communication systems.

CERN

Centre Européen de Recherche Nucléaire. Of interest here as the developer of the World Wide Web. *See* 3.11.

CIX

Commercial Internet Exchange. Originally developed as a commercial Internet as the original government-funded networks *AUP* forbade commercial use. *See* 2.2.

client

The software running on the local computer which is used to access facilities on a remote computer through the network. *See also client-server* and 3.2.

client-server

The networking architecture in which a *server* provides services to a remote *client. See* 3.2.

commercial access provider

A company which provides an Internet connection for a fee.

CREN

Corporation for Research and Educational Networking. *See Bitnet* and 2.2.

CSNet

Computer and Science Network. Merged with *Bitnet* in 1989 to form *CREN. See* 2.1.

D

DARPA
(U.S.) Defence Advanced Research Projects Agency. The agency of the U.S. Department of Defence which funded the original network research which established *ARPAnet. See* 2.1.

directory
Computer files on many systems are organised by being grouped together in directories and subdirectories. In some systems directories are called 'folders'.

discussion group
An ongoing information exchange on a specific subject. *ListServ* (*see* 3.5) organises discussion groups as mailing lists. An alternative, using a different format and protocol is *Usenet* newsgroups (*see* 3.4).

distribution
In *Usenet*, the area to which a message is to be sent: it may be institutional, local, regional, continental or global.

DNS
Domain Name System. The system that translates human readable names (e.g. strath.ac.uk) into numeric *IP addresses. See* 2.6.

DOD
(U.S.) Department of Defence. Funder of the original network research through *DARPA*.

DOE
(U.S.) Department of Energy.

domain
A part of the *DNS* naming hierarchy. *See* 2.6

domain name
See DNS.

E

EFF
Electronic Frontier Foundation. 'A foundation established to address social and legal issues arising from the impact on society of the increasingly pervasive use of computers as a means of communication and information distribution.' (*RFC* 1392). *See* 2.7.

e-journal

a journal distributed by *e-mail. See* 5.1, 5.3.

e-mail

electronic mail. The computer-based exchange of messages between individuals through the network. *See* 3.3.

F

FAQs

Frequently Asked Questions. A document containing information (in the form of questions and answers) that new members of *mailing lists* or *newsgroups* would find of use. *See* 2.7.

field

A portion of a record set aside for a particular kind of data. For example, in *e-mail* there are 'To', 'From' and 'Subject' fields to be filled by the user and the mail delivery system adds several more. *See* 3.3.

file server

A computer that stores files and allows network access to them.

file transfer

The copying of a file from one computer to another.

FTP

File Transfer Protocol. The protocol (and programs implementing that protocol) which enables a user on one computer to access lists of files on a remote computer and transfer selected files, *See* 3.6.

flame

'A strong opinion and/or criticism of something, usually as a frank inflammatory statement, in an electronic message.' (*RFC* 1392). To avoid being flamed read the *FAQs.*

FQDN

Fully Qualified Domain Name. The complete, formal and unique name by which a *host* computer is identified on the Internet. *See* 2.6.

G

GIF

Graphical Interchange Format. The file format in which many images are stored.

Gopher
A menu-based information retrieval system. *See* 3.8.

H

header
'The portion of a packet, preceding the actual data containing source and destination addresses, and error checking and other *fields*.' (*RFC* 1392).

hierarchical file system
A method of storing files in a 'tree' fashion with subdirectories and files branching off (or nesting within) a root *directory*.

homepage
The entry point of a *WWW* site.

host
The computer system which provides files, programs and communications to its users. It may be local or remote.

host name
The portion of the *fully qualified domain name* that refers to the specific host computer. *See* 2.6.

hotlist
A list of *bookmarks* providing easy access to frequently accessed sources.

HTML
Hyper-Text Mark-up Language. The coding used to format documents for the *WWW*.

HTTP
Hyper-Text Transfer Protocol. The standard method for moving documents in the *WWW*.

I

IAB
Internet Architecture Board. 'The technical body that oversees the development of the Internet suite of protocols.' (*RFC* 1392). *See* 2.2, 2.3.

IANA
Internet Assigned Numbers Authority. *See* 2.3.

IAP

Internet Access Provider.

IESG

Internet Engineering Steering Group. 'It provides the first technical review of Internet standards and is responsible for day-to-day management of the *IETF*.' (*RFC* 1392).

IETF

Internet Engineering Task Force. 'The IETF ....purpose is to co-ordinate the operation, management and evolution of the Internet, and to resolve short-range and mid-range protocol and architectural issues.' (*RFC* 1392). *See* 2.3.

interest groups

Also known as 'special interest groups' (SIGs). Usually refers to the organisation of the *ListServ* mailing lists or *Usenet* newsgroups.

Internet

The world-wide system of interconnected computer networks using technical standards defined by Internet Activities Board (IAB) and the Internet Engineering Task Force (*IETF*). Other networks (such as *Bitnet*) which can exchange messages with computers on the Internet, but cannot connect for other services such as *FTP,* are considered part of an even larger network referred to as the 'Matrix'. *See* 2.4.

Internet Society

A non-profit organisation established to further the development of the *Internet.*

IP

Internet Protocol. The general set of rules for formatting and routing *packets* across the various networks on the *Internet.*

IP address

Internet Protocol Address. Each computer connected to the *Internet* has its own unique IP address, represented by a 32 bit numeric string. For convenience, this is usually represented as the human-readable *DNS* address. *See* 2.6.

IR

Internet Registry. The central repository for *Internet* information. Provides the central allocation of network and autonomous system identifiers. *See* 2.3.

IRTF

Internet Research Task Force. The IRTF is chartered by the *IAB* to consider Internet issues from a theoretical point of view. It has Research Groups, similar to *IETF*

Working Groups, but where the IETF concentrates on creating short-term practical solutions, the IRTF takes a longer-range theoretical view. *See* 2.3.

ISDN
Integrated Services Digital Network. The digital telephone technology which combines voice and data services in a single line. ISDN standards are specified by *CCITT*.

ISO
International Standards Organisation. Responsible for the *OSI* suite of protocols.

J

JANET
Joint Academic Network. The U.K. academic and research network.

K

Knowbot
A 'knowledge robot'. Typically used to automatically assess the size of the *Internet* or index *WWW* sites.

L

ListServ
List Server. An automated mailing-list distribution system. *See* 3.5.

lurking
Used to describe 'listening in' on a mailing list, newsgroup, etc. without actually participating in the discussion. Recommended as away for new users to become familiar with a given group (to avoid being *flamed* for posting a basic or foolish question).

M

mailbox
The file or directory in which a users incoming *e-mail* messages are stored.

mailing list
A list of *e-mail* addresses. Used by a 'mail exploder' to allow a message to be delivered to several addresses simultaneously. Mail exploders are used to implement mailing lists and enable users to send a message to a single address where the exploder then delivers the message to the individual *mailboxes* in the list.

mail server
Software that distributes files in response to *e-mail* requests.

MIME
Multipurpose Internet Mail Extensions. A protocol for Internet *e-mail* which allows the transmission of non-textual data such as graphics, sound, and other types of binary files.

N

name resolution
'The process of mapping a name into its corresponding address.' (*RFC* 1392).

nameserver
The software that maintains lists of host names and IP addresses. In the Internet Domain Name System, no single nameserver maintains all names and addresses – addresses are distributed among many nameservers which are interlinked.

netiquette
'network etiquette'. Socially acceptable behaviour on the network. *See* 2.7, 3.4.2.

network
A group of computers that exchange data or communications.

NFS
Network File System. A protocol developed by Sun Microsystems which allows computers to access files over a network as though they were on a local disk.

newsfeed
The host which provides the Usenet news.

newsgroup
A discussion group managed by Usenet. Articles are read and posted by means of a Newsreader client. *See* 3.4.

NIC
Network Information Centre. Provides information and services to network users. *See* 2.3, 2.7, 4.2.

NNTP
Network News Transfer Protocol. 'A protocol ... for the distribution, inquiry, retrieval, and posting of news articles.' (*RFC* 1392).

node

A device with a network address attached to a computer *network*.

NSF

National Science Foundation. The U.S. government agency which funded *NSFnet*.

NSFnet

National Science Foundation Network. A 'network of networks' which formed a major part of the U.S. *Internet*.

O

OSI

Open Systems Interconnect. A suite of protocols, developed by the *ISO*, to connect different types of computers and networks.

P

Packet

A self-contained bundle of data transmitted over a connectionless (packet-switching) network.

POP

(1) Point of Presence. A connection point in a *network* with the necessary equipment that will allow other computers, networks or dial-up users to connect to it.
(2) Post Office Protocol. 'A protocol designed to allow single user hosts to read mail from a *server*.' (*RFC* 1392).

port

A specific connection on a host computer which will allow direct connection to an application (e.g. *WWW* page) rather than connecting to the computer and then loading the application.

PPP

Point-to-Point Protocol. Allows a computer running *TCP/IP* to connect to the Internet over standard telephone lines using a high speed modem. Defined in *RFC* 1171.

protocol

A standardised procedure or format for exchanging data between computers.

R

RFC
Request For Comments. 'The document series, begun in 1969, which describes the Internet suite of protocols and related experiments.' (RFC 1392). *See* 2.3, 2.7.

S

server
A program running on a network computer which provides resources or services to users. Accessed by client software. *See* 3.1, 3.2.

service provider
An organisation which provides access to the Internet.

signature
Data appended at the end of e-mail messages, usually giving the *snail-mail* address, phone number, etc. of the sender. *See* 3.3.

SIG
Special Interest Group.

SLIP
Serial Line Internet Protocol. Defined in *RFC* 1055, the protocol used to run *IP* over serial lines (for example, to connect a home PC to an Internet access provider via ordinary telephone lines).

SMTP
Simple Mail Transfer Protocol. A protocol, defined in *STD* 10, *RFC* 821, used to transfer electronic mail between computers. It is a server-to-sever protocol, so other protocols, such as *POP*, are used to access the messages in client-server mail systems.

snail mail
The ordinary, non-electronic, mail service.

STD
'A subseries of RFCs that specify Internet standards. The official list of Internet standards is in STD 1.' (*RFC* 1392).

T

TCP

Transmission Control Protocol. A transport layer protocol for the Internet defined by *RFC* 793.

TCP/IP

Transmission Control Protocol/Internet Protocol. The basic Internet protocol suite. *TCP* breaks a message down into *packets* for transmission by *IP*; once the packets are received, *TCP* reassembles them at the source. *See* 2.2.

Telnet

A facility which allows users to log-in remotely from one computer to another. *See* 3.10.

U

Unix

An operating system, originally developed by Bell Laboratories, that is used by many of the computers connected to the Internet.

URL

Uniform Resource Locator. The unique descriptor which identifies documents in the *WWW*. *See* 3.11.1.

Usenet

A computer-mediated conferencing system. *See* 3.4.

V

VERONICA

Very Easy Rodent Oriented Net-wide Index to Computerised Archives. *See* 3.9.

W

WAIS

Wide Area Information Servers. *See* 3.12.

WWW

World Wide Web. A system of hypertext-linked documents that are linked through the Internet. *See* 3.11.

X

X25

A data communications interface specification for passing data into and out of public data communications systems.

X400

The CCITT and ISO standard for electronic mail.

X500

The CCITT and ISO standard for electronic directory services.